Interdisciplinary Perspectives on
Health, Illness and Disease

At the Interface

Dr Robert Fisher
Series Editor

Advisory Board

Dr Margaret Sönser Breen
Professor Margaret Chatterjee
Dr Salwa Ghaly
Professor Michael Goodman
Professor Asa Kasher
Mr Christopher Macallister

Professor Diana Medlicott
Revd Stephen Morris
Professor John Parry
Dr David Seth Preston
Professor Bernie Warren
Revd Dr Kenneth Wilson, O.B.E

Volume 21

A volume in the *Probing the Boundaries* project
'Making Sense of: Health, Illness and Disease'

Probing the Boundaries

Interdisciplinary Perspectives on Health, Illness and Disease

Edited by

Peter L. Twohig and Vera Kalitzkus

Amsterdam - New York, NY 2004

52.00

Illustrations on pages 184-193
©2003 Kunsthaus Zürich. All rights reserved

The paper on which this book is printed meets the requirements of "ISO
9706: 1994, Information and documentation - Paper for documents -
Requirements for permanence".

ISBN: 90-420-1973-5
©Editions Rodopi B.V., Amsterdam - New York, NY 2004
Printed in The Netherlands

Contents

Welcome to a *Probing the Boundaries* Project

Interdisciplinary Perspectives appears within the *Making Sense of: Health, Illness and Disease* project series of publications. These projects conduct inter- and multi-disciplinary research aiming to explore the processes by which we attempt to create meaning in health, illness and disease. The projects examine the models we use to understand our experiences of health and illness (looking particularly at perceptions of the body), and evaluate the diversity of ways in which we creatively struggle to make sense of such experiences and express ourselves across a range of media.

Among the themes these projects explore are:

- the 'significance' of health, illness and disease for individuals and communities
- the concept of the 'well' person; the preoccupation with health; the attitudes of the 'well' to the 'ill'; perceptions of 'impairment' and disability; the challenges posed when confronted by illness and disease; the notion of being 'cured'
- how we perceive of and conduct ourselves through the experiences of health and illness
- 'models' of the body; the body in pain; biological and medical views of illness; the ambiguous relationship with 'alternative' medicine and therapies; the doctor-patient relationship; the 'clinical gaze'
- the impact of health, illness and disease on biology, economics, government, medicine, politics, social sciences; the potential influences of gender, ethnicity, and class; health care, service providers, and public policy
- the nature and role of 'metaphors' in expressing the experiences of health, illness and disease - for example, illness as 'another country'; the role of narrative and narrative interpretation in making sense of the 'journey' from health through illness, diagnosis, and treatment; the importance of story telling; dealing with chronic and terminal illness
- the relationship between creative work and illness and disease: the work of artists, musicians, poets, writers. Illness and the literary imagination - studies of writers and literature which take health, disability, illness and disease as a central theme

Dr Robert Fisher
Inter-Disciplinary.Net
http://www.inter-disciplinary.net

Permissions

We are grateful to the Image Resources and Copyright Management, Kunsthaus, Zurich for their permission to reproduce the photographs of works by Ferdinand Hodler which appear in Chapter 12.

Introduction: Interdisciplinary and International Perspectives on Health, Illness and Disease

Vera Kalitzkus and Peter L. Twohig

The study of health, illness and disease has grown enormously in recent decades and many aspects of health care are the subject of intense debate, including the sustainability of health care systems, biomedicine and its alternatives, emerging infectious diseases, drug-resistant bacteria and the seemingly intractable problem of improving health in many settings. In some countries, such as Canada or Germany, the public perception is that the system is faltering. Other countries struggle to provide even basic services under the weight of economic burdens or political instability.

Health is, of course, linked to broad questions of economic development, social order and culture and there are many ways to 'make sense' of health, illness and disease. In many countries, teams of academic researchers, including clinicians, social scientists and humanists, have been put together to explore the tapestry of health. Collaborative efforts, particularly those that cross disciplines and borders, can be perilous. But these efforts can also be wonderfully liberating, generating new conversations and pushing the boundaries of scholarship. In some ways, interdisciplinary health research has transcended the traditional gulf between the world of the scientist and clinician and that of the social scientist and humanist. The interplay between illness and disease, patient and provider, treatment and healing is at the centre of this volume and the Making Sense conference project, which began in 2002. The first collection of essays, *Making Sense of Health, Illness and Disease* contained a selection of papers presented at St Catherine's College, University of Oxford.[1] Cumulatively, the essays in that volume help reveal the many ways to 'make sense' of health, illness and disease and highlight the socio-cultural norms embedded in health practices, as well as the symbolic nature of those practices.

The effort to extend and deepen the conversations among researchers interested in health, illness and disease was renewed at the second international Health, Illness and Disease conference in July 2003. How appropriate that the second conference met in the Jacqueline du Pré building at St. Hilda's College, Oxford University, named in honour of the brilliant cellist. Du Pré's career as a performer was cut short because multiple sclerosis sapped her physical strength and she gave her last performance in 1973.

The story of Jacqueline du Pré, recounted in several biographies,[2] illustrates in a dramatic and well-known way how the encounter with illness shapes the lives of individuals and their social networks. The only distinctive element in du Pré's story is that her social network was more extensive than that of most other affected persons. Her personal encounter with illness also did much to highlight the need for research and understanding into multiple sclerosis in the UK. For most of us, our engagement with health, illness and disease is a more personal and private encounter.

The papers in this volume shed light on many aspects of the encounter with illness and disease. The contributions use different research approaches and methodologies to investigate health and healing. Some use the analytical tools of the social sciences, while others draw on personal experiences. This volume has been organized into four sections. The first section establishes a frame of reference in which we can explore philosophical issues around the nature of our bodies and of life itself. Taken together, these essays challenge us to always rethink the nature of our analytical categories and therefore serve as an essential starting point. With the exploration of Jewish medical ethics, Michael Weingarten draws our attention to the religious and cultural implementations of ethical views. In an increasingly connected world, we need to come to an mutual understanding of various ethical viewpoints, whether they are informed by religious or cultural aspects. In his essay, Richard A. Ingram demonstrates how Nietzsche's personal experience and subjective views shape his philosophy and his writing. Ingram analyses the way Nietzsche's thinking has been shaped by his state of health. But instead of branding this as subjective and non-scientific, he shows the potential of this subjective stance – rooted in bodily experience – as a tool for fresh insights. James A. Marcum is exploring body metaphors and their implications for the actual encounter with patients in the biomedical setting. He draws our attention to the effects of the medical model on the patients life world.

The second section brings together essays that draw on narratives of disability, media portrayals of mothers and madness and the introduction of humour into the clinical setting by the work of clown-doctors. Nicola Goc shows the role of mass media in the social definition of the sane and the insane. Post partum psychosis is of interest for the media only in case of 'horrific details' such as infanticide or child murder. This links the public perception of post partum psychosis closely to crime. Goc pleads for "a discursive space within the news media" thus opening up ways to educate the public about this mental disorder and helping affected people to seek help. But not only the perception of lay people is influenced by the media portrayal. Goc shows that also judicial, medical and welfare decisions are influenced by this distorted view. Brett Smith and Andrew Sparkes pursue the complex interplay between narratives of sport and disability. It becomes evident how metaphors of body, health and illness in a specific culture (or sub-culture) can be problematic, insofar as they may hinder the articulation of new metaphors to live by. Clown doctors provide a space for hope, by recasting the experience of hospitalization for both patients and health care providers. Bernie Warren describes how the artistry of clown doctors in the clinical setting can affect both the mood and attitude of hospital staff as well as lighten the burden of illness for those in hospital.

Narrative and literature now occupy an important place within medical discourse and the selection of papers in section three illustrate how patient and literary narratives add new dimensions to our interpretations of clinical encounters. Increasingly, people experiencing illness are carving out intellectual space and demanding that their voices be also heard and considered. There is now a vast literature of first-person accounts of illness, the most famous of which might be the works of Susan Sontag.[3] These accounts are now so numerous that they have been labelled "pathographies" and are studies on their own terms.[4] There is also a rich literature that has explored the "healing function" of storytelling.[5]

These analytical paths are followed in the third section of this volume. Jarmila Mildorf highlights how physicians have embraced the possibility of story through their creation of literary texts. Through these pursuits, physicians write not only for themselves but the larger community and, through their writing, there exists the possibility of greater understanding between physicians and patients and the acknowledgement of the interests of one another. In her essay, Betty Bednarski explores the "possibilities of story" through Jacques Ferron's short story "Le petit William." Stories are, of course, an important aspect of medical education and practice. The *British Medical Journal* frequently publishes brief accounts of memorable patients or other stories "conveying instruction, pathos, or humour." That such stories are a regular feature of a prestigious medical journal signifies the important place of story within medicine. Bednarski extends this to the literary realm. Through her exploration of the three central characters in "Le petit William," she reveals much about the interaction between midwives and physicians, between health care providers and their patients and, importantly, about social order in 20th century Quebec. Taken together, Mildorf and Bednarski agree that the stories of medicine, whether the fiction of Jed Mercurio or the short stories of Jacque Ferron, create space through which greater understanding between physicians and patients can occur.

Karen Christopher and Gregory Makoul extend this analytical path by exploring what happens when people experiencing illnesses are given the opportunity to tell their story through video. The artists, the patients themselves, are given the opportunity to identify what they feel are the most important aspects of their narratives. In a model of dissemination, these stories are then shown to a diverse audience. As Christopher and Makoul highlight, the opportunity for patients to recount their experience is significant, because the stories of health, illness and disease "frame the way patients are seen and treated." The contribution from Ottomar Bahrs and colleagues is also concerned with this question. This project explores the potential of two interdisciplinary quality circles, which use video documentation of clinical encounters to understand and improve patient-doctor communication. Ultimately, the authors hope to identify the elements that will promote a salutogenic orientation in clinical encounters with chronically-ill patients. In this way, the quality circles seek to reframe clinical encounters in terms of the resiliency of patients, rather than focusing on the pathology of disease.

The final section deals with life's final chapter. Studies of death and dying are an important aspect of explorations of health, illness and disease. Elisabeth Kübler-Ross gave us not only the well-known five stages of death but also a deep appreciation of how death brings hope to the terminally ill person's family and caregivers. Through the analysis of death we can learn not only about the funerary customs and rituals that surround death but also about the attitudes of people toward death, its various representations, and what the study of death reveals about our contemporary values. Jon Cutler provides a very personal account of his encounter with his father's impending death and unpacks a number of issues concerning the art of dying. In his elegant essay on the depiction of Valentine Godé-Darel's struggle with ovarian cancer, Harold Schweizer highlights how the artistry of Ferdinand Hodler and its unflinching depiction of suffering invites us to experience it at some level.

Taken together, essays in this volume help us to rethink health, illness and disease and, as Christopher and Makoul note, to reframe individuals "not as diseases but as people living with disease." The translation from patient's stories into medical stories is not straightforward or unproblematic. As Bahrs, et al. highlight, the physician reinterprets the patient story and thereby transforms it from one rooted in experience into one grounded in ideas of disease. We hope that the essays in this volume become part of a conversation that will permit the stories of patients to re-enter the clinical encounter.

Notes

[1] Peter L. Twohig and Vera Kalitzkus, eds. *Making Sense of Health, Illness and Disease* (Amsterdam and New York: Rodopi, 2004).
[2] See Elizabeth Wilson, *Jacqueline du Pré: Her Life, Her Music, Her Legend* (New York: Arcade, 1999); Piers du Pré and Hilary du Pré, *A Genius in the Family: An Intimate Memoir of Jacqueline du Pré* (London: Vintage, 1997); and Carol Easton, *Jacqueline du Pré: A Biography* (London: Hodder & Stoughton, 1989).

³ Susan Sontag, *AIDS and its Metaphors* (New York: Farrar, Straus, Giroux, 1989) and Sontag, *Illness as Metaphor* (New York: Farrar, Straus, Giroux, 1988).
⁴ G. Thomas Couser, *Recovering Bodies: Illness, Disability and Life Writing* (Madison: University of Wisconsin Press, 1997) and Anne Hunsaker Hawkins, *Reconstructing Illness: Studies in Pathography* (West Lafayette: Purdue University Press, 1993).
⁵ Arthur Frank, *The Wounded Storyteller: Body, Illness and Ethics* (Chicago: University of Chicago Press, 1995); Arthur Kleinman, *The Illness Narratives: Suffering, Healing and the Human Condition* (New York: Basic Book, 1988); and Howard Brody, *Stories of Sickness* (New Haven: Yale University Press, 1987).

Bibliography

Brody, Howard. *Stories of Sickness*. New Haven: Yale University Press, 1987.

Couser, G. Thomas. *Recovering Bodies: Illness, Disability and Life Writing*. Madison: University of Wisconsin Press, 1997.

du Pré, Piers and Hilary du Pré. *A Genius in the Family: An Intimate Memoir of Jacqueline du Pré*. London: Vintage, 1997.

Easton, Carol. *Jacqueline du Pré: A Biography*. London: Hodder & Stoughton, 1989.

Frank, Arthur. The Wounded Storyteller: Body, Illness and Ethics. Chicago: University of Chicago Press, 1995.

Hawkins, Anne Hunsaker. *Reconstructing Illness: Studies in Pathography*, West Lafayette: Purdue University Press, 1993.

Kleinman, Arthur. *The Illness Narratives: Suffering, Healing and the Human Condition*. New York: Basic Book, 1988.

Sontag, Susan. *AIDS and its Metaphors*. New York: Farrar, Straus, Giroux, 1989.

Sontag, Susan. *Illness as Metaphor*. New York: Farrar, Straus, Giroux, 1988.

Twohig, Peter L. and Vera Kalitzkus, eds. *Making Sense of Health, Illness and Disease*. Amsterdam and New York: Rodopi, 2004.

Wilson, Elizabeth. *Jacqueline du Pré: Her Life, Her Music, Her Legend*. New York: Arcade, 1999.

Acknowledgement

The editors would like to thank all the contributors to this volume and the conference participants. We would also like to acknowledge the production assistance provided by Jackie Logan, Gorsebrook Research Institute, Saint Mary's University, and of Claire Rillie, who is now chasing tallships up the North American coastline.

Part 1

Philosophical Approaches to
Health, Illness and Disease

The Sanctity of Life or the Sanctification of Life?
A Critical Re-assessment of Jewish Medical Ethics

Michael Weingarten

1. Introduction

The immensity of the value of life in the Jewish tradition is forcefully expressed in a talmudic source[1]: "He who saves a single life is as if he saved the entire world, and he who destroys a single life is as if he destroyed the entire world."[2] Three different reasons have been proposed for this special value. The first, an argument from ownership,[3] is that since life is given by God, it may only be taken by God; creation confers ownership rights on the creator. The prophet Jeremiah put these words into God's mouth (or vice versa!): "as clay in the potter's hand, so are you in My hands" (Jer 18:6). Maimonides (1135-1204), the most prominent of all post-talmudic Jewish scholars and jurists, derived from this a positive duty to protect life as long as we possess it.[4] The second argument, the argument from infinity, is that because life was created by God, who is by definition infinite, therefore every fraction of human life is of infinite value, every human life is equal in value, and no smallest part of life may be disposed of. Rabbi Jakobovits, the founder of modern studies of Jewish medical ethics,[5] was the first contemporary Jewish authority to argue that life itself is of infinite value and therefore indivisible, each fraction of life possessing infinite sanctity. It is this view that has been taken as an authoritative Jewish endorsement of the 'right to life' position in the contemporary Western debate. The third reason posited for the sanctity of human life in Jewish thought, is that every human being is created in God's own image;[6] we will return to examine this theme later on.

'Sanctity of life' is a term that is used widely in medical ethics to contrast with the approach that emphasizes the quality of life. According to Helga Kuhse's definition "it is absolutely prohibited intentionally to terminate life because all human life irrespective of its quality or kind is equally valuable and inviolable."[7]

Non-religious thinkers, as well as religious ones, have also subscribed to a 'sanctity of life' doctrine.[8] Dworkin finds this difficult to conceive. He interprets the notion of sanctity as an intrinsic, as opposed to an instrumental, dimension of life, and moreover one which is not incremental, like knowledge, but simply exists once. He sees this as an essentially religious view.[9] The secular arguments that have been put forward to support the absolute value of human life, include: the special cognitive and emotional capacity of the human species; the amazing and unparalleled complexity of the human organism, and especially the brain;

the irreplaceable value of a life of accumulated good actions and good experiences; and, the continuous creative investment that makes a life what it becomes. Others have argued that life is a pre-condition for the experience of all those other things that we find good and valuable, therefore life itself must be inherently most valuable. McMahan has challenged all these ideas systematically, and has further shown that even if the secular notion survives criticism, it cannot logically form the basis for a right to life position simultaneously in questions of abortion on the one hand and euthanasia on the other hand.[10]

Among the influential Jewish ethicists who have promoted the sanctity of life as the basis for all medical ethics, we may cite Leon Kass,[11] chairman of President Bush's Council on Bioethics, the American medical-*halakhic* (*halakha* is Jewish religious law) authorities Bleich and Rosner,[12] and, as we have already noted, the late Lord Jakobovits, who was the British Chief Rabbi. Interestingly, the leading Israeli medical ethicists have not used the phrase as such, although some, such as Rabbi Eliezer Waldenberg, Chief of the Jerusalem Rabbinical Court,[13] certainly subscribe to a doctrine of the absolute value of human life. In sharp contrast to the theoretical position taken by the ethicists, it is noteworthy that in America, the Jews, physicians and lay people alike, are in practice among the most liberal in their attitudes toward the withdrawal of treatment in terminal care.[14]

In this chapter, I will join those who challenge the common assumption that one of the central and necessary features of Jewish philosophy as applied to medical ethics is 'the sanctity of life'. Some orthodox writers have already pointed out that this assumption is difficult to square logically with the *halakhic* position on the treatment of the dying, which is that at the very final stage of life, nothing should be done to delay the end.[15]

2.   Holiness in Judaism

We must first clarify our terms. What does sanctity or holiness (Hebrew *qedushah*) mean in Judaism? What in Judaism is considered sacrosanct if not life?[16] Surprisingly at first glance, it is certain times, places, texts and events that are termed holy. The Sabbath Day is holy; the Temple Mount is holy. So is the Bible. What characterizes this attribute of holiness is that these times and places and texts are designated, intrinsically and exclusively, to all eternity and inviolably, for the purpose of the service of God.[17] In this they are distinguished from secular endeavours and it is this distinction that constitutes holiness. If some society were to introduce a sort of leap-week, occasionally inserting an extra day into the week, then the Sabbath would move from Saturday to Friday, and so on. The seventh day is holy. Although the Jewish service of God on the Temple Mount in Jerusalem is not currently possible while others occupy it, the Mount is nonetheless still holy in that its specified function is dedicated to the service of God alone. Matrimony too is holy, in that only sexual relations within marriage comply with God's command to populate the earth with families. Holiness implies both dedication and distinctiveness. In this sense man's life as such is not holy; its use is not by definition restricted to the service of God, for Judaism admits of the secular in human matters.

Holiness as a biblical concept is ascribed first and foremost to God and to His Name. In the Bible, man is adjured to become holy, in imitation of God in whose image he is formed: "Be you holy, for I your Lord God am holy" (Lev 19:2). The common Christian understanding of this is that because God is holy, therefore Man, created in His image, is also holy. The Jewish understanding is different, in that Man is created merely in the image of God, but is never to be identified with God. Holiness, an attribute of God, is not to be identified automatically in those created in His image. Man's holiness, then, is not so much a state as an achievement. The challenge is for the Jew to sanctify life as far as possible by such superior behaviour as makes a moral person distinct from other people. Similarly, at a collective level, the Jewish People has to aspire to its claim to holiness, just like each of its individual members.

The term 'sanctity of life' (*qedushat ha-hayim*) does not appear in any of the classical rabbinic Jewish sources,[18] and in its first recorded use, by the former Israeli Chief Rabbi Uziel (1880-1953), it was in the biblical sense of a state of holiness towards which man should aspire.[19] Only recently has an Ashkenazi Chief Rabbi of Israel, Israel Meir Lau, used the term repeatedly in its vernacular sense, and this was in the context of the care of the terminally ill, although even he has stressed that the value of any prolongation of life is in the opportunity it might afford for repentance before death.[20] Among rabbinical writings, the Israeli Rabbinical High Court has also gone on record with a purely metaphysical usage of the phrase:

> this ruling is based upon the natural urge to live, and the sanctity of life which is deeply entrenched within every Jew, *qua* Jew, and for this reason we do not believe that any member of Israel has committed suicide unless we have witnessed the very deed by ourselves.[21]

Moreover, a recent book, edited by two orthodox Jerusalem scholars, one a philosopher and the other an historian, is entitled *Sanctity of life and martyrdom*, indicating the shift of usage from the traditional idea of holiness as a human aspiration to the modern idea of holiness as a property of life itself.[22]

3.   The sanctification of life

Let us turn now to examine the implications of a sanctity-of-life doctrine
as compared with a doctrine of the sanctification of life. There are obvious
problems with the limits of the requirements of the sanctity of life: for
example, what about other forms of life, equally created by the same God
in his infinite wisdom? Are they as sacrosanct as human life? And if not,
why not? We may note that after the Flood, God's Bible specifically
permits Noah to eat animal meat. Subsequently, sacrificing animal lives is
sometimes even required, not just permitted, for temple rituals. The fact
that this permission to kill animals for food was only given after the Flood,
but not earlier in the ideal state of the Garden of Eden, was taken by Rabbi
Avraham HaKohen Kook (1865-1935), the first Chief Rabbi of the Jews in
the land of Israel in modern times, to imply that indeed in the ideal
condition, animal life would be as sacrosanct as human life, sacrifices
would be only of plant origin and man's diet would be vegetarian.[23] So, at
least from a philosophical position, the concept of the sanctity of life, even
if for the time being not its full implementation, can withstand this
challenge from the question of animal life.[24]

    The most severe punishment in Jewish law is reserved for
desecration of the holy Sabbath – in biblical times it was the death penalty.
Even the sin of eating on the holy fast of Yom Kippur is not so severely
punished, but only by the penalty of *karet* (divine "cutting off," whatever
that might mean). Nonetheless, where Sabbath observance might endanger
life, for example by suspending the medical care of a seriously ill patient
or of a woman in childbirth, there the preservation of life takes precedence
over observing the Sabbath.[25] By implication, the preservation of life
supercedes every other obligation too. The rabbis, always trying to hang
their rulings on biblical exegesis, associate this particular idea with
Leviticus 18:5: "Keep my statutes....and live by them." The exegesis is
that although the Bible adjures man to live by its precepts, obedience to
the law is not required in circumstances where so doing would cost a
person his life: "live by them – but do not die because of them."[26] The
Bible provides a code to live by, not to die for. So there seems to be a
strong rabbinic tradition that establishes a clear ranking order for moral
principles – the preservation of life is the ultimate principle, next comes
Sabbath observance, and then all the rest of the laws. In a similar vein, the
biblical injunction 'Thou shalt not murder' (often wrongly translated as
'thou shalt not kill') has earned its place in western civilization as a self-
evident, or independently credible, moral principle that appears in every
version of moral theory. It is an *a priori* duty, or a rule with a supreme
degree of utility, or a universally agreed feature of the social contract, or
the best rule for survival of the species, all depending on your school of
philosophical thought.

So it is initially surprising to find that some of the discussants in the relevant talmudic passages, while accepting that preservation of life takes precedence over Sabbath observance, do not utilize the same exegesis. For it is in the exegesis, and not directly in the ruling, that we find expression of the meta-principle of the sanctity of life. The alternative rationale proposed for the ruling is that it is preferable to desecrate today's Sabbath in order to be able to observe next week's Sabbath.[27] In other words, it is not life as an end in itself that has such positive value as to supercede the value of the Sabbath, but Sabbath observance is the end and the aim, and life is only the means towards it. A life without Sabbath observance is a pointless life, and perhaps indeed not worth preserving, or at least, not at the expense of desecrating the Sabbath. This is clearly an intelligible and potent challenge to the idea of the sanctity of life but it does have its problems. Does that mean that a patient who is in a terminal coma and will not survive the week should not be treated on Sabbath, where the treatment involves technical desecration of the Sabbath as it usually does? What about those exempt from Sabbath observance, such as children or people with severe learning disorders? And what about non-Jews? All of these questions have been asked and answered in one way or another, and this is not the place to go into the answers. For there is a far more interesting consequence of this dichotomy of approach to the relationship between the two principles; the preservation of life on the one hand, and the service of God on the other hand, exemplified here by Sabbath observance. If the preservation of life is the supreme value, an end in itself and not just a means to an end, then where it conflicts with the Sabbath, the Sabbath must be deemed not to exist at all.[28] The seventh day of the week exists, in such circumstances, but for the particular parties involved in this fight for life, it is devoid of its sanctity as a Sabbath day, for the sanctity of life supervenes. However, if the preservation of life is merely a means to the end of enabling the service of God, then the Sabbath day still exists in all its sanctity, but its desecration is permitted, even required, insofar as this is needed in order to preserve the endangered life. In purely practical terms this means that those attending the patient may only do what is immediately and absolutely necessary for saving life, but no more.[29] In contrast, if the first view is followed, the view that represents the sanctity of life with the Sabbath suspended, then the attendants and the patient may do anything that is normally forbidden on the Sabbath, even though it may not be directly life-saving, but merely contributes, say, to the comfort of the patient.[30] Another consequence of the distinction is whether the attendants are required to minimise the extent to which their actions desecrate the Sabbath, for example, by using a machine or a non-Jew to act on their behalf, on condition of course that the treatment is equally effective given in this way. Technically, such actions mediated by an agent are deemed less flagrant breaches of the Sabbath rules. If preserving the sanctity of the Sabbath is the ultimate aim, then surely it would be best to minimise its desecration while still preserving the patient's life.[31] But if it is life itself that is sacrosanct, resorting to such devious devices would be unnecessary and irrelevant.[32] Somewhat unusually for Talmudic discussions, this argument was actually left unresolved.

The mediaeval scholars continued the debate, and Maimonides was in sympathy with the life-as-an-end-in-itself attitude. Life is a supreme value for Maimonides and its preservation is a basic virtue. It is clear to Maimonides that there is a positive duty to heal the sick. Although this duty is incumbent on everyone, as a physician himself he makes it quite clear, however, that one should defer to those most skilled and experienced in such matters.[33] Nahmanides (1194-1270), another highly influential mediaeval scholar, takes a rather different approach to illness, stressing that there is metaphysical meaning to human experience, including illness, and while the physician certainly has license to heal (Nahmanides too is thought to have been a physician, though the evidence for this is shaky), the patient should not rely purely on the doctor's skill, but should use the illness as an opportunity to repent his ways, and to turn to God for salvation.[34] Whereas Maimonides perceives of illness as an imbalance in God's nature that we are required to endeavour to correct, Nahmanides sees illness as a signal to intensify one's service of God. Life itself is not an end for him, rather it is the service of God that is the uppermost value. Later Jewish legislation through the centuries has done nothing to resolve the issue and we are still faced with the tension between the two schools of thought today.[35]

There is however, one further challenge from within rabbinic law to the idea of life as the absolute and sacrosanct value. For there are three circumstances where a Jew is enjoined to sacrifice his life – when challenged to worship pagan gods, or to commit adultery or to kill another man.[36] The last of the three is the easiest to cope with, for if both lives are equally holy, and one has to end, there is a good moral case to be made for your dying without committing the sin of murder rather than his dying and you sinning as well. Therefore this situation does not in fact challenge the idea of the sanctity of life. However, the other two situations are seemingly more problematic. As for the worship of pagan deities, since this action would deny God and his sanctity, assuming that the worship was sincere, it would in itself deny the sanctity of life which it its turn is predicated on a belief in the one God, the creator. So, again, we survive the challenge to the idea of the sanctity of life. We are left with enforced adultery, which the Talmud does not attempt to explain but cites as a tradition. If life is infinitely sacrosanct, why should it be forfeited when faced with the alternative of committing the sin of adultery in particular? Adultery, like the desecration of the Sabbath, was punishable by death, but in contrast to the Sabbath this law is not suspended in order to preserve life. The answer would seem to lie in the concept of marriage in Judaism as a sacred covenantal relationship, as well as a contractual one. And party to this covenant are three – man, woman and God.[37] Breach of this covenant is in itself a denial of God's part in it. Adultery becomes similar to idolatry, in its denial of God and his sanctity. There is no better example than this to demonstrate the difference in the weight given to certain values in Judaism, as compared to western secular values. If the sanctity of life seems to have found its place at the summit of western morals, Judaism may be seen to place the integrity of the family even higher.

4.   Conclusion

There is, then, at least a good case to be made for a central trend in Jewish philosophy that stresses the sanctification of a person's life by its dedication to the service of God, rather than seeing the sanctity of life as a property of life itself, without at the same time denying the immense value of life. This formulation can indeed be seen as a rather weak form of the sanctity of life principle and it has been espoused as such by some non-Jewish philosophers. Kurt Baier says "there is a goal to which every rational being is committed and which is sacrosanct", making the goal holy, which he calls "the sacred essence," but not the life. Creighton Peden calls this a "sacred natural process" where "the goal of every person is to lead the life that is optimal."[38] It is not at all clear in what sense the term sacred is being employed in this context, and this sort of sanctity certainly cannot be understood as equivalent to the Hebrew *qedushah*.

The practical implications of this Jewish concept of life for medical ethics are very clear and quite startling. There is no right to life – on the contrary, the finitude of life is starkly recognised in the Bible – from dust to dust. There are only the duties of life. These duties do not devolve on foetuses or on people in terminal comatose states. If abortion and euthanasia are wrong, it must be for some other reasons, but not just because the extinction of life is wrong *prima facie*. For example, the destruction of a foetus might be seen to contradict God's command to populate the world with people who may serve Him.[39] It is also wanton destruction of part of God's creation and, if even the wanton destruction of a fruit tree is forbidden, surely the wanton destruction of a foetus is also wrong.[40] This is much weaker than a sanctity-of-life principle, and is indeed overridden in certain circumstances, such as where pregnancy constitutes a serious threat to the mother's well-being. This position is predicated on the assumption that a foetus is not yet a person and, indeed, Jewish law only ascribes the rights and duties of personhood from the moment of birth but not before. In the case of euthanasia, however, where we are certainly dealing with killing a person, the prohibition against murder most definitely applies even when the terminally ill person has little time to live. On the other hand, where pain makes life not worth living, and the person is already on the path to imminent death, Jewish law will not require that efforts be made to prolong that life, and will also accept the use of medication that puts life at risk where it is needed in order to alleviate suffering.[41] A strong form of the sanctity of life principle could not possibly reach such a conclusion.

Notes

[1] The talmudic literature, compiled between the first and sixth centuries, is the central corpus of Jewish law, and its major components are Mishna, Tosefta, Babylonian Talmud, and Jerusalem Talmud.

[2] Mishnah *Sanhedrin* 4:5.

[3] Baruch Brody, "Morality and religion reconsidered," in: *Readings in the philosophy of religion: an analytic approach*, ed. Baruch Brody (Englewood Cliffs NJ: Prentice Hall, 2nd ed 1992), 491-503.

[4] Moses Maimonides, *Mishneh Torah*, Laws of Murder 1:4.

[5] Immanuel Jakobovits, *Jewish Medical Ethics* (New York: Bloch, 1959).

[6] The vitalists understand life as an entity that shares God's metaphysical holiness. DM Carr, *The erotic word: sexuality, spirituality and the Bible* (Oxford: Oxford University Press, 2003) thinks that the Hebrew reading of the *imago dei* motif is that God created humans with the ability to create new life and guard the creation. Others, e.g. Avi Sagi and Daniel Statman, *Religion and Morality*. (Amsterdam-Atlanta: GA. Rodopi, 1995), 156-164, read into *imago dei* the human capacity for moral judgement.

[7] H Kuhse, *The sanctity of life doctrine: a critique* (Oxford: Clarendon, 1987).

[8] For a discussion of the basic differences between Jewish and Christian ethics on the one hand and the Hippocratic approach on the other hand, see: Danuta Mendelson, "The Medical Duty of Confidentiality in the Hippocratic Tradition and Jewish Medical Ethics", *Journal of Law and Medicine* 5 (1998): 227-238. (Added to bibliography)

[9] R Dworkin, *Life's dominion* (New York: Alfred Knopf, 1993), 73.

[10] J. McMahan, *The ethics of killing: problems at the margin of life* (Oxford: Oxford University Press, 2002).

[11] L Kass, "Death with dignity and the sanctity of life," in *A time to be born and a time to die: the ethics of choice*, ed. BS Kogan (New York: Aldine de Gruyter, 1991), 117-145.

[12] F Rosner F and JD Bleich, ed.,, *Jewish Bioethics* (New York: Ktav Hebrew Publishing Co, 1999).

[13] Avraham Steinberg, *Encyclopedia of Medicine and Jewish Law* (Jerusalem: 1998, Hebrew; English translation, F Rosner 1999-) sv "*Noteh La'mut*" ("Terminal states"). (Added to bibliography)

[14] D Davis, "A question of context: a response to Fred Rosner", *Journal of Clinical Ethics* 6 (1995):232-6, n.16. (Added to bibliography)

[15] Baruch Brody, "A historical introduction to Jewish casuistry on suicide and euthanasia,", in *Suicide and euthanasia,* ed. B Brody (Dordrecht: Kluwer, 1989), 39-75; Daniel Sinclair, *Tradition and the biological revolution: the application of Jewish law to the treatment of the critically ill* (Edinburgh: Edinburgh University Press, 1989).

[16] Natan Rotenstreich, "On the sanctity of life," in *Sanctity of life and martyrdom,* ed. IM Gafni and A Ravitzky (Jerusalem: The Zalman Shazar Center for Jewish History, 1992).

[17] Unlike Mount Sinai, since the revelation was a once-off event never to be repeated, so that the mount reverted to its previous secular function and status.

[18] This statement relies on a search of the Bar-Ilan Responsa database version 10+, 2002, and is supported by Rabbi HD Halevi, "Sanctity of life and martyrdom: are they mutually exclusive?" in *Sanctity of life and martyrdom,* ed. IM Gafni and A Ravitzky (Jerusalem: The Zalman Shazar Center for Jewish History, 1992) 15-25 (in Hebrew).

[19] Responsa *Mishpetei Uziel* vol. 2 *Orah Hayyim* #23.

[20] Responsa *Yahel Yisrael* #62, 87 (Jerusalem 1992).

[21] Rulings of the Rabbinical High Court, Jerusalem, vol 1;164.

[22] IM Gafni and A Ravitzky eds, *Sanctity of life and martyrdom* (Jerusalem: The Zalman Shazar Center for Jewish History, 1992).

[23] AI Kook, *The vision of vegetarianism and peace: the Torah's point of view,* ed. D. Cohen (Jerusalem: Nezer David, 1983); Y M Barilan, "The vision of vegetarianism and peace: Rabbi Kook on the ethical treatment of animals" (forthcoming). (Added to bibliography)

[24] See too Maimonides' argument that killing animal life is permitted only in order to preserve human life: FJ Leavitt, "The idea of nature in Maimonides' philosophy of medicine: Jewish or Greek?" *Korot* 13 (1998-99): 102-21.

> Since God commanded animals to exist, they have as much right to exist as we have...It follows that we may kill or destroy other creatures only if our survival is threatened, or when God explicitly commands us to do so. (page 120)

[25] Joseph Karo, *Beth Yosef,* commentary on Asher ben Yehiel, *Tur Shulkan Arukh , Orah Hayyim* 228;2 (printed in standard editions).

[26] Babylonian Talmud, *Yoma* 84b; Moses Maimonides, *Mishneh Torah*, Laws of Sabbath 2:3.

[27] Babylonian Talmud, *Yoma* 85b.

[28] Moses Maimonides, *Mishneh Torah*, Laws of the Sabbath 2:2.

[29] Joseph Karo, *Kesef Mishne,* commentary on Moses Maimonides, *Mishne Torah*, Laws of the Sabbath 2:14; and *Bet Yosef,* commentary on Asher ben Yehiel, *Tur Sulkhan Arukh, Orah Hayyim* 328.

[30] *'RAVAD"* (Rabbi Abraham of Posquieres) cited in *Magid Mishneh* on Moses Maimonides, *Mishneh Torah*, Laws of the Sabbath 2:14.

[31] Nahmanides, *Torat Ha-Adam*, sv "Danger".

[32] *Turei Zahav* commentary on Asher ben Yehiel, *Tur Sulkhan Arukh, Orah Hayyim* 328:5.

[33] Moses Maimonides, *Mishneh Torah*, Laws of the Sabbath 2:1.

[34] Nahamanides commentary on Exodus 21:19 and Leviticus 27:11.

[35] *Encyclopedia Talmudit,* sv "*Holeh*" ("Sick person") notes 267-269. Noam Zohar, *Alternatives in Jewish Bioethics* (Albany NY: SUNY, 1997) Daniel Sinclair, *Tradition and the biological revolution: the application of Jewish law to the treatment of the critically ill* (Edinburgh: Edinburgh University Press, 1989); N Solomon, "From folk medicine to bioethics in Judaism" in *Religion, health and suffering*, ed. J.R. Hinnells and R. Porter (London; New York: Kegan Paul International 1999), 166-186.

[36] Babylonian Talmud, *Sanhedrin* 74a; Babylonian Talmud, *Pesahim* 25b; A Ravitsky, "Introduction" in *Sanctity of life and martyrdom,* ed. IM Gafni and A Ravitzky (Jerusalem: The Zalman Shazar Center for Jewish History, 1992) 11-12.

[37] Jerusalem Talmud, *Berakhot* 9:1, 12d.

[38] K Baier, "The sanctity of life", *Journal of Social Philosophy* 5 (1974): 1-6. C Peden, "The sacred natural process interpretation", *Journal of Social Philosophy* 5 (1974): 6-8. (Added to bibliography)

[39] Genesis 9:6-7 links the three concepts - the prohibition of bloodshed, *imago dei*, and procreation. Isaiah 48:18. Babylonian Talmud, *Yevamot* 63b compares celibacy with bloodshed. Rabbi Yair Bachrach (Germany, 17th cent., YH Bachrach, *Havot Ya'ir*. Lemberg 1894 #31) compares abortion to onanism - the wasting of seed.

[40] Deuteronomy 20:19; *Sefer HaHinukh* 529.

[41] Eliott Dorff, *Matters of life and death. A Jewish approach to modern medical ethics* (Philadelphia: Jewish Publication Society, 1998); Abraham Steinberg, "The terminal patient: a comparative view of democratic and halakhic values" in *Moral dilemmas in medicine,* ed. Raphael Cohen-Almagor (Jerusalem: Van Leer Institute / Hakibbutz Hameuchad Publishing House, 2002):290.

Bibliography

Baier, K. "The sanctity of life", *Journal of Social Philosophy* 5 (1974): 1-6.

Barilan, Y.M. "The vision of vegetarianism and peace: Rabbi Kook on the ethical treatment of animals" (forthcoming).

Brody, Baruch . *Suicide and euthanasia.* Dordrecht: Kluwer, 1989.

Brody, Baruch. *Readings in the philosophy of religion: an analytic approach.* Englewood Cliffs NJ: Prentice Hall, 2nd edition 1992.

Carr, DM. *The erotic word: sexuality, spirituality and the Bible.* Oxford: Oxford University Press, 2003.

Cohen-Almagor, Raphael. *Moral dilemmas in medicine.* Jerusalem: Van Leer Institute / Hakibbutz Hameuchad Publishing House, 2002.

Davis, D. "A question of context: a response to Fred Rosner", *Journal of Clinical Ethics* 6 (1995):232-6.

Dorff, Eliott. *Matters of life and death. A Jewish approach to modern medical ethics.* Philadelphia: Jewish Publication Society, 1998.

Dworkin, R. *Life's dominion.* New York: Alfred Knopf, 1993.

Gafni, IM and Ravitzky, A. *Sanctity of life and martyrdom.* Jerusalem: The Zalman Shazar Center for Jewish History, 1992.

Hinnells, JR and R Porter, R. *Religion, health and suffering.* London; New York: Kegan Paul International, 1999

Jakobovits, Immanuel . *Jewish Medical Ethics.* New York: Bloch, 1959

Kogan, BS. *A time to be born and a time to die: the ethics of choice.* New York: Aldine de Gruyter, 1991.

Kook, AI. *The vision of vegetarianism and peace: the Torah's point of view.* Jerusalem: Nezer David, 1983.

Kuhse, H. *The sanctity of life doctrine: a critique.* Oxford: Clarendon, 1987.

Mendelson, Danuta. "The Medical Duty of Confidentiality in the Hippocratic Tradition and Jewish Medical Ethics", *Journal of Law and Medicine* 5 (1998): 227-238.

McMahan, J. *The ethics of killing: problems at the margin of life.* Oxford: Oxford University Press, 2002.

Peden, C. "The sacred natural process interpretation", *Journal of Social Philosophy* 5 (1974): 6-8.

Rosner, F and Bleich, JD. *Jewish Bioethics*. New York: Ktav Hebrew Publishing Co, 1999.

Sagi, Avi and Statman, Daniel. *Religion and Morality*. Amsterdam-Atlanta: GA. Rodopi, 1995.

Sinclair, Daniel. *Tradition and the biological revolution: the application of Jewish law to the treatment of the critically ill.* Edinburgh: Edinburgh University Press, 1989.

Steinberg, Ayraham. *Encyclopedia of Medicine and Jewish Law* (Jerusalem: 1998, Hebrew; English translation, F Rosner 1999) sv "*Noteh La'mut"* ("Terminal states").

Zohar, Noam. *Alternatives in Jewish Bioethics*. Albany NY: SUNY, 1997.

Note on Contributor

Michael Weingarten is Professor of Family Medicine at Tel-Aviv University, and a practicing physician in Rosh Haayin, Israel. His research is in clinical ethics and medical anthropology. He has written *Changing Health and Changing Culture*. Westport: Praeger, 1992.

Beyond the Body Beautiful:
The Uses and Dangers of Nietzsche's Rethinking of Health and Illness

Richard A. Ingram

Why write an essay about Friedrich Nietzsche for a book devoted to making sense of health, illness and disease? There are two main reasons. First, Nietzsche challenges us to rethink many of our common assumptions about the nature of health and illness. By taking life as his one great cause, Nietzsche's philosophy of health puts into perspective the illnesses of individuals through an investigation of the ways that illnesses can be experienced as transformative and life-enhancing events. Second, Nietzsche acts as a diagnostician of the modern age, urging us to face up to a crisis in our ability to make sense of anything and everything. It is this diminished creative capacity that Nietzsche identifies as a more fundamental illness than any recognized by medicine or psychiatry.

In assessing Nietzsche's ideas, certain biographical and historical factors demand attention. Appointed as a professor at the age of twenty-four, Nietzsche experienced frequent bouts of serious illness, which led to him applying for, and being granted, retirement just ten years later. Although Nietzsche's health problems persisted, he believed that they afforded him a level of insight that was, quite simply, unique in human history: "I have a subtler sense of smell for the signs of ascent and decline than any other human being before me; I am the teacher *par excellence* for this - I know both, I am both."[1] Such was the strength of this conviction that Nietzsche made the mistake of announcing that, according to the report of a Turinese medical doctor, "he is a famous man." After his death in 1900, Nietzsche was to become a famous man; but in 1890 this erroneous self-representation was interpreted by the doctor as a sign of "mental degeneration," and Nietzsche was duly despatched to a psychiatric clinic.[2]

Nietzsche's extraordinary output as an author was thereby brought to a dramatic and sudden end just as he was beginning to gain a wide readership. In his correspondence, Nietzsche had occasionally expressed anxieties concerning the misuses to which his writings might be put. In June 1884, he confided to his sister: "I am frightened by the thought of what unqualified and unsuitable people may invoke my authority one day."[3] These premonitions were to prove well founded, as Nietzsche's legacy was claimed by Benito Mussolini and Adolf Hitler, both of whom were endorsed by Nietzsche's sister. The adoption of Nietzsche by fascist leaders inevitably provoked controversy over whether his thought anticipates the theory and practice of fascism, and these debates show no sign of losing their intensity.[4]

Armed with information of this kind, Nietzsche's accusers often dismiss his work either on the grounds that he is better classified as a clinical case than read as a philosopher or out of the belief that he is a proto-fascist. Daniel White and Gert Hellerich have exposed a major flaw with the first of these objections by showing that instead of seeing Nietzsche's "philosophy of health" as "symptomatic of his physical condition," we may approach it as "a challenge to the cultural assumptions underlying the science of medicine."[5]

Consider this entry from Nietzsche's notebooks, dated around 1885-86:

> Health and sickliness: be careful! The yardstick remains the body's efflorescence, the mind's elasticity, courage and cheerfulness - but also, of course, *how much sickliness it can take upon itself* and *overcome* - can *make* healthy. What would destroy more tender men is one of the stimulants of *great* health.[6]

Rather than accepting the judgements of medicine about whether individuals are healthy or ill, Nietzsche's advice is to adopt a different standard. An energetic disposition that does not succumb to pessimism can conquer certain illnesses by incorporating setbacks and using them to grow stronger. In order to distinguish his revaluation of health and illness from the standard applied by medicine, Nietzsche coins the phrase "great health."

Within a year of composing this note, Nietzsche wrote a second preface for his 1882 book, *The Gay Science*, in which he described the latter as the fruit of a protracted struggle:

> Gratitude flows forth incessantly, as if that which was most unexpected had just happened - the gratitude of a convalescent - for *recovery* was what was most unexpected. 'Gay Science': this signifies the saturnalia of a mind that has patiently resisted a terrible, long pressure - patiently, severely, coldly, without yielding, but also without hope - and is now all of a sudden attacked by hope, by hope for health, by the *intoxication* of recovery.[7]

The "cheerfulness" that Nietzsche prescribes for coping with illness excludes maintaining hope for improvement. Indeed, it is precisely at the moment when unanticipated recovery occurs that hope for that which is commonly called health – the standard of health promoted by medical science – confronts the convalescent as an obstacle to great health. Even as he enjoys and gives thanks for his return to health, Nietzsche wants to avoid being like the character in the verse, "Dialogue," whose amnesia ensures that all the lessons from the struggle with illness are lost:

> A. Was I ill? Have I recovered?
> Has my doctor been discovered?
> How have I forgotten all?
> B. Now I know you have recovered:
> Healthy is who can't recall.[8]

What, then, is the wisdom that Nietzsche gleans from enduring long periods of poor health? In the first section of his autobiography, "Why I Am So Wise," Nietzsche recalls discovering that his cognitive powers were often heightened at these times:

> In the midst of the torments that go with an uninterrupted three-day migraine, accompanied by laborious vomiting of phlegm, I possessed a dialectician's clarity *par excellence* and thought through with very cold blood matters for which under healthier circumstances I am not mountain-climber, not subtle, not *cold* enough.[9]

Far from accepting the passive role of the patient, Nietzsche explores the terrain of his illness, and finds himself better equipped for tackling intellectual questions that he would otherwise be unable to negotiate. With this shift from passivity to activity, Nietzsche becomes more perceptive: "Everything in me became subtler – observation itself as well as all organs of observation." Having acquired new sensory techniques, Nietzsche's unprecedented capacity for insight flows from the realisation of the uses to which these skills can be put: "Now I know, have the know-how, to *reverse perspectives*: the first reason why a 'revaluation of values' is perhaps possible for me alone."[10]

In developing his ability to reverse perspectives, Nietzsche made a leap that was both the basis for his philosophy of health, and the source of many of his more alarming ideas. It is once again in the section "Why I Am So Wise" that he discloses the connection between his poor health and his philosophical breakthroughs:

> Freedom from *ressentiment*, enlightenment about *ressentiment* - who knows how much I am ultimately indebted, in this respect also, to my protracted sickness! This problem is far from simple: one must have experienced it from strength as well as from weakness. If anything at all must be adduced from being sick and being weak, it is that man's really remedial instinct, his

> *fighting instinct* wears out. One cannot get rid of
> anything, one cannot get over anything, one cannot
> repel anything – everything hurts. Men and things
> obtrude too closely; experiences strike one too deeply;
> memory becomes a festering wound. Sickness itself *is* a
> kind of *ressentiment*.[11]

To his illness, Nietzsche credits the discovery of the phenomenon of
ressentiment, the resentment that consists of hyper-sensitivity and that
overtakes the body when negative impacts cannot be forgotten.
Ressentiment cuts across medicine's division of the healthy and the sick,
enabling Nietzsche to arrive at his diagnosis of the fundamental illness of
rationalist cultures: nihilism.

Seizing the position of doctor, Nietzsche lays bare an epidemic of
ressentiment in which his patients are everyone who suffers from an
inability to create new ways of making sense. This failure befalls both the
healthy and the sick, as these categories are defined by regular doctors.
This failure is succinctly expressed in the maxim: "He who does not know
how to put his will into things at least puts a *meaning* into them: that is, he
believes there is a will in them already (principle of 'belief')."[12] To
interpret events as containing particular meanings is, for Nietzsche, to
have assumed that meanings are inherent to events, and, therefore, to have
surreptitiously infused events with meanings at the outset. Nietzsche is
showing that interpretation amounts to the repetition of old ways of
making sense that have solidified as beliefs. The unchallenged meanings
of belief constitute a beyond, an other-world that devalues life in this
world.

How does this other-world develop? The crucial contrast is
between our "remedial instinct" to fight, overcome, and forget pain and
suffering, and the rationalist tendency to search for the underlying
meanings of pain and suffering, an illness for which Gilles Deleuze and
Félix Guattari have since supplied the term "interpretosis."[13] Nietzsche
traces the victory of rationalism over instinct back to Socrates: "Socrates
is recognized ... as an instrument of Greek disintegration, as a typical
decadent. 'Rationality' *against* instinct. 'Rationality' at any price as a
dangerous force that undermines life."[14] Being seduced into valuing
rationality as higher than bodily instinct marks the onset of the illness of
nihilism. Through the figure of Zarathustra, Nietzsche effects a reversal of
perspectives that relegates rationality to a subordinate position in relation
to bodily instinct: "The body is a great reason," states Zarathustra in the
section of *Thus Spoke Zarathustra* entitled "The Despisers of the Body,"
"a plurality with one sense, a war and a peace, a herd and a shepherd. An
instrument of your body is also your little reason, my brother, which you
call 'spirit' – a little instrument and toy of your great reason."[15]

Nietzsche's judgement is that when the self cannot do what Zarathustra tells us "it would do above all else," that is, "to create beyond itself,"[16] it is mired in nihilism and would do best to pass away quietly. The aphorism "A moral code for physicians" sees the eugenicist potential of Nietzsche's new medical order reach its nadir:

> The invalid is a parasite on society. In a certain state it is indecent to go on living. To vegetate on in cowardly dependence on physicians and medicaments after the meaning of life, the *right* to life, has been lost ought to entail the profound contempt of society. Physicians, in their turn, ought to be the communicators of this contempt – not prescriptions, but every day a fresh dose of disgust with their patients ... To create a new responsibility, that of the physician, in all cases in which the highest interest of life, of *ascending* life, demands the most ruthless suppression and sequestration of degenerating life – for example in determining the right to reproduce, the right to be born, the right to live ...[17]

Anyone who is incapable of following Nietzsche's example, in other words, forfeits the right to live and the right to reproduce. By failing to learn how to experience illness as a way for the self to undergo transformation through the expansion of creative powers, such people are shown to be part of descending life. As such, they become a burden to individuals who are capable of self-transformation, or self-overcoming, and should be disposed of forthwith.

Where does Nietzsche's philosophy of health go astray? How can it be that this genealogist of morals, the most patient unraveller of moralities, ends up proposing such an abhorrent moral code? These questions can be answered by retracing the path that leads Nietzsche from his self-transformation during a time of poor health to the revaluation of all values in which nihilism is overcome.

While he is sick, Nietzsche discovers that sense and intellect can be heightened by illness, thereby opening up perspectives that would otherwise remain inaccessible. The myth of the body beautiful crumbles as the idea that a healthy body is required to view the world correctly gives way to the perspectivism of the sublime, self-overcoming body. The problem is that Nietzsche then comes to value the operation of reversing opposed perspectives ahead of the vast array of perspectives that illness allows him to glimpse. When the sublime body is no longer understood by Nietzsche as a process but rather as a goal, it is declared to be the standard of the "great health." Having dismantled one illusion, Nietzsche erects another in its place.

Nietzsche teaches us that the standard of health advanced by medicine devalues life by closing off access to the multiple perspectives that become visible through illnesses. The experience of illness is considered by medicine to bring only negative impacts to bear on the body, and recovery is therefore presumed to consist of the restoration of health. Nietzsche's illnesses permitted him to uncover their positive impacts, and to view the concepts of health and illness from different angles. As the decade of the 1880s reached its end, Nietzsche came to believe that his "great health" was impregnable. He had overcome all illness, he concluded, by reversing the common understandings of health and illness. It is in this context that Nietzsche's descent (or ascent) into madness at the end of 1889 can be read as the final act in the drama of his philosophy of health. For Nietzsche's body rebelled against his hubris with a reminder that within one lifetime, only a finite number of illnesses, and a finite number of perspectives can be experienced. Nietzsche's body supplemented his philosophy of health with the observation that there are certain illnesses that bring the activity of writing to an end, and resist the reversal of health and illness.

For a period in his life, Nietzsche did overcome illness by undoing the duality of health and illness without reversing its opposed terms. It could be said that he started to capitulate to illness when he constructed a new duality of great health, or ascending life, and degeneration, or descending life. Having diagnosed a cultural crisis in creating new ways of making sense, Nietzsche rushed to cure himself of the illness of nihilism. With the benefit of knowing the outcome of this precipitate action, it can recognized that Nietzsche would have been wise to heed the advice of the following aphorism from the book that he published at the beginning of his last decade of creating new ways of making sense, *Daybreak*:

> Thinking about Illness! – To calm the imagination of the invalid, so that at least he should not, as hitherto, have to suffer *more* from thinking about his illness than from the illness itself – that, I think, would be something! It would be a great deal! Do you now understand our task?[18]

Having charted the trajectory of Nietzsche's philosophy of health, the implications of the diagnosis of nihilism can be considered more closely. If thinking about an illness causes greater suffering than the illness itself, it is because the imagination strains to find meanings in corporeal events that have no meaning other than that which is created from them. With the concept of *ressentiment*, Nietzsche highlights the repetitive movement of passing through the same sensations to which we are condemned when we cannot raise the strength to abandon the rationalist sense-making imperative. These sensations have often been accorded the highest value by the intellect, thereby separating them from their lowly origins. Yet, as Nietzsche warned in an essay that remained unpublished within his lifetime, the distance from the highest values conceived by the intellect to the lowest values is never further than the length of the digestive tract:

> Does nature not remain silent about almost everything, even about our bodies, banishing and enclosing us within a proud, illusory consciousness, far away from the twists and turns of the bowels, the rapid flow of the blood stream and the complicated tremblings of the nerve-fibres? Nature has thrown away the key, and woe betide fateful curiosity should it ever succeed in peering through a crack in the chamber of consciousness, out and down into the depths, and thus gain an intimation of the fact that humanity, in the indifference of its ignorance, rests on the pitiless, the greedy, the insatiable, the murderous - clinging in dreams, as it were, to the back of a tiger.[19]

The activity of thought remains self-deceiving until it acknowledges that fierce currents of corporeal desire drive all our pursuits, even those which proceed under the privileged sign of "reason."

Nietzsche's rethinking of health and illness in the lives of individuals is part of his intervention in the wider social malaise. Just as he contemplates the situation of individuals who suffer from thinking about their illnesses, so he reflects on cultures that seek refuge from cycles of birth and death in illusory ideas of human destiny. At all levels, Nietzsche aims to sweep aside the notion that pain serves a purpose. Neither the lives of individuals nor the histories of cultures move towards the achievement of particular or universal ends. There is no possibility of making sense of pain and suffering as necessary sacrifices contributing to the attainment of a world in which they will no longer arise. Far from being a cause for further sorrow, however, the absence of purpose enables endless experimentation by removing obstructions to new ways of making sense.

Nietzsche's revaluation of all values can therefore be understood as an attempt to subordinate hermeneutics to aesthetics. A close reading of the aphorism "Beautiful and ugly" from *Twilight of the Idols* will provide a clearer view of the sublime body on which Nietzsche's aesthetics are centred.[20] It is here that Nietzsche shows that the cost of the rationalist sense-making imperative is the cultivation of resentment towards life. Only by overcoming this imperative will the sublime body release itself.

In the aphorism "Beautiful and ugly," Nietzsche contests the philosophy of history that Kant derives from an aesthetics of the sublime.

By resorting to the concept of the sublime, Kant is tacitly admitting that the previously highest value of the beautiful cannot be sustained. Nietzsche spells out what Kant can only hint at, namely that the beautiful has crashed from the heavens down to earth: "Nothing is so conditional, let us say *circumscribed*, as our feeling for the beautiful. Anyone who tried to divorce it from man's pleasure in man would at once find the ground give way beneath him."[21] The beautiful is inseparable from the corporeal delights that ascetic moralities believe to be ugly and evil, and will not allow itself to be raised into an abstraction. For Nietzsche, Kant's approach to beauty is shown to be vacuous: "The 'beautiful in itself' is not even a concept, merely a phrase."[22] What Nietzsche finds objectionable is Kant's insistence on stripping away desire from the feeling of pleasure or displeasure that accompanies judgements regarding beauty, a move that Kant justifies on the basis that we "like the beautiful without any interest,"[23] whereas desiring entails an object in which we have an interest.

Nietzsche discerns a will to power at work in Kant's cerebral perspective on aesthetics, and believes that Kant overlooks this point: "[Man] alone has bestowed beauty upon the world – alas! only a very human, all too human beauty."[24] At stake is Kant's desire to preserve an experience that will reassure us of our ability to supply history with a goal that surpasses human understanding: the goal of achieving freedom governed by moral law. Kant identifies this experience with a mental event that occurs during our apprehension of the sublime, and finds a contemporaneous example in the qualified enthusiasm of people like himself who observed the French Revolution from a distance.[25]

The French Revolution confirms for Kant that there are objects of such magnitude that imagination is incapable of comprehending them. In contrast to the restful appreciation of the beautiful, the failure of imagination when confronted with the sublime produces displeasure and unease at the chasm between sensibility and reason. Yet in the same instant that we feel revulsion towards an object in relation to which "even the greatest power of sensibility is inadequate,"[26] the object also exerts an attraction over us.

The paradox of a simultaneous pleasure and displeasure arises because imagination operates under the direction of reason to strive towards an objective that it is not yet capable of attaining. Dissonance gives way to consonance once it dawns on us that an object first perceived as overwhelming becomes "small when compared with ideas of reason."[27] The feeling of the sublime affords us a glimpse of a disembodied perspective of reason that provides the only vantage point from which the progressive nature of human history can be confirmed.

Nietzsche does not reject Kant's opposition of the beautiful and the sublime, but reconfigures it. He starts by applying a tuning fork to Kant's "ideas of reason," and through their hollow ring exposes them as empty idols from which meaning has drained away.[28] Kant's feeling of the sublime is considered "reactive" by Nietzsche because it calls for the body to submit to a view from nowhere that has always already been evaluated as superior to all embodied perspectives. Kant detaches reason from its corporeal base, elevates it to the position of highest principle, and proposes that we genuflect to it. For Nietzsche, Kant's "ideas of reason" are forms, images, or idols demanding to be worshipped, and still belong to an "all too human beauty." Hence Nietzsche's concise appraisal of the beautiful: "In the beautiful, man sets himself up as the standard of perfection; in select cases he worships himself in it."[29]

Kant's concept of the sublime barely manages to conceal the ascetic ideal according to which the forces of the desiring body are instructed in self-denial. In return for acquiescing to the devaluation of life, humans are offered the consolation of belief in historical progress towards a moral order. But when the body is deprived of the outlet of recreation and re-creation, what is cultivated is *ressentiment*: resentment towards life. In place of the joyous affirmation of life as a work of art, what remains is a pallid hope for the future that sanctions a disciplinary regime for bodies in the here and now.

Nietzsche, on the other hand, wearing the mask of Zarathustra, urges us to dance, laugh, and forget the weighty demands of moralists: "We should consider every day lost on which we have not danced at least once. And we should call every truth false which was not accompanied by at least one laugh."[30] Zarathustra's message could be summed up with the phrase: "It's the body, stupid!"

> I want to speak to the despisers of the body. I would not have them learn and teach differently, but merely say farewell to their own bodies—and thus become silent.
> 'Body am I, and soul'—thus speaks the child. And why should one not speak like children?
> But the awakened and knowing say: body am I entirely, and nothing else; and soul is only a word for something about the body. ...
> There is more reason in your body than in your best wisdom.[31]

In contrast to despisers of the body such as Kant, the way of Zarathustra is the festival of life in which Dionysian ecstasy completely overtakes the senses. "It is only in the Dionysian mysteries, in the psychology of the Dionysian condition," writes Nietzsche at the end of *Twilight of the Idols*, "that the fundamental fact of the Hellenic instinct expresses itself—its 'will to life.'"[32]

In the same section of *Twilight of the Idols* as the aphorism, "Beautiful and ugly," Nietzsche asks: "What is the meaning of the antithetical concepts Apollonian and Dionysian, both conceived as forms of intoxication, which I introduced into aesthetics?" The Apollonian artist is a creator of beautiful images, statues, and narratives, of stable modes of being. Whereas:

> In the Dionysian state … the entire emotional system is alerted and intensified: so that it discharges all its powers of representation, imitation, transfiguration, transmutation, every kind of mimicry and play-acting, conjointly.[33]

The body formed through the discipline of the ascetic ideal, that is, the body beautiful, capitulates as the sublime body comes to the fore. The body beautiful opens out into the formless, into that which cannot be represented in an image, preserved in a statue, or symbolized in a narrative: the unstable sublime body.

Notes

[1] Friedrich Nietzsche, *On The Genealogy of Morals, and, Ecce Homo*, ed. and trans. Walter Kaufmann (New York: Vintage, 1989), 222.
[2] Avital Ronell, *Finitude's Score: Essays for the End of the Millennium* (Lincoln: University of Nebraska Press, 1994), 81.
[3] Friedrich Nietzsche, *Selected Letters of Friedrich Nietzsche*, ed.and trans. Christopher Middleton (Indianapolis: Hackett, 1969), 227.
[4] For a collection of essays that provide a balanced and well-informed analysis of the plausibility of such claims, see Jacob Golomb and Robert S. Wistrich, eds., *Nietzsche: Godfather of Fascism? On the Uses and Abuses of a Philosophy* (Princeton: Princeton University Press, 2002).
[5] Daniel White and Gert Hellerich, *Labyrinths of the Mind: The Self in the Postmodern Age* (Albany: State University of New York Press, 1998), 129.
[6] Friedrich Nietzsche, *Writings from the Late Notebooks*, ed. Rüdiger Bittner, trans. Kate Sturge (Cambridge: Cambridge University Press, 2003), 78.
[7] Friedrich Nietzsche, *The Gay Science*, ed. Bernard Williams, trans. Josefine Nauchkoff (Cambridge: Cambridge University Press, 2001), 3.
[8] Ibid., 12.
[9] Nietzsche, *Ecce Homo*, 222-223.
[10] Ibid., 223.
[11] Ibid., 229-230.
[12] Friedrich Nietzsche, *Twilight of the Idols, and, The Anti-Christ*, trans. R.J. Hollingdale (New York: Penguin, 1990), 34.

[13] "In truth, signifiance and interpretosis are the two diseases of the earth or the skin, in other words, mankind's fundamental neurosis." Gilles Deleuze and Félix Guattari, *A Thousand Plateaus: Capitalism and Schizophrenia*, trans. Brian Massumi (Minneapolis: University of Minnesota Press, 1987), 114.

[14] Nietzsche, *Ecce Homo*, 271.

[15] Friedrich Nietzsche, *Thus Spoke Zarathustra: A Book for None and All*, trans. Walter Kaufmann (New York: Penguin, 1978), 34.

[16] Ibid., 35.

[17] Nietzsche, *Twilight of the Idols*, 99.

[18] Friedrich Nietzsche, *Daybreak: Thoughts on the Prejudices of Morality*, ed. Maudemarie Clark and Brian Leiter, trans. R.J. Hollingdale (Cambridge: Cambridge University Press, 1997), 53.

[19] Friedrich Nietzsche, "On Truth and Lying in a Non-Moral Sense," in *The Birth of Tragedy and Other Writings*, ed. Raymond Guess and Ronald Speirs, trans. Ronald Speirs (Cambridge: Cambridge University Press, 1999), 142-143.

[20] Nietzsche, *Twilight of the Idols*, 89.

[21] Ibid.

[22] Ibid.

[23] Immanuel Kant, *Critique of Judgement*, trans. Werner S. Pluhar (Indianapolis: Hackett, 1987), 127.

[24] Nietzsche, *Twilight of the Idols*, 89.

[25] Immanuel Kant, "An Old Question Raised Again: Is the Human Race Constantly Progressing?" trans. Robert E. Anchor, in *On History*, ed. Lewis White Beck (New York: Macmillan, 1963), 143-146.

[26] Kant, *Critique of Judgement*, 115.

[27] Ibid.

[28] Nietzsche gives *Twilight of the Idols* an alternative title, *How to Philosophize with a Hammer*. Rather than using his hammer to smash idols, however, Nietzsche wields it test ideas and reveal them to be hollow illusions: "This little book is a *grand declaration of war*; and as regards the sounding-out of idols, this time they are not idols of the age but *eternal* idols which are here touched with the hammer as with a tuning fork." Nietzsche, *Twilight of the Idols*, 32.

[29] Nietzsche, *Twilight of the Idols*, 89.

[30] Nietzsche, *Thus Spoke Zarathustra*, 210.

[31] Ibid., 35.

[32] Nietzsche, *Twilight of the Idols*, 120.

[33] Ibid., 84.

Bibliography

Deleuze, Gilles and Félix Guattari,. *A Thousand Plateaus: Capitalism and Schizophrenia*, trans. Brian Massumi. Minneapolis: University of Minnesota Press, 1987.

Golomb, Jacob, and Robert S. Wistrich, eds. *Nietzsche: Godfather of Fascism? On the Uses and Abuses of a Philosophy*. Princeton: Princeton University Press, 2002.

Kant, Immanuel. "An Old Question Raised Again: Is the Human Race Constantly Progressing?" trans. Robert E. Anchor, in *On History*, ed. Lewis White Beck. New York: Macmillan, 1963, 137-154.

_____. *Critique of Judgement*, trans. Werner S. Pluhar. Indianapolis: Hackett, 1987.

Friedrich Nietzsche. *Selected Letters of Friedrich Nietzsche*, ed. and trans. Christopher Middleton. Indianapolis: Hackett, 1969.

_____. *Thus Spoke Zarathustra: A Book for None and All*, trans. Walter Kaufmann. New York, Penguin, 1978.

_____. *On the Genealogy of Morals, and, Ecce Homo*, trans. Walter Kaufmann and R. J. Hollingdale. New York: Vintage, 1989.

_____. *Twilight of the Idols, and, The Anti-Christ*, trans. R.J. Hollingdale. New York: Penguin, 1990.

_____. *Daybreak: Thoughts on the Prejudices of Morality*, ed. Maudemarie Clark and Brian Leiter, trans. R.J. Hollingdale. Cambridge: Cambridge University Press, 1997.

_____. "On Truth and Lying in a Non-Moral Sense," in *The Birth of Tragedy and Other Writings*, ed. Raymond Guess and Ronald Speirs, trans. Ronald Speirs, 1999, 139-153.

_____. *The Gay Science*, ed. Bernard Williams, trans. Josefine Nauckhoff. Cambridge: Cambridge University Press, 2001.

_____. *Writings from the Late Notebooks*, ed. Rüdiger Bittner, trans. Kate Sturge. Cambridge: Cambridge University Press, 2003.

Ronell, Avital. *Finitude's Score: Essays for the End of the Millennium*, Lincoln: University of Nebraska Press, 1994.

White, Daniel R., and Gert Hellerich. *Labyrinths of the Mind: The Self in the Postmodern Age*. Albany: State University of New York Press, 1998.

Note on Contributor

Richard A. Ingram is a PhD Candidate in Interdisciplinary Studies at the University of British Columbia, Vancouver, Canada. He wishes to acknowledge financial support from the Peter Wall Institute for Advanced Studies, provided through the major project, "An Interdisciplinary Inquiry into Narratives of Disease, Disability and Trauma," and intellectual support from fellow members of the Ephemeral Theory Collective, a group of interdisciplinarians whose work is informed by the ideas of Gilles Deleuze and Félix Guattari.

Mechanized Bodies or Embodied Persons? Alternative Models of the Patient's Body in Modern Medicine

James A. Marcum

1.   Introduction

In modern Western medicine, the human body can be perceived simply as a material object completely reducible to a collection or system of physical parts that can be fixed or even replaced with new parts, when broken or lost. From this perspective, then, the patient's body is a machine composed of individual body parts. Obviously such a model of the body has had a profound impact on how the patient, and the society in which the patient resides, interprets illness, as well as on the patient-physician relationship. According to this model, illness is construed as a diseased body part separate from the overall integrity of the patient's body and lived context.

Utilizing this mechanical model of the body, today's physician functions primarily as a mechanic or technician, whose clinical gaze is often focused exclusively on the diseased body part and not on the patient as a whole, including the patient's social milieu. Modern medical technology has played a critical role in the development of this model of the patient's body and in the transformation of the patient-physician relationship, by providing the necessary instrumentation and techniques for treating the patient as a mechanized body. According to this model, the patient's body is part of a machine-world, a collection of interconnected machines that are used to diagnose and to treat the patient as body parts often separate from a lived context.

Competing or alternative models have been proposed to account for the patient's body, especially models that attempt to capture the wholeness or integrated unity of the patient's body within a lived context. Many of these models of the human body are based on Eastern philosophical and religious traditions.[1] For example, Harriet Beinfield and Efrem Korngold propose a model that reflects the garden-like nature of human embodiment based on the Chinese notion of *ch'i*, with the physician as gardener: "Like a gardener, the doctor observes the patient and perceives the signs and symptoms to determine the nature of the problem at hand."[2] Besides these models, there have also been attempts to reform the Western mechanical model of the body by humanizing it. Specifically, the phenomenological tradition of the twentieth century has been utilized to transform the mechanized body into a lived one. [3]

The phenomenological model of the patient as embodied person reclaims the wholeness or integrated unity of the body, especially with respect to the patient's experience of illness. The body is not reducible or explainable simply in terms of body parts; rather the patient's body is embedded in a life-world, composed of the patient's everyday (bodily) experience within a lived context. The patient is or exists as an integrated body, not simply as a collection of separate body parts. From a phenomenological perspective, the language and concepts used to describe the inanimate world are inadequate to account for the patient as an embodied person. Labouring under this phenomenological model, the physician cares for the patient's health through an empathetic clinical gaze, in which the physician is genuinely aware of and compassionately concerned for the patient's illness and suffering. This awareness and concern is based on a common 'uncanny' experience of the body. According to this model, the patient interprets illness and suffering in terms of the disruption of the embodied person's life-world and not simply in terms of an isolated, dysfunctional body part.

In this paper, I explore the impact of these two models of the patient's body on modern medical practice. I briefly examine the origins of the models and the trajectory of the models for envisioning and understanding the human body in the future. I also examine the effect these two models have had on the patient-physician relationship and on the healing process, especially in terms of both the machine-world and the life-world in which the patient's body is located. Finally, the paper concludes with a discussion of how these two models of the body affect the patient's interpretation of the meaning of illness.

2.   Mechanized Body in a Machine-World

Descartes is considered the traditional source for the mechanization of the human body. He split the mind from the body, and on the one hand imparted to the mind a person's identity and vitality, while on the other hand he compared the body to a machine made from inanimate material. For example, he states in the *Treatise on Man*: "I suppose the body to be just a statute or a machine made of earth."[4] Drew Leder compares the Cartesian body to a corpse and argues that the comparison has had an acute impact upon the practice of modern medicine: "Modern medicine, profoundly Cartesian in spirit, has continued to use the corpse as a methodological tool and regulative ideal."[5] The acme of the human body's mechanization vis-à-vis medical practice was achieved by physicians motivated by Isaac Newton's mechanical philosophy. For example, Archibald Pitcairn, one of the earliest physicians to appropriate Newton's mechanical philosophy, argued for a "mathematical physick" or medicine, in which "Physicians ought to propose the method of Astronomers as a pattern for their Imitation."[6]   After Newton, iatromechanism became the dominant approach to medical practice and has increasingly influenced its practice until the present. Today, the standard medical model for knowledge and practice is simply an extension and application of the Newtonian mechanical worldview.

Based on this mechanical worldview, the body has been transformed into a scientific object that has been reduced to a collection of separate body parts. In other words, it is simply a machine with interchangeable components. As Fredrik Svenaeus observes: "The body becomes a hierarchical structure – an organism framed in a special language."[7] Thus, the body as parts is made of different anatomical systems, such as the respiratory and cardiovascular systems. These systems are, in turn, made up of various organs, such as lungs and hearts, which are made up of epithelial, muscular, nervous, and glandular tissues. Finally, to complete the reduction, these tissues are composed of different cellular types that are made up of a variety of molecules. Moreover, it is critical to note that the mechanized body is generally stripped of its lived context: for the mechanized scientific body is an abstract, universal thing that obeys or is subject to the physical and chemical laws of the natural sciences.

The impact of this model of the body for medical knowledge and practice is all too familiar. The patient's body as a machine is separated from the patient's self.[8] The aim of scientific medicine vis-à-vis the mechanized patient's body is to fix or replace the broken or missing part, without reference to the patient's lived context, since all patients' bodies are nearly or essentially the same. By reducing the patient to a collection of body parts, argues Alasdair MacIntyre, the patient as a person vanishes before the physician's gaze: "to view the human being as an assemblage of bodily parts and processes is to deprive the patient qua patient of every moral as well as every social dimension."[9] Patients as body parts become cogs in a machine-world, a world of interconnected machines in which the patient's body is but another anonymous and exchangeable component. For example, a kidney dialysis machine is used to treat multiple patients under similar conditions; for patients are exchangeable mechanical devices within a machine-world.

An important component of the development of the mechanized body is the rise of medical technology. Modern medical technology provides important objective and quantitative data concerning the patient's disease state. According to Ian McWhinney, "a constant theme [for medical technology] is the tendency for medicine to be dominated by the mechanistic values of objectivity, precision, and standardization."[10] This tendency has fostered mechanization of the patient's body on two counts. First, it has provided the artificial parts and pieces that have replaced or substituted for the macro parts (organs) or micro parts (molecules) of the patient's body. Second, it has provided a cadre of machines to which the patient's body can be connected, forming body-machine hybrids. The result of this technology is a machine-world. Physicians utilize this world to diagnose the diseased body part and to mend or replace it through pharmaceutical drugs or surgery: "modern medicine has now evolved to the point where diagnostic judgments based on 'subjective' evidence – the patient's sensations and the physician's own observations of the patient – are being supplanted by judgments based on 'objective' evidence, provided by laboratory procedures and by mechanical and electronic devices."[11]

Since the patient as separate body parts is just one more component of the machine-world, the patient becomes disembodied or invisible as the patient's body recedes into the background. Rather than being an embodied person, the patient becomes, for instance, a collection of test results derived from medical technology. The machine-world in which the patient's body is located has advanced tremendously over the last half of the twentieth century, from the stethoscope and microscope of an earlier era. Machines such as the heart-lung machine, the dialysis machine, and computerized tomography or positron emission tomography, have all redefined the patient's body in terms of mechanization, with three results. We have already encountered the first result, that of the fragmented body resulting from the division of the body into individual, isolated parts. The second is the standardization of the body. The standardized body is a generic body to which the patient's body *qua* clinical data is compared. The final result of mechanization is the estranged body, the alienation of the patient's body from the patient's self and lived context or other people.

The medical model of the mechanized body has also profoundly shaped the patient-physician relationship. Diagnosis and treatment of a patient's diseased body parts are puzzles that concern the physician-scientist as mechanic or technician. As Michael Bayles remarks, "The occupation of auto mechanic has arisen in society almost simultaneously with the progress of medicine…Despite one's initial aversion to this analogy [physician as mechanic], it soon seems a very strong and informative one for the concepts of health and illness as well as the ethical relations involved."[12] Employing this model, the physician's clinical gaze is myopic. It becomes focused only on the diseased body part, often to the exclusion of the patient's overall experience of illness and suffering within a lived context. In addition, as Kay Toombs explains, "the 'medical gaze' is directed to the inside of the body" so that the "physician in a sense renders the outer appearance of the physical object-body transparent."[13] She also notes that often this gaze is accompanied by the "gaze" of the machines used to diagnose and treat the patient's body.[14] Diagnosis of the diseased body part depends on a technology that represents the patient's body parts as a set of quantitative, objective, clinical data and observations. And from that diagnosis, the physician then chooses the appropriate therapeutic modality, sometimes with little patient consultation. The concern of the physician is to save the patient's body from the disease state and ultimately from death. Accordingly, bodily death is defeat and is generally avoided at all costs, both financially and biologically.

Under the mechanized model of the body, the physician's concern for the patient's body and its parts is detached from the emotions of either the patient or physician; for machines do not have emotions. If emotions enter into the patient-physician relationship, they too are reduced to a molecular mechanism. For example, Candace Pert has championed the role of biochemical molecules in the expression of emotions and the maintenance of health: "biochemicals are the physiological substrates of emotion, the molecular underpinnings of what we experience as feelings, sensations, thoughts, drives, perhaps even spirit or soul."[15] The final impact of the mechanized model on the patient's relationship to the physician is passivity on the part of the patient and dominance on the part of the physician. The physician is an authority figure with the technological knowledge, power, and expertise to save the patient's body or body part. Thus, the physician's relationship to the patient is one of dominance or superiority, both in terms of medical technology and access to that technology.

The trajectory of the modern mechanized body is towards two hybrid forms of the human body: the molecular body and the cyborg body. As mentioned above, the patient's body has not only been reduced to individual macro parts (organs) but also to micro parts (molecules). Of course the most important molecule, which has achieved iconic stature in Western society, is the macromolecule responsible for the transfer of genetic information, DNA. The analysis of DNA and of the genes it composes, especially in terms of the human genome project, has ushered in the new era of genomic medicine.[16] Medical scientists can now introduce foreign genes into the body to produce bodies that are genetic hybrids. Besides these hybrids, there are also the hybrids that are cyborgs, part machine and part human. Both these hybrid body forms represent the future of the mechanized body.

3.   Embodied Person in a Life-World

During the twentieth century, phenomenologists, such as Edmund Husserl, Martin Heidegger, Jean-Paul Sartre, Maurice Merleau-Ponty, and others, attempted to radicalize our every day experiences of life by making them explicit and by so doing explicate the meaning of such experiences through an analysis of their intentional structure. According to Husserl, Western science faced a major crisis: positivist natural science failed to answer or even to address fundamental questions about human nature and existence. He argued that we must return to the "things themselves", i.e., to concrete phenomena, instead of to their scientific abstractions, in order to uncover their meaning. For what makes possible scientific abstraction is the concrete world in which we live daily. This daily world or life-world is the ground or foundation upon which the meaning of human existence rests. According to Richard Baron, "phenomenologists seek to reunite science with life and to explore the relationship between the abstract world of the sciences and the concrete world of human experience."[17]

Since modern medicine is grounded in modern science, it too is facing a crisis similar to that faced earlier by science. However, for medicine this crisis revolves around the distance between the patient's concrete world and the physician's abstract scientific world. This has led to a crisis of care in modern medicine; for the clinician's stance and gaze are generally toward the patient's disease state and only derivatively toward the patient's suffering. The current crisis in medical care is also due partly to the machine model of the human body and can be addressed by resituating the body within the context of the everyday life-world, instead of thrusting it into an artificial machine-world. Again to quote Baron: "If we can adopt a phenomenological perspective, we can try to enter the world of illness as lived by patients rather than confining ourselves to the world of disease as described by physicians."[18]

Rather than reducing the person to atomic elements or abstracting the person in terms of universals, phenomenologists embrace the person as creating a life-world, in Husserlian terms, or as being-in-the-world, in Heideggerian terms.[19] A person, then, is physically embodied as a self in a unique life-world. As Michael Schwartz and Osborne Wiggins note, "The lifeworld is the sphere of prescientific activity…the realm of everyday social interaction and practical projects…The human being who inhabits and acts in the lifeworld is the embodied subject."[20] The life-world is not the physical universe that science depicts; rather, it is the world of the everyday that is made up by our personal activities and projects. It is the world that is lived bodily, through which we impart meaning to our lives. The person, then, is embodied concretely in the here and now and not abstractly in a universal world that occupies no specific place and occurs at no particular time.

As embodied persons, we create our individual life-worlds. The body is personalized in a lived context or environment. The person is not composed of separate body parts or of a mind-body dualism, according to the Cartesian model, but is an integrated bodily unit that is situated in a specific location and time. To quote Eliot Deutsch: "Persons have bodies to the degree to which they appropriate the physical conditions of their individuality and become integrated (and not merely unified) psychological beings."[21] At the pre-reflective level, the person 'ex-ists' the body: "I am 'embodied' in the sense…that I *am* my body."[22] In other words, the body is the medium in which the person carries out intentionally daily tasks and activities, and we come to know the body not through abstracting but by living the body. The body is not some thing that the person possesses as an object; rather, it is a lived, integrated unity that is not readily discernable into a body on the one hand and a mind (or even self) on the other. At the reflective level, the body may be grasped as an object distinct from the self; but it is still an object within a life-world. It is not an object in terms of being a scientific object, i.e., as a theoretical or an abstract thing. In other words, we do not experience our bodies as molecules, cells, tissues, etc. Rather, the body is an integrated unity through which a person 'in-habits' a life-world.[23]

The phenomenological model of the human body has important implications for the patient's experience of illness. Illness is not so much a dysfunction of a mechanized body or body part within a machine-world as it is a disruption of an embodied person's life-world: "illness must be understood not simply as the physical dysfunction of the mechanistic, biological body but as the disorder of body, self and world (of one's being-in-the-world)."[24] At the pre-reflexive level, illness results in an awareness of the body as separate and foreign that stands out over and against ('ek-stasis') the normal course of life.[25] No longer does the suffering patient go about everyday life without conscious awareness of the ill body's constraints. That body in terms of its spatial and temporal dimensions imposes itself upon the patient. Illness often expands the temporal scale and collapses the spatial domain in which the body is lived. For example, a routine activity, such as combing one's hair, which took little time, takes relatively longer, when an arm is broken.

At the reflective level, the body announces itself objectively in terms of its disruption of the normal course of the life-world. As a broken tool thwarts the builder's plans so the ill body disrupts the patient's plans. This is not to say that the body is a tool and that the ill body is a broken tool, but the analogy of the ill body as a broken tool does capture the impact illness has on the patient's experience of the body: "it would be wrong to call the body parts tools since they are also part of *Dasein* as self. They are not only a part of the totality of tools, but also, as lived (*leibliche*), they belong to the projective power of the self."[26] The objectification of the ill body at the reflective level differs from the objectification credited to science. In the former the patient is an object but one that is situated in a unique life-world as an embodied person, while in the latter the patient is an object located in a common machine-world as a disembodied person.

The phenomenological model of the human body also has important implications for the patient-physician relationship and the act of healing. The physician's clinical gaze is one of empathetic care for the patient's suffering. The physician is able to accomplish this empathetic gaze because of a shared human condition in which we all participate in the "uncanniness" of both our bodies and life-worlds.[27] Although our bodies and life-worlds are our own, there is a sense in which they are independent of us. In other words they are not always controllable. We are, after all, contingent beings. Even though we may not be ill, our bodies often announce themselves through moments that disrupt our lives. Through these experiences, we become aware of the limitations of the body: "Some reflection on this apprehension of the body as 'uncanny' under normal circumstances provides a clue as to the profound sense of bodily alienation which is intrinsic to the experience of illness."[28]

Toombs utilizes the above feature of our common experience in which the uncanny body announces itself, to examine features of the patient's illness and to address the patient-physician relationship.[29] These features include losses of wholeness, certainty, control, freedom to act, and the familiar world. The loss of wholeness is reflected in the breakdown of the patient's bodily integrity, which often leads to a loss of control over bodily functions and of the patient's life. Besides these losses, illness is also associated with a loss of freedom to do many of the activities the patient was once accustomed to doing. The loss of certainty pertains to the acknowledgement of the patient's mortality. Finally, illness leads to a loss of the familiar world in which the patient lives. By being made aware of these features of illness and how they influence the patient's life, physicians can more adequately attend to the patient's suffering rather than simply to the patient's pain caused by a diseased body part.

The trajectory of the embodied person is two-fold. The first is towards transformation of the mechanized body, whether in its molecular or cyborg manifestations, into a lived body. The notion of embodiment is stretched to include the artificial enhancements of or additions to the body. As the mechanical body becomes more artificial, the embodied person strives to incorporate modifications of and additions to the body into a unique life-world. Patients must reclaim their bodily identity as embodied not abstracted persons, i.e., as integrated bodily units embedded in unique life-worlds.

A second trajectory is to transform the textual body, as represented by the texts obtained from the medical history and exam, into a lived body. Besides reducing the patient to a mechanized body, scientific medicine has also reduced the patient to a textual body that often replaces the physical presence of the patient.[30] The medical history represents the patient as a text in which the physician asks the questions and the patient answers them, with little extraneous input from the patient. The medical exam also represents the patient as a set of numbers obtained from laboratory tests and as a set of written descriptive phrases obtained from the physician's prodding and poking the patient's body. As Svenaeus argues: "If the body is a meaningful phenomenon...this is so because it is *lived*, an aspect of our being-in-the-world, and not because it is written."[31]

4. The Meaning of Illness

As we have seen, the type of model used to represent the patient's body has a significant impact on the clinical encounter between the patient and the physician, including the healthcare system. For the mechanized body model, the patient is a machine and the physician a mechanic, who attends to the pain associated with a broken or missing body part in order to relieve that pain by mending or replacing the part. Both the patient and physician are cogs within a medical machine-world. For the embodied person model, the patient is an integrated bodily unit within a life-world, as is the physician, who attends empathetically to the patient's illness and suffering. Curiously, under this latter model the patient may be healed without necessarily having the diseased body part cured.

This curious state of affairs is the result of the profound impact these models have upon the meaning patients attach to their illnesses. For the mechanized body model, the self as mind is separate from and above the experience of the body's disease state; and, the pain associated with the disease state, as experienced by the patient, is imposed from outside by the damaged or broken body part. The ultimate impact of this model upon the patient is fragmentation, both in terms of the patient's personhood and relationship to a lived context. For the mechanized body, the meaning of the disease is confined simply or exclusively to the defective or impaired body part. The result of this fragmentation is alienation and estrangement of the diseased body part both from the patient's self and from the patient's life-world. Moreover, the physician generally provides the meaning for the patient's disease state, especially in terms of body parts, as a dysfunction of the body-machine. Unless the diseased body part is cured, the physician has failed and cannot heal the patient; for healing is equated with curing the diseased body part.

Certainly the manipulability of the mechanized body is important for addressing the material issues, such as pain, associated with disease; but it is inadequate for understanding the suffering associated with the patient's illness. An important question that the physician must address is: Why does *this* patient suffer? The answer revolves around the meaning the patient attaches to illness. It is the patient as an embodied person who provides the meaning of the illness and suffering rather than the physician or the medical profession. That meaning is situated in terms of the disruption in the patient's life-world and the meaning structure associated with it; for illness is not simply a diseased body part isolated from the patient's self or life-world. The aim of the healthcare system, including physicians, should not be confined to curing the patient's diseased part but should also extend to helping the patient resolve the disruption in his or her life-world and the anxiety associated with suffering from an illness. This can only be achieved by taking into account the meaning attached to illness and suffering by the patient.

The physician enters the patient's world of illness and suffering and what it means through listening to the patient's illness narrative. Arthur Kleinman has championed the importance of the patient's narrative and the responsibility of the physician to take it into account, during the healing process: "The work of the [healthcare] practitioner includes the sensitive solicitation of the patient's and the family's stories of the illness."[32] The meaning that a patient attaches to illness and suffering, especially chronic or terminal illness, is critical for the healing process and that meaning is accessible through the patient's illness story. Consequently, it is imperative that the physician take seriously this story when diagnosing and treating the patient: "narrative medicine can give physicians and surgeons the skills, methods, and texts to learn how to imbue the facts and objects of health and illness with their consequences and meanings for individual patients and physicians."[33]

I would like to illustrate the impact these two models of the body on the patient's experience and meaning of illness, with a discussion of Frank's illness narrative as recorded in his book *At the Will of the Body*. He begins the chapter, entitled "The Body as Territory and as Wonder", with the words spoken to him by the physician initially testing Frank for the presence of cancer. According to Frank the physician claimed that the test results indicated that "This will have to be investigated."[34] Frank correctly assesses that the word 'this' was not addressed to Frank as a person but to the body part that was a disease candidate. Frank then explores two stories concerning the patient's body: one of territory and one of wonder. As territory, the patient's body is generally envisioned as the property of the medical profession. According to Frank, the patient or the patient's body becomes colonized by physicians: "When a person becomes a patient, physicians take over her body, and their understanding of the body separates it from the rest of life."[35] Besides the colonization in which the physician assumes "centre stage", according to Frank, the patient is also disembodied: "the person within my body was sent out into the audience to watch passively."[36] The end result of colonization and passivity is loss of the patient's self. How does the patient regain that self? According to Frank, it is through wonderment at the body.

In contrast to the story of territory, and the mechanized body it assumes, Frank asserts that the approach to the patient's body should be one of wonder. Rather than trying to control the body, especially through the medical profession's attempt to manage the diseased body parts through its technology, Frank tells us that the "[o]ne lesson I have learned from illness is that giving up the idea of control, by either myself or doctors, made me more content."[37] "Wondering at the body," for Frank, "means trusting it and acknowledging its control."[38] Frank does not mean to contrast wonder over and against therapy, but he seeks to reorient the relationship between the two: "wonder is an attitude in which treatment can best proceed."[39] It is through this wonderment at the body that Frank regains his embodiment: "Illness taught me that beyond anything I can do, the body simply is. In the wisdom of my body's being I find myself, over and over again."[40] Through wonderment at the body, Frank realizes that he is an embodied person who brings meaning to his life-world, whether in health or in illness. To reduce the body at any time to a body part is to lose the integrity of lived experience as an embodied person.

At root, the meaning of illness is an ontological issue, i.e., illness involves making possible or articulating a patient's life-world or being-in-the-world. In terms of Heidegger's notion of *Sorge* (care), the meaning-structure of illness as being-in-the world is made possible or articulated with respect to a person's concern as a being thrown into a world that is often strangely unfamiliar or unhomelike (*Unheimlich*).[41] This is certainly the case, when a person is diagnosed with a fatal illness or must live with a debilitating illness. As an embodied person, the patient comes to know the authentic and genuine self as limited and finite, especially in the face of death or chronic illness.[42] The face of death or illness and the anxiety (*Angst*) over them are the bases of the patient's *life*-world or *being*-in-the-world. By resolving the anxiety surrounding the patient's illness through reestablishing the homelikeness (*Heimlichkeit*) of the patient's world, the patient is healed even though the diseased body part is not cured. Physicians must learn to utilize effectively in the healing process the patient's anxious care about bodily existence.

5.   Conclusion

In modern Western medicine, the patient's body is often perceived as a material object that can be reduced to a system of physical parts. The patient is viewed as a machine composed of individual body parts, which can be fixed or exchanged with new parts, when broken. By reducing the patient's body to an assemblage of body parts, the patient *qua* person vanishes. Such a model of the patient's body has had a profound impact on the patient-physician relationship. Physicians are mechanics or technicians, whose clinical gaze is often focused exclusively on the diseased body part and not on the patient as a whole. Modern technology has played a critical role in the development of this model of the patient's body and in the transformation of the patient-physician relationship, by providing the necessary instrumentation and techniques for reducing the patient to a mechanized body. Alternative models have been proposed to account for the patient's body, models that attempt to capture the wholeness of the patient as an embodied person. The phenomenological model of the patient as embodied person reclaims this wholeness as a significant component of the patient's experience of illness. Specifically the patient's body is embedded in a life-world, composed of the patient's everyday bodily experience within a lived context. According to this model the patient is an embodied person, in whom the body and self influence the behaviour and state of each other, in a reciprocal fashion. Labouring under this model, the physician cares for the patient's health through an empathetic clinical gaze, in which the physician becomes aware of the impact illness has upon the patient's daily life, including losses of wholeness, certainty, control, freedom to act, and the familiar world. Finally, these two models of the body have a profound impact on the patient's interpretation of illness. For the mechanized body the medical profession supplies the meaning for the patient's diseased part, while for the embodied person the patient supplies meaning in terms of a disrupted life-world. The question facing us today is whether it is too late to humanize the mechanized body in terms of the embodied person, in order to address the crisis of care facing modern medical practice.

Notes

[1] An important assumption underlying work on the medical body is Drew Leder's notion of a "positive feedback loop" between a culture and its conception of the body: "The body's practices and self-interpretations are always already shaped by culture. Conversely, culture is always shaped out of the stuff of bodies, arising in response to corporeal needs and desires." Drew Leder, *The Absent Body* (Chicago: University of Chicago Press, 1990), 151.

[2] Harriet Beinfield and Efrem Korngold, *Between Heaven and Earth: A Guide to Chinese Medicine* (New York: Ballatine Books, 1991), 38.

[3] Although phenomenology may appear to be incommensurable with more analytic traditions in philosophy, there are important connections between them. See Leder, 155.

[4] René Descartes, *The World and Other Writings*, ed. and trans. Stephen Gaukroger (Cambridge: Cambridge University Press, 1998), 99.

[5] Leder, 146.

[6] Archibald Pitcairn, *The Works of Dr. Archibald Pitcairn* (London: F. Noble, 1715), 14, quoted in Theodore Brown, *The Mechanical Philosophy and the 'Animal Oeconomy'* (New York: Arno Press, 1981), 216.

[7] Fredrik Svenaeus, *The Hermeneutics of Medicine and the Phenomenology of Health: Steps Towards a Philosophy of Medical Practice* (Boston, Kluwer, 2000), 49.

[8] The notions of self and person, although not identical, are taken as similar and unproblematic for the present discussion. For further discussion of the self, especially in terms of phenomenology, see Richard M. Zaner, *The Context of Self: A Phenomenological Inquiry Using Medicine as a Clue* (Athens, OH: Ohio University Press, 1981).

[9] Alasdair MacIntyre, "Medicine Aimed at the Care of Persons Rather than What . . .?", in *Changing Values in Medicine*, ed. Eric J. Cassell and Mark Siegler (United Publications of America, 1979), 83-96, 90.

[10] Ian R. McWhinney, "Medical Knowledge and the Rise of Technology," *Journal of Medicine and Philosophy* 3 (1978): 293-304, 299.

[11] Stanley J. Reiser, *Medicine and the Reign of Technology* (Cambridge: Cambridge University Press, 1978), ix.

[12] Michael D. Bayles, "Physicians as Body Mechanics," in *Concepts of Health and Disease: Interdisciplinary Perspectives* ed. Arthur C. Caplan, H. Tristram Engelhardt, Jr., and James J. McCartney (Reading, MA: Addison-Wesley, 1981), 665-675, 665. Bayles eventually does critique the analogy between auto mechanic and physician and argues that the patient-physician relationship should be founded on a fiduciary model.

[13] S. Kay Toombs, *The Meaning of Illness: A Phenomenological Account of the Different Perspectives of the Physician and Patient* (Boston: Kluwer, 1993), 78-79.

[14] Ibid., 94.

[15] Candace B. Pert, *Molecules of Emotion: The Science Behind Mind-Body Medicine* (New York: Simon & Schuster, 1997), 130.

[16] Alan E. Guttmacher and Francis S. Collins, "Genomic Medicine–A Primer," *New England Journal of Medicine* 347 (2002): 1512-1520.

[17] Richard J. Baron, "An Introduction to Medical Phenomenology: I Can't Hear You While I'm Listening," *Annals of Internal Medicine* 103 (1985): 606-611.

[18] Baron, 609.

[19] Svenaeus, 84.

[20] Michael A. Schwartz and Osborne Wiggins, "Science, Humanism, and the Nature of Medical Practice: A Phenomenological View," *Perspectives in Biology and Medicine* 28 (1985), 341.

[21] Eliot Deutsch, "The Concept of the Body," in *Self as Body in Asian Theory and Practice*, ed. Thomas P. Kasulis (Albany, NY: SUNY Press, 1993), 5.

[22] Toombs, 52.

[23] Leder makes a similar point: "[skills and habits] are enveloped within the structure of the taken-for-granted body from which I in*habit* the world." Leder, 32.

[24] Toombs, 81.

[25] For further discussion on the "ecstatic body", see Leder, *The Absent Body*, 11-35.

[26] Svenaeus, 109.

[27] For further discussion of uncanniness, see Zaner, 47-66.

[28] Toombs, 100.

[29] Ibid., 90-8.

[30] Stephen L. Daniel, "The Patient as Text: A Model of Clinical Hermeneutics," *Theoretical Medicine* 7 (1986): 195-210.

[31] Svenaeus, 139.

[32] Arthur Kleinman, *The Illness Narratives: Suffering, Healing and the Human Condition* (New York: Basic Book, 1988), 10.

[33] Rita Charon, "Narrative Medicine: A Model for Empathy, Reflection, Profession, and Trust," *Journal of the American Medical Association* 286 (2001), 1898.

[34] Arthur W. Frank, *At the Will of the Body: Reflections on Illness* (Boston: Houghton Mifflin, 2002), 50.

[35] Ibid., 52.

[36] Ibid., 53.

[37] Ibid., 59.

[38] Ibid.

[39] Ibid.

[40] Ibid., 63

[41] For further discussion of unhomelikeness and homelikeness, see Svenaeus, 90-100.

[42] See Leder for a similar discussion but in terms of the "dys-appearing body", 69-99.

Bibliography

Baron, Richard J. "An Introduction to Medical Phenomenology: I Can't Hear You While I'm Listening," *Annals of Internal Medicine* 103 (1985): 606-611.

Bayles, Michael D. "Physicians as Body Mechanics," in *Concepts of Health and Disease: Interdisciplinary Perspectives*. Ed. Arthur C. Caplan, H. Tristram Engelhardt, Jr., and James J. McCartney, 665-75. Reading, MA: Addison-Wesley, 1981.

Beinfield Harriet and Efrem Korngold, *Between Heaven and Earth: A Guide to Chinese Medicine*. New York: Ballatine Books, 1991.

Brown, Theodore. *The Mechanical Philosophy and the 'Animal Oeconomy'*. New York: Arno Press, 1981.

Charon, Rita. "Narrative Medicine: A Model for Empathy, Reflection, Profession, and Trust," *Journal of the American Medical Association* 286 (2001): 1897-1902.

Daniel, Stephen L. "The Patient as Text: A Model of Clinical Hermeneutics," *Theoretical Medicine* 7 (1986): 195-210.

Descartes, René. *The World and Other Writings*, ed. and trans. Stephen Gaukroger. Cambridge: Cambridge University Press, 1998.

Deutsch, Eliot. "The Concept of the Body," in *Self as Body in Asian Theory and Practice*. Ed. Thomas P. Kasulis, 5-19. Albany, NY: SUNY Press, 1993.

Frank, Arthur W. *At the Will of the Body: Reflections on Illness*. Boston: Houghton Mifflin, 2002.

Guttmacher, Alan E. and Francis S. Collins, "Genomic Medicine–A Primer," *New England Journal of Medicine* 347 (2002): 1512-1520.

Kleinman, Arthur. *The Illness Narratives: Suffering, Healing and the Human Condition*. New York: Basic Book, 1988.

Leder, Drew. *The Absent Body*. Chicago: University of Chicago Press, 1990.

McWhinney, Ian R. "Medical Knowledge and the Rise of Technology," *Journal of Medicine and Philosophy* 3 (1978): 293-304.

Pert, Candace B. *Molecules of Emotion: The Science Behind Mind-Body Medicine*. New York: Simon & Schuster, 1997.

Reiser, Stanley J. *Medicine and the Reign of Technology*. Cambridge: Cambridge University Press, 1978.

Schwartz, Michael A. and Osborne Wiggins, "Science, Humanism, and the Nature of Medical Practice: A Phenomenological View," *Perspectives in Biology and Medicine* 28 (1985): 331-361.

Svenaeus, Fredrik. *The Hermeneutics of Medicine and the Phenomenology of Health: Steps Towards a Philosophy of Medical Practice.* Boston, Kluwer, 2000.

Toombs, S. Kay. *The Meaning of Illness: A Phenomenological Account of the Different Perspectives of the Physician and Patient.* Boston: Kluwer, 1993.

Zaner, Richard M. *The Context of Self: A Phenomenological Inquiry Using Medicine as a Clue.* Athens, OH: Ohio University Press, 1981.

Acknowledgement

This paper was supported in part by funds from the Baylor University Research Committee and by a Baylor University Summer Sabbatical Award.

Part 2

**Representations of Health, Illness, and Disease:
Personal, Public and Institutional Perspectives**

Mothers and Madness: The Media Representation of Postpartum Psychosis

Nicola Goc

The dominant media narrative of postpartum psychosis is as a judicial narrative. From the media's perspective postpartum psychosis only has currency, and therefore newsworthiness, when it is seen as essential to a reading of the court discourse of a mother defending a charge of infanticide or child murder. Beyond the rigid constraints of the courtroom discourse, deconstructed into a court reportage of infanticide, there is little media discourse on postpartum psychosis. The media narrative is driven by the desire to make sense of an abhorrent criminal act rather than to bring to the public an attempt to make sense of a mental illness. It aims to reassure its readers that the act of a mother murdering her child is the result of the individual woman's psychosis – it does not attempt a discourse on the role of society in infanticide. This simplistic discourse reassures readers that family life and the structure of the community is under no threat. Murdering mothers are an aberration, and postpartum psychosis is the demon. But what happens when the madness defence fails? Within the judicial postpartum discourse another dominant narrative is inevitably threaded – popular assumptions of the nature of motherhood.

Mass media informs the public about a multitude of social issues, including mental health and deviance, and in so doing serves as an important reference point for our definition of the sane and the insane, the normal and the abnormal, the good and the bad, the acceptable and the unacceptable, the legal and the illegal. A large percentage of news text is given over to deviance discourses and this representation is inextricably linked to the media's role in informing public policy. The news media claims to establish a discursive space for public deliberations of social issues, yet this space is firmly under their control. The rigid construction of news texts, dictated by imperatives that adhere to a news-making formula, does not allow for significant public input or for a contextual understanding of social issues beyond the immediate narratives of an individual news events. In terms of mental health issues the news construct predominantly dichotomises mental illness into a deviance discourse.

Postpartum depressive illnesses are not uncommon - postpartum depression affects more than one in ten women and one in every 600 women experience a psychosis.[1] Women are more vulnerable to psychosis in the post-birth period than at any other time during the female life cycle. In the first thirty days after birth a woman is 21.7 times more likely to develop psychosis than in the two-year period prior to childbirth. Because postpartum psychosis frequently represents a bipolar spectrum disorder, mood stabilisation and antipsychotic intervention are often necessary. Postpartum psychosis is associated with hallucinations and delusional beliefs, often about the infant, and is a psychiatric emergency requiring hospitalisation. The mother must be evaluated and the family informed of the potential dangers of infanticide impulses. This is the personal drama that plants the seed of sensationalised journalism. In media terms, the cogent fact that the majority of women suffering from postpartum psychosis do not harm their children is from this point ignored.

Despite considerable research there is still no clear medical consensus on what causes postpartum psychosis and how it should be treated. Add to this a dearth of references for the legal and medical professions on the subject of mothers with postpartum psychosis who kill their children and the way is left open for the news media to restrict its discourse to judicial and infanticide narratives of the "Mad Mother Kills Baby" paradigm and to speculate and posit opinion as fact. Media attention rarely moves beyond sensationalised infanticide reportage. While there is no doubt that the recent high profile media cases of Andrea Yates, Melissa Drexler ("The Prom Mom"), Paula Sims, Angela Cannings, Kathleen Folbigg and others have increased public awareness, the focus continues to be on the high drama of infanticide and judicial discourses. In terms of media representation and media analysis of postpartum psychosis the topic is predominantly restricted to a judicial analysis. Rarely does the subject of postpartum psychosis, or the more common and milder postpartum depression, receive news coverage beyond the infanticide discourse. Most people outside of the mental health profession, when thinking of postpartum psychosis, think of women as protagonists in a judicial news discourse. Through media narrative, postpartum psychosis has become inextricably linked to infanticide in the public's mind.

Journalism plays a central role in the formation of public opinion. By adhering to a rigid news-making formula that focuses on sensational and emotive aspects of mental illness, and in this case postpartum psychosis, no room is left for a contextual understanding of the medical and social issues beyond the immediate news narrative. The news construct dichotomises mental illness into a deviance discourse and pejorative headlines abound, as these Australian examples illustrate:

"Murder in the Nursery," *Daily Telegraph*, (Sydney), 23 May 2003, p.5.
"Sick Mother Killed Baby," *Herald Sun* (Melbourne), 1 July 1997, p.9.

"Child-killer mum goes free," *The Mercury*, (Hobart), 5 July 1997, p.6.

"Baby Kill Mum Freed," *Herald Sun*, (Melbourne), 5 July 1997, p.3.

This should not come as a surprise. Ward's 1997 investigation into United Kingdom newspaper coverage of mental health-related stories examined 1035 articles and found that "almost half of the coverage related to violence and crime" and that "negative items were given greater prominence."[2] A discourse that accentuates the negatives and refracts the complexities of such issues as postpartum psychosis into a judicial discourse reduces the public's understanding of the issue and affects the individual's capacity to make informed decisions. Ward's report also found that articles providing advice and guidance on mental health subjects accounted for less than eight per cent of the coverage. Within this highly-charged news reportage information is reduced to an adversarial judicial discourse where knowledge becomes "evidence" to be scrutinised, rejected or accepted, tailored and reconstructed in terms of a legal paradigm and then disseminated through the news rubric of court reportage. Dr Park Dietz, a prominent Californian forensic psychiatrist who was an expert witness for the prosecution in the Andrea Yates case, says "psychiatric expert witnesses are fixtures of the criminal justice system today and nowhere more so than in trials involving pleas of insanity to explain and excuse a crime."[3]

One journalist who has attempted to redress the balance in the reportage of postpartum psychosis within the judicial paradigm is British journalist Clare Dyer, who writes for *The Guardian* and *The British Medical Journal*. When a woman was charged with murdering three of her children and the attempted murder of a fourth in 2002 Dyer wrote:

Last week an unnamed woman was bailed on charges of murdering three of her children and the attempted murder of a fourth. Yet the media debate seems to focus on only two possibilities: murder or cot death. That may have been understandable in the context of the Clark and Cannings cases, because neither raised infanticide as a defence. Both insisted they had not killed their babies. But now that the verdicts have been delivered, their murder convictions – the only ones open to the juries if they were sure the babies died at their mothers' hands – should not obscure the fact that there is another alternative; a loving mother can kill her baby and yet not be responsible for that baby's death.[4]

In the case of Angela Cannings, Dyer reported her belief that the "most obvious explanation – one which was never put before the judge or jury – is that she acted while in the grip of a severe post-partum depression." Judge Mrs Justice Hallet also believed Cannings killed her children when suffering from postpartum depression or psychosis. In her summation, Justice Hallet told Cannings:

> It's no coincidence, in my view, that you committed these acts in the weeks after their births. It is not my decision when you will be released, but I intend to make it known in my remarks that in my view you will never be a threat to anyone in future.[5]

Clare Dyer interprets these comments as Justice Hallet saying Cannings should have been convicted of the lesser crime of infanticide – the killing by a mother of her own child under the age of one year. Dyer's alternative viewpoint is a rarity in the press discourse on infanticide.

When Andrea Yates killed her five children on a Texas summer morning in June 2001 the media world-wide was conducting a public trial long before she had her day in court. As Yates was being transported in handcuffs in the back of a police car to the police station a Houston radio-talk-show host, "who had just heard the gruesome news, began railing about how a horrible thing had happened in Houston, how a 'bitch' had killed her kids."[6] The policeman driving the vehicle, Frank Stumpo, looked in his rear-view mirror at Yates.

> She was looking out the window, and this guy was just ripping her apart, saying, "Let's just shoot her," Stumpo recalled to NEWSWEEK. "It was the only time I saw her display any emotion. Her lip was quivering. I said to her, "you're a celebrity."[7]

From the outset public opinion drove the news discourse and the central question was is she mad or is she bad? While Yates waited in the Harris County gaol's psychiatric unit, after pleading not guilty by reason of insanity, the news media was putting on trial the defence of postpartum psychosis. Within hours of the news of the killings KPRC, a Houston TV station, opened a website discussion forum with the question: "If Yates had postpartum depression should her penalty be lessened?" Within four days the site had run to 37 pages and among the hundreds of messages left, the calls for Yates' execution by lethal injection outnumbered those against it by approximately 15 to 1.[8] Two comments from another news forum website, FreeRepublic.com, on 25 June 2001, reflected the general tone of the public discourse:

> "Crazy or not this post-partum stuff looks like one huge cop out to excuse 5 MURDERS."
> "The situation is that she KILLED her children. Her children were not killed by someone else. I do not understand why anyone would want to go easy on a woman who KILLED her own children for any reason. She, in Hannibal Lecter fashion, should be locked up and studied. No excuses for a murderer of 5 children."[9]

Postpartum psychosis, in combination with social isolation, were critical factors in Yates' case. Yates had attempted suicide several times when suffering postpartum depression after the birth of previous children. Andrea Yates had five children under the age of seven, the youngest six months old. Yates was prescribed a cocktail of anti-psychotic and anti-depressive drugs including Haldol, commonly used to treat schizophrenia, and Wellbutrin, and had made the decision to stop taking the medication just prior to killing her children. Dr Park Dietz, called by the state of Texas as a rebuttal witness, said Yates suffered from a severe mental illness at the time she drowned her five children, but that she knew her actions were wrong.[10] Dietz "thought Yates was probably suffering from schizophrenia" but because under US law for an insanity defence to be successful the defence must be able to prove that the defendant did not know that her/his actions were wrong, Yates' insanity plea failed.

The Yates case put the public spotlight on postpartum psychosis as never before, but still the spotlight remained firmly upon the punitive judicial narrative. With the surfeit of text, image, audio and internet material, only a small proportion of media space was given over to an informative discourse on postpartum psychosis and its impact on families and society. The theme running through the news texts was the concomitant dualistic representation and analysis of mothers who kill their children, within the framework of madness versus badness. Eighteen months after the Yates tragedy a feature article "Moms who kill – when depression turns deadly" in *Psychology Today,* written by Mark Levy, Deborah Sanders and Stacy Sabraw, told its readers

> The focus of a lot of media attention recently, this illness gained a voice largely due to the story of Andrea Yates, the woman found guilty of drowning her five children in a bathtub in Texas last year. Yates, who has a long history of mental illness, confessed to jurors that Satan had ordered her to kill her children. Though diagnosed with postpartum

psychosis, she was judged capable of discerning right from
wrong and sentenced to life in prison.

Despite the sensationalised heading this largely informative magazine
article told readers that despite considerable research into the nature of
postpartum mood disorders, there is "still no clear medical consensus on
what causes it and how it should be treated."

> If the 'baby blues' persist, depression can escalate to
> dangerous levels, influencing some women to experience
> psychosis and - in rare and tragic cases - to kill their
> offspring.[11]

When the Andrea Yates hard news discourse moved momentarily
away from the judicial sphere it stepped straight into a global discourse on
motherhood and became the subject of an emotive, opinion-driven media
debate about good versus bad mothers. At one end of the spectrum there
was Bernadette Galiano's *Cornell Review* editorial:

> Andrea Yates will be eligible for parole in 40 years, but
> her five children will still be dead. Although the jury found
> her guilty of murder, Andrea Yates has been portrayed as
> the victim in this horrific crime. She has become the poster
> child of postpartum depression. [12]

At the other end of the spectrum Anna Quindlen's *Newsweek*
article "Playing God on no Sleep - Isn't motherhood grand? Do you want
the real answer or the official Hallmark-card version?" moved beyond the
madness/badness dichotomy to examine modern motherhood and to
suggest that society itself may play a significant part in such tragedies.[13]
Quindlen wrote that the "insidious cult of motherhood" is summed up by
the psychic weight of the sampler displayed on the wall of her general
practitioner's waiting room: "God could not be everywhere so he made
mothers." Quindlen wrote:

> We are meant to be all things to small people, surrounded
> by bromides and soppy verse and smiling strangers who
> talk about how lucky we are. And we are lucky. My
> children have been the making of me as a human being,
> which does not mean they have not sometimes been an
> overwhelming and mind-boggling responsibility. That last
> is the love that dare not speak its name, the love that is
> fraught with fear and fatigue and inevitable resentment.
> But between the women who cannot have children and

sometimes stare at our double strollers grief-stricken, and
the grandmothers who make raising eight or 10 sound like
a snap and insist we micromanage and overanalyze, there
is no leave to talk about the dark side of being a surrogate
deity, omniscient and out of milk all at the same time.

She told readers that she had read with "horrified fascination" the story
of Andrea Yates:

A onetime nurse suffering from postpartum depression
who apparently spent a recent morning drowning her five
children in the bathtub.
There is a part of my mind that imagines the baby, her
starfish hands pink beneath the water, or the biggest boy
fighting back, all wiry arms and legs, and then veers
sharply away, aghast, appalled.

Quindlen, as a journalist and mother of young children, was able to look
beyond the madness/badness judicial paradigm and write about the
broader social issues of the pressures of modern-day motherhood and
examine where postpartum psychosis might fit within this much more
complex paradigm. In looking for answers, or at least in establishing a
discourse in which Andrea Yates' actions could be examined beyond the
judicial paradigm, she wrote candidly of the compounded stresses of a
sleep-deprived mother coping with the incessant demands of toddlers and
babies.

Every mother I've asked about the Yates case has the same
reaction. She's appalled; she's aghast. And then she gets
this look. And the look says that at some forbidden level
she understands. The looks say that there are two very
different kinds of horror here. There is the unimaginable
idea of the killings. And then there is the entirely
imaginable idea of going quietly bonkers in the house with
five kids under the age of seven.

Quindlen discussed her own first-hand experience of motherhood in the
twenty-first century where women are isolated from traditional support
networks, telling readers "the weight was not always so heavy" and once
the responsibility was spread around extended families, even entire
towns. She brought sociologist Jessie Bernard into the discourse:

The way we institutionalise motherhood in our society
assigning sole responsibility for child care to the mother,

cutting her off from the easy help of others in an isolated
household, requiring round-the-clock tender, loving care,
and making such care her exclusive activity – is not only
new and unique, but not even a good way for either
women or – if we accept as a criterion the amount of
maternal warmth shown - for children. It may, in fact, be
the worst.

Journalist Michael Duffy responded to Quindlen's article on
Andrea Yates with an attack on what he saw as the US media's penchant
for blaming infanticide on the oppression of mothers. He told readers of
Sydney's *The Daily Telegraph* "basically, some US middle-class feminists
have decided to use the murders to further their argument that motherhood
equals oppression."[14]

Feminism might have changed the way most of us think
and act, but the urge to think of men and women
differently still runs deep. We are seeing this in the
reactions to Andrea Yates killing her five children in
America. The simple fact is that Yates was crazy, and if
she was a man, I suspect, we would just accept that as fact.
Yet in Yates's case, there have been all sorts of attempts to
'explain' what she did by reference to post-natal
depression, the pressures of motherhood, the medication
she had just come off, possession by the devil, and so on.
She is a woman, you see, and while we expect many men
to act badly, even to their own children, it is unnatural for
a woman to do so.

The *London Spectator's* Mark Steyn responded to Quindlen in
similar vein asking readers: "What do you have to do to get bad press
these days?" He said "by comparison with the lives of their grandmothers
and great-grand-mothers, women today enjoy a Hallmark greeting-card
version of motherhood":

Though life's a bitch (for female journalists) with the job
and the school-run and collecting 'em from day care and
picking up takeaway on the way home, the average woman
cares for fewer kids and fewer aged demanding relatives,
has more mechanical assistance and more mobility, and
does less physical labour and housework than any
generation in human history. But boomer narcissism
knows no bounds. So, for the new generation of sob

sisters, infanticide is an understandable by-product of the burdens of contemporary lifestyle.
Sometimes people will go mad and do evil things.
To try to use such events to further one's own cause is dishonest and potentially dangerous. It would be tragic if large numbers of women with post-natal depression came to view themselves as a potential Andrea Yates. [15]

Australian journalist Janet Albrechtsen's response to this global media postpartum psychosis debate returned to the judicial paradigm with the biological determinism argument, telling her readers that "playing the biology card is dangerous".[16]

If women argue raging hormones caused them to kill, men might argue raging testosterone caused them to rape. If women want special dispensations for hormone imbalance in the courtroom, employers might impose special conditions for hormone imbalance in the workplace.

Albrechtsen called for the scrapping of infanticide laws which exist in many countries including Australia and the United Kingdom. "Scrapping infanticide laws would send a message that women cannot trade on frailty," she said. According to Albrechtsen infanticide laws transform a woman's badness into madness, much in the way Shakespeare transformed Lady Macbeth's badness into madness when she spoke of dashing her child's brains out.

Infanticide laws achieve the same result. A mother who kills a child under the age of one may be charged with the lesser offence of infanticide or can rely on the defence of infanticide. These laws allow a mother to escape criminal responsibility if childbirth or breastfeeding has left 'the balance of her mind disturbed'. The NSW [New South Wales] Law reform Commission found that courts and medical experts do not generally require proof of a severe or persisting psychiatric disorder. And, remarkably, the mother doesn't have to show her disturbed mind caused her to kill her child.
In 1999, Sydney woman Karen Diana Pope drowned her fully clothed three-month-old daughter Rachel in a baby bath. Earlier this year she pleaded guilty to infanticide and walked free. If insane, Pope should have relied on the insanity defence to the original charge of murder. Instead,

our lax laws of infanticide allow bad choices such as hers
to be written off as momentary lapses of judgement.
A Victorian Law Reform Commission study revealed that
those found guilty of infanticide rarely go to jail and some
women claiming postnatal depression are not even
prosecuted. By contrast, last year Texan woman Andrea
Yates was sentenced to 40 years' jail for murdering her
five young children by drowning them, one by one, in the
bathtub of her home. In the absence of infanticide-type
laws, Yates tried to argue insanity. The heavier burden of
the insanity defence meant she failed.
MANY called Yates's conviction a tragedy. A child dying
of leukaemia is a tragedy. Yates made a choice. She made
that same choice five times, not changing her mind even as
her eldest boy gasped, 'I'm sorry' while she drowned him.

In response to Albrechtsen's article, Associate Professor Anne
Buist, Director of the Australian National Postnatal Depression Program,
said the article showed "no understanding of the key issues that brought
about the alternative of an infanticide charge to murder."[17]

This stems from an historical attempt to explain a marked
increase in mental illness in the postpartum period: 1 in
600 women experience a psychosis and more than 1 in 10
women experience postnatal depression. There is little
current evidence that this is hormonal – or at least not
purely hormonal – and we are still researching this area in
order to explain the phenomena in more detail. A vast
majority of women with a mental illness do not harm their
children.

Part of the problem for the poor quality media coverage postpartum
psychosis - and postpartum depression - receive is the lack of a consensus
on its causes and treatment within the medical profession. While postnatal
depression is more common than gestational diabetes, pre-eclampsia and
pre-term delivery, it has received much less attention in contemporary
medical literature, training and clinical practice.[18] The US does not
include postnatal depression as a defence for murder and there is no
formal recognition of postpartum depressive illnesses. The American
Psychiatric Association Diagnosis and Statistical Manual of Mental
Disorders does not include conditions relating to childbirth in its clinical
classification system the DSM-111-R.
This confusion is further exacerbated by the refraction of the news
discourse into multiple social and medical issues. Recently the postpartum

depression news discourse shifted focus onto fathers. A June conference of the Royal Australian and New Zealand College of Psychiatry in Hobart heard that first-time fathers suffered "postnatal blues" after the birth of their child due to poor sexual relations with their partners during pregnancy. "The most powerful predictor of a good psychological outcome for first–time fathers at six months was high sexual satisfaction during pregnancy," Professor John Condon from Flinder's University told the Hobart *Mercury*.[19] Professor Condon was reported as saying that if sex during pregnancy "is robust - the outcome will be good for fathers." This much-publicised finding was one of the few news stories to come out of the conference and is the result of a study of 300 first-time fathers "recruited" during their partner's pregnancy and followed up at three, six and 12 months after the birth of their children. They were, according to Professor Condon, "willing because they felt a lot had been done on post-natal depression in women but no one had looked at blokes." Professor Condon said that analysis of the data showed 25 per cent of men did not suffer postnatal depression and 25 per cent suffered "badly."

Dr Jennifer Kunst says the lack of public understanding of postpartum psychosis compounds the problem and impacts on the number of mothers who do kill their infants. In her clinical work she has been pained to discover that

> ... too often a woman who killed her infant had been turned away by health care professionals, law-enforcement officers, or family members just before the crime, despite her obvious psychiatric disorganisation and violent impulses.[20]

According to Associate Professor Buist a lack of understanding is "what kept the asylums open for many years." She believes this lack of understanding is "probably why the family of Andrea Yates was not able to talk openly about her problems and get the assistance that could have averted this tragedy."[21]

Conclusion

Media texts inform public opinion, which in turn shape public policy. When misinformation, conflicting information, subjective commentary and personal opinion are put forward as fact the public's knowledge is compromised and unsound judicial, medical and welfare decisions are made. In terms of postpartum psychosis it is important that an open discourse finds a discursive space within the news media. As Dr Margaret Spinelli says, education is an important instrument in the treatment of these disorders.[22] While the postpartum psychosis news discourse remains refracted into sensationalised judicial reporting the public will not reach a clearer understanding of the issues and unsound judicial decisions will continue to be made, reacting to superficial and all-too-often uninformed media coverage. University of Houston law professor, David Dow, told the *Houston Chronicle* that the decision by the district attorney to "go for death" in the Andrea Yates case cannot be removed from the context of the unprecedented media coverage the case had generated. "Andrea Yates by any rational measure is not a death-penalty case," Dow said. "I don't think there can be any other explanation other than the high degree of publicity it has gotten." [23]

Journalists have a role to play in the process of change. Public journalism, with its idealistic aims to inform the public; to protect the public from duplicitous or biased journalism; to eschew emotional or slanted reporting; and to raise the credibility of the profession of news reporting, may offer the way ahead.[24] Through the conduit of public journalism the reporter's actions

> ...should try to create the conditions in which the public can learn its business and find solutions to its problems. Public politics, public discussion, public involvement by public-minded citizens – these are the announced goals.

Award-winning investigative journalist Phillip Knightly, who exposed the thalidomide tragedy, recently told an Australian audience "Each individual journalist carries, at any one moment, an unknowable share of the responsibility for what happens next."[25] Journalists have the responsibility to bring to the postpartum psychosis public discourse news reporting that will inform the public, reportage that will lead to finding ways in which to prevent tragedies like that of Andrea Yates and her five young children from ever being repeated.

Notes

[1] Associate Professor Anne Buist, "Media Release: College Statements. Letter to the Editor, The *Australian* 15 November 2002," The Royal Australian and New Zealand College of Psychiatrists Media Release, 15 November 2002.
[2] Catherine Francis, et al., *Mental Health and Illness in the Media*, (Canberra: University of Canberra Press, 2001), 5.
[3] Anastasia Toufexis, "A Conversation with Park Dietz; A psychiatrist's Eye View of Murder and Insanity," *New York Times*, 23 April 2002, sec.F, p.5.
[4] Clare Dyer, "Not guilty as charged," *The Guardian*, 14 May 2002.

[5] Clare Dyer, "Cause of death: unknown," *The Guardian*, 4 February 2003.

[6] Evan Thomas, "Motherhood and Murder," *Newsweek*, 2 July 2001, p.20.

[7] Ibid.

[8] Anna Picard, "Could you too be a killer mummy?" *New Statesman*, 9 July 2001, p.20.

[9] FreeRepublic.com "A Conservative News Forum," 25 June 2001, (16 May 2003). <www.freerepublic.com/forum/a3b37aee045df.htm>.

[10] Dr Park Dietz, quoted in "US woman may face death penalty in postnatal depression case," *Psychminded.co.uk*, 15 March 2002, (23 May 2003). <psychminded.co.uk.html.>

[11] Levy, Mark et al., "Moms who kill when depression turns deadly," *Psychology Today*, December 2002, 60-66.

[12] Bernadette Galiano, Editorial, *Cornell Review*, 27 March 2002.

[13] Anna Quindlen, "Playing God on no sleep – Isn't Motherhood Grand? Do you want the real answer or the official Hallmark-card version?" *Newsweek*, 2 July 2001, p.62.

[14] Michael Duffy, "Tragedy no time for point-scoring," The *Daily Telegraph,* 15 July 2001, p.19.

[15] Mark Steyn, "Mums defend a baby-killer," *London Spectator*, 30 June 2001.

[16] Janet Albrechtsen, "Let's get tough with killer mums," The *Australian*, 13 November 2002, p.13.

[17] Buist, 2002.

[18] Leopold, Kathryn et al., ""Postpartum Depression," *The Female Patient – A Peer Reviewed Journal*, August 1997, (26 April, 2003). <http:// www.obgyn.net/femalepatient/default.asp?page=leopold>.

[19] Margareta Pos, "Post-natal blues don't spare dads, says study," The *Mercury*, May 2003, p.9.

[20] Dr Jennifer Kunst, "Editorial Reviews," *New England Journal of Medicine*, Massachusetts Medical Society, 20 March 2003.

[21] Buist, 2002.

[22] Dr Margaret Spinelli, "Antepartum and Postpartum Depression," The *Journal of Gender-Specific Medicine* 1998, 1 (2): 33-36.

[23] Mike Tolson, "Unequal Justice," *Houston Chronicle*, 10 September 2001.

[24] Rosen, J. et al., *Public Journalism: Theory and Practice*. (Dayton: Kettering Foundation, 1994) p.7.

[25] Phillip Knightly, "Reflections of a Warhorse," The Evatt Foundation Speech, Sydney June 2003, Broadcast ABC Radio National, *The Media Report*, 19 June 2003.

Bibliography

Francis, Catherine, Jane Pirkis, David Dunt and R.Warwick Blood. *Mental Health and Illness in the Media – a Review of the Literature – 2001*. Canberra: Commonwealth Department of Health and Aged Care, 2001.

Rosen, J. and D. Merritt. *Public Journalism: Theory and Practice*. Dayton: Kettering Foundation, 1994.

Spinelli, Margaret G. "Antepartum and Postpartum Depression," The *Journal of Gender-Specific Medicine* 1998, 1 (2): 33-36.

Note on Contributor

Nicola Goc is a lecturer in Journalism and Media Studies at the University of Tasmania. Her postgraduate thesis is on the representation of infanticide in the popular press.

Becoming Disabled Through Sport: Narrative Types, Metaphors and the Reconstruction of Selves

Brett Smith and Andrew C. Sparkes

1.   Introduction

Metaphor, or the means by which one thing is described in terms of something else a ubiquitous and important feature of everyday speech that affects the ways in which people perceive, think, and act.[1] Yet, metaphor is not simply about cognitive patterns of thought and action. It can also be understood as culturally and historically contingent and related to the linguistic structures and forms that are available to individuals. Thus, as El Refaire (2001) notes, metaphors cannot be viewed in isolation from the interests and motivations of the main story told by people and it should be recognised that the "social, historical, and political circumstances can have an important influence on the choice and specification of metaphors."[2]

Similar sentiments seem to inform the work of Low (1994) who points out that metaphors, which are embedded in our culture, are important linguistic resources that people draw on to help make meaning and sense of the world.[3] As such, they are central to the way people compose selves and significantly, they can be both illuminating and restrictive. This understanding of metaphor as a key resource in how people constitute their lives is also embodied. Indeed, metaphors can be generated by the experience of the body as well as culture. Hence, as Low notes, "body metaphors provide a possible solution for the expression of lived experience that can communicate bodily sensation, as well as social, culture and political meaning."[4] In view of all this, researchers might usefully consider analysing the inextricable connection between metaphors, stories, selves, and bodies.

Accordingly, we draw on data from a project that explores the life histories and stories of a small group of men (n=14), who have experienced a spinal cord injury (SCI) through playing the aggressive, contact sport of rugby union football and who now define themselves as disabled. Our intention is to highlight the salient and most common metaphors utilised by the men in the telling of their life stories and to illustrate how, post SCI, these are shaped by three powerful narrative types that circulate in Western cultures. We also consider the implications of this dynamic process for their identity reconstruction as disabled men.

2.   Methodology

Details of the methodology that underpins this project has been described in detail elsewhere so a brief summary is provided.[5] This article focuses on the confidential, thematic, informal, life history interviews conducted with fourteen participants in their homes by the primary investigator (Brett Smith), who acted as an 'active listener' in an attempt to assist the participant to tell their life story in their own way and in their own words. Each participant, none of whom are involved in sport now, was interviewed at least three times, with each interview lasting from two to seven hours. All interviews were tape-recorded and transcribed, and analysed reflexively, utilising multiple forms of narrative analysis. Of specific relevance to this chapter are the holistic analysis of form, and the categorical-form analysis.[6] Our analyses first bring to focus the metaphors used within the restitution narrative. Next, the metaphors associated with the chaos narrative are considered. Finally, the metaphors drawn on in the quest narrative are examined.

3.   Metaphors and the Restitution Narrative

The restitution narrative framed and shaped eleven of the men's life stories. According to Frank (1995), the plot of the restitution narrative has the basic storyline: "Yesterday I was healthy, today I'm sick, but tomorrow I'll be healthy again."[7] For these men, this translates to, "Yesterday I was able-bodied, today I'm disabled, but tomorrow I'll be able-bodied again." This 'master' or metanarrative, we would suggest, has an affinity for the *restored* self and the *entrenched* self that lock the individual into their past body-self relationships and ways of being in the world with the hope that they will return to this state.[8]

Furthermore, for the participants who told restitution narratives, sporting or 'war' metaphors were foregrounded in their stories. These are guiding metaphors in the men's stories of restitution and the construction of self. This is perhaps not surprising given the men's history of participating in sport, a source or domain of practice that seems to actively cultivate and celebrate this metaphorical language while other forms are marginalised and silenced. As has been noted, while sport is *not* war, sporting contexts are redolent with military language.[9] Therefore, on occasions there appears to be a conflation and convergence of the vocabularies of sport and war. Importantly, this privileged and institutionalised struggle language may, in turn, seep into a person's consciousness, becoming a powerful way of talking that helps to frame and shape their self stories.

With respect to the restitution stories told by eleven of the men, the most common metaphorical resource that helped shape their self stories was linked with *a fight to make a comeback*. The 'fight' metaphor with sporting connotations, and the sporting metaphor of a 'comeback', is displayed in the following comments by Phil:

> Brett: What did rugby mean to you?
> Phil: It meant everything. Rugby taught me so much and I'm so glad that I played. I mean, well, it taught me to never stop *fighting*, not to give up even when the odds might be stacked against you, and that a *comeback* is always possible. And I've taken that way of looking at life into how I see disability. I won't stop *fighting* and I'll make a *comeback*, to, y'know, walk again and return to my real self... I won't stop *fighting* until that happens. And it's a man's prerogative to do that, otherwise what type of a man would I be?

The metaphors of the participants' disability experience – related to cultural constructions of gender discussed below – are not confined to sporting struggles. On occasions, fight and comeback metaphors were also connected to medicine. For example, consider the comments by Matthew: "I'll *fight* to make a *comeback* which means walking again and being cured, and medicine will find one, a cure that is. So until one is found, I'll keep *fighting*. What else can I do?"

In restitution, another common metaphor that strongly shaped the participants senses of self involved the terms *winning is being cured of disability*. For example, framed by the demands of the restitution narrative for themes relating to the technology of a biomedical cure and the restorable body-self, Paul made a narrative connection to the metaphorical struggle associated with winning the war and being cured of disability:

> Brett: Can you tell me what you do during the day?
> Mark: My day to day existence isn't anything really to talk about. Why? Because I really don't do a lot. And my life is really on hold until a cure is found. So, it's about not giving in. It's about *beating* this. And *winning* is being cured of disability and walking again. To be myself.

A further prevalent metaphorical strand in all the eleven men's stories was one where disability and impairment was defined as an *enemy that must be beaten*. This is evident, for example, in the following comments by Rob:

> Rugby isn't a game for wimps. Very physical...And I think that what I learnt from playing was that you never go into something thinking that you can be *beaten*. So, y'see, that's how I look at my situation now ... Because I

want to walk again, and I think that I will, the situation is
clear. Disability for me is an *enemy* that must be *beaten* ...
And I think that to look at it any other way wouldn't be
very manly ... and there would be too much emotional
stuff involved. So it's better to keep a clear head and just
get on with it. Wait until the doctors find a cure, and not
let myself be *beaten*.

Several metaphors were foregrounded in all the men's stories of
restitution, including disability and impairment as an enemy that must be
beaten, being cured of disability as a victory, and the fight to make a
comeback. In addition, the metaphor *the body as a battleground* was also
common. For example, the language of battles to regain the body's former
predictability, and attempts to outdistance mortality by rendering disability
transitory through a biomedical model, is displayed by Jacob in the
following comment:

Brett: How do you feel about your body now?
Jacob: I don't like it. It's not who I am, or what I want to
be. It's a *battleground*. I'm always *fighting* it, trying to
regain some control. And I always want more control ...
That's why I say I want to walk. I want to, well, because
it's a long, constant *battle* against the body and trying to
exert control over it, and with doctors and medical
research being the only solution, I can't see me walking
within the next 10 years, but after that, I think people will
be able to cure spinal injury, a cure will be found ... But
in the meantime, I won't shed any tears or reveal any of
my worries. No, I'll *battle* this ... I don't think that's
unusual. It's what real men do.

The comments given above signal the powerful ways in which
metaphors operate within a specific narrative to shape the experiences of
the men we spoke to. Their comments also reveal how these metaphors
and narrative draw on particular models of body, identity, and disability
supplied by the cultures and sub-cultures that people inhabit. Importantly,
these internalised metaphors and the restitution narrative are often taken-
for-granted and used unreflexively. Moreover, despite being coherent and
eminently plausible in that they help make sense of what the people
involved are experiencing, they may be problematic, counterproductive,
and constraining when it comes to reconstructing or restorying new body-
self relationships following a major disruptive life event.

For example, with regard to sport and war metaphors chosen, it
may be argued that storying SCI as a fight, battle, and/or enemy, helps
create, and perpetuates an idealised prototype of a good, medicalised,

recovery story. Yet, as Frank (1995) argues, a problem of this restitution plot "is the obvious but often neglected limitation of the modernist deconstruction of mortality: when it doesn't work any longer, there is no other story to fall back on."[10] When restitution does not work, and when a person can no longer fight to make a comeback, win the war to return to their former body-self, or beat disability and impairment, other stories and metaphors have to be prepared or narrative wreckage will ensue.

Further, years after from the event, the sport and war metaphors chosen by the men is indicative of the cultural resources they currently have at their disposal and the acceptable norms of storytelling that operate in relation to gender. Accordingly, men, and particularly sporting men, in Western cultures are often expected to be stoic in the face of adversity - the 'classic' non-expressive male. For such men, concealing emotions, emotional reticence, and the nondisclosure of emotions, all operate to mask vulnerabilities as part of a control strategy that is a key signifier of hegemonic masculinities. To admit to *not* battling, *not* fighting, and *not* wanting to make a comeback, for example, is to relinquish control and thus to put the masculine self at risk.

Others have also suggested that in specific circumstances and in certain contexts sport and/or military metaphors may be problematic, counterproductive, prohibit change, and constraining to live by. For example, Kleiber and Hutchinson (1999) who, talking about men and SCI, suggest that sport and military metaphors invoke a sense of heroic struggle that can be particularly problematic when it comes to restorying the self after becoming disabled as it links into singular and inherently limiting patterns of masculine behaviour and ideals.[11] Specifically, Western culture loves heroes, and sporting stories in general are replete with heroic metaphors that indicate how men are supposed to override their needs and limitations and learn instead to fight or push onward toward victory over one's body despite disability, illness, pain, fatigue, hardship, danger, or desire. At the same time, breaking down, giving up, not fighting, refusing to make a comeback, being needy, showing fear or weakness, or being sad, are normally sources of shame within hero narratives. However, this heavily gendered plot when operating as a narrative map may be limiting to live by. As Kleiber and Hutchinson argue, portraying recovery as aligning one's actions with those of the physically heroic not only generates "an unrealistic ideal that most individuals cannot live up to, it also directs the course of recovery in personally limiting ways."[12]

That the majority of the men in our study have an affinity for this story many years beyond SCI is not surprising given that Western cultures, and sporting subcultures in particular, treat health and being able-bodied as the 'normal' and 'desirable' condition that people should not only want to have, but ought to have restored when lost. Yet, the combined effect of the restitution narrative, and sport and war metaphors, problematises the ability of participants to narratively reconstruct their sense of self. This can be done, for example, by reducing their access to, and flexibility to engage with, the wider cultural repertoire of stories that are available for synthesis into personal or ontological stories. As such, future possible selves might be ignored and the potential for these men to explore other identities as disabled men is limited.

Of course, this is not to propose that these men should be denied the right and the opportunity to attempt to restore their previous senses of self and achieve their former performance levels following SCI. Likewise, it is not to suggest that they should be denied the opportunity to tell or listen to restitution stories containing sport and war metaphors. Struggle language can be important in developing and maintaining a sense of concrete hope that is associated with restoring the body-self following a disruptive life event. It needs to be acknowledged, however, that problems can arise when people become fixated on one kind of body and sense of self in circumstances where the restitution narrative and its associated metaphors of sport and war are not appropriate. As the words of men make clear, under such circumstances individuals find it hard to remind themselves that alternative body-self narratives might have to be found and told.

4.   Metaphors and the Chaos Narrative

According to Frank (1995), the plot of the *chaos narrative* imagines life never getting better and so it is the opposite of the restitution narrative. Such stories are chaotic in their absence of narrative order and lack of plot. They are anxiety provoking and threatening both for the teller and the listener. Jamie, an ex-dock-yard crane driver who experienced a SCI eight years ago and breathes using a ventilator, was the only person in our sample whose life was, and remains in chaos after SCI. As he volunteered:

> I don't know how I could describe my life. It's, I don't know. Life, it's nothing. I've gone. And, I don't know, then, then I'd say that I quite like looking outside at the garden. I'm nothing. I can't do one thing about my life. It's over.

Following SCI, Jamie's world was and remains unmade. With no narrative map to use as a guide, and with no foreseeable replacement, biographical time stops and the future is perceived as a foregone conclusion. Moreover, the over determination of his situation is extended, or compounded, by the "loss of control of the bowels," "excruciating pain," "a wife that left about seven months after the injury happened," and "the lack of involvement with my three children…who I see once a fortnight." Against such issues, Jamie often drew on different expressions of *choking* to depict his experiences of SCI and everyday life. For instance, in response to being asked, "how would you describe your life now", he replied: "I don't know. Nothing to describe. My life is, is, choking. I'm choking...I'm *suffocating* and there no let up. Day after day. My life is falling away, being *choked* to death."

Another prevalent rhetorical construction of life in chaos, for Jamie, is connected to the imagery of *solid darkness*. When asked, what he thought the future might hold for him, he replied: "I can't see anything. My situation won't change, only worsen. Only get *darker*. It's, it's, *darkness* closing in. All around me. Thick *black*. I'm in *darkness*." Furthermore, in descriptions of living in chaos, *emotional selves* are revealed as *brittle objects*. This is evident in the following comments:

> Brett: How do feel now, so many years after the accident?
> Jamie. I'm not sure. The same I'd say. I was *shattered* by the accident, and I'm still *shattered*. There is nothing left. Everything has *crumbled away* from *underneath* me. It's still *crumbling*. My life has *fallen apart*. I've got nothing. My emotions are *shattered*. No one to turn to. Nothing.

In chaos, for Jamie, another common resource concerning how one may intelligibly talk about and perform embodied emotions is the metaphorical idea that *emotions are entities within a person*. For him:

> I'm *consumed* with these feelings of "What's the point of being here?" I can't answer that. I wish I were even *filled with anger*. But I'm not. Nothing inside me. I'm ... seven second silence] I can't do anything. *Darkness* is *consuming* me. And I can't even move my fingers. What can I do?

The combination of metaphors Jamie draws on operate to help convey and actively compose the disorder, distortion, fragmentation, threat, anguish, uncontrollability, and disconnection from other bodies he feels when living in chaos. As Low (1994) argues, metaphors can provide a flexible, creative, and strategic language for the expression or communication of otherwise senseless and unspeakable suffering and emotion.[13] They also invite others, including the interviewer, to bear witness to the affects and consequences of SCI on one's body-self and life. In this sense, the metaphors Jamie utilises are not just cultural resources for ways of talking, but also embodied performances and a call of the chaotic body.

Having said this, since lived chaos makes reflection impossible, storytelling is difficult for chaotic bodies. Yet, for Jamie, because stories help frame and structure meaning, it might be proposed that metaphor and narrative, act as entrapments in the chaos he tells. That is, rather than working through chaos or keeping chaos at bay, narration and the associated metaphors of choking, darkness, emotional selves as brittle objects, lead to the cyclical experience of chaos: chaos begets chaos; the story goes this way, not that. Further, one's life story may come to be experienced as effectively over when entrapped in chaos, thereby leading to narrative foreclosure. As such, the notion of entrapment within narratives and metaphors of chaos emphasises their constraining aspects and raises the issue of how the chains that bind the chaotic body-self to one particular storyline and set of repetitive metaphors might be loosened or cast aside. For Frank (1995), this partly entails people telling their stories and having them witnessed.[14] Here, opportunities may be created to re-imagine the past and future, develop new relations of reciprocity within a community that affords recognition, and honours the chaotic body without forcing it within cultural preferred plot structures where it should be simply fixed.

5.   Metaphors and the Quest Narrative

In terms of experiencing SCI via sport, *quest stories* meet suffering head on; they accept impairment and disability and seek to *use* it. Just what the quest is may never be wholly clear, but the quest is defined by the person's belief that something is to be gained from the experience. Two of the men in our study told this kind of story about themselves during the interview process.

Within a quest narrative, for both David and Doug, journey metaphors coalesced and were common. As they came to realise a sense of purpose, like Frank (1995) argues, the idea that disability has been, and is, a journey emerges: "The meaning of the journey emerges recursively: the journey is taken in order to find out what sort of journey one has been taking."[15] In particular, for the two men in this study, the most prevalent journey metaphor they used invoked the image of being *reborn*. For example, David, who "virtually grew up at the rugby club" where his father, a headmaster at the local school, was the chairman, often commented: "I've been *reborn*, and have become a much better person due to the injury, and everything that has happened to me on this *journey* that I'm on." Likewise, Doug who before SCI often worked at two jobs, but who now studies part-time and "is a full-time father after splitting amicably from my wife," frequently suggested that, for him, SCI leads to new opportunities and a chance to remake a life that has past:

> Brett: Could you describe where you are in your life now?
> Doug: Well, firstly, as I say, I've been *reborn*. Again, I don't mean in a religious sense. But I've developed a new life and have become a different person I think. Certainly

much more open, and I'm taking a very different *path* and *journey*....Being disabled has been an opportunity to explore myself and develop as a person. Hearing people, including non-disabled, talk about their lives, and knowing that it's not me individually, but a societal issue, including the barriers we face, whether that's access to buildings or equal rights for employment, has helped. Yeah, knowing that it's not me had a major lift, and helped me to change, to be *reborn*.

As these comments suggest, counter-narratives linked with a political narrative and the liberating and empowering potential of the *social model* of disability, which locates disability within society and is concerned with the things that impose restrictions on disabled people, can play a significant role in teaching people how to interpret their own and others' disability experiences. They are also one road to restorying the self over time, re-embodying the self, and developing a more communicative relationship with bodies. Yet, this process of acceptance and engagement, of transcending one's narrative resources, and reconstructing body-self relationships via counter-narratives, is not easy and should not be romanticised. Accordingly, both men acknowledged that these strategies for reconstructing selves are not necessarily useful or pertinent to all people. They also frequently peppered their stories with journey metaphors involving imagery of the *distance travelled* (e.g., advancements) and *difficulties with travelling* (e.g., ups, and downs) that offset what might seem a too-rosy picture of life in wheelchair. Combining these metaphors, Doug noted the following:

> When I look back now on my life, I think I've made a lot of *advancements,* and have *moved forward* since breaking my neck. But, I don't want to paint my life as perfect, because it isn't. Y'see, on the *journey* that I'm on, just like anyone, be they disabled or not, I have *ups* and *downs*, good days, and bad one's. It isn't easy being disabled, and *along the way* there are a lot of problems, such as access issues, still, and new laws need implementing. So, while yes I wouldn't change *back* to who I was before the injury, and I should stress that accepting disability and not wanting to return to your old life isn't an easy thing to get your head around … As I've said, there are lots of *ups* and *downs along the way*, but once you accept it and understand that disability isn't, or shouldn't be a tragedy, then it's a *movement toward* being positive about yourself.

David offers similar reflections:

Brett: How do you feel about your life now?
David. I feel very positive about my life, about myself,
and the *journey* that disabled people are on *toward* being a
valued and accepted group in society. Certainly I've
covered a lot of ground in the years since my injury ...
But, don't get me wrong, there are days when I feel very
shitty about my life, and ... being disabled is about
dealing with the *ups*, and *downs*, and when I just *lose my
way* I realise just how hard it all it is. Y'know, there are
occasions when you feel you've taken a *step back*
because, for example, there are times when I can't get seat
at a restaurant or pop into a hairdresser because they aren't
disability friendly. They just don't realise that it isn't us
that is the problem, but access policies and society as well.
So it isn't a *smooth path* ... And, well, I'm just grateful
that I've had people to *guide* me *along the way* and to
show me that, while yes my life, like anyone's won't be
perfect, disability doesn't necessarily have be a disaster.
And, for me, with the help of others, being injured turned
into a positive experience in which I've been able to
develop myself, love my body, and accept it has
limitations, like all bodies. ... The *advice* and *guidance*
from some disabled people has also helped me deal with
the practical aspects of disability, and learn to understand
the limits of what my body can do and cannot do.

As these comments reveal, David and Doug make narrative
linkages on their respective journeys to a metanarrative of progress and
highlight how, partly via the metaphors associated with *distance travelled*
and *difficulties with travelling*, this complex aspect of journeying is not
without uncertainties, descents, risks, and difficulties. Indeed, the
comments confirm the point that the various structural or access issues
created by society can be experienced as disabling. They also indicate that
they can be restrictive and constraining when it comes to restorying and
re-embodying the self.

Importantly, towards the end of David's statement, he clearly
signals what is, for him, useful in terms of restorying the self and
developing differently valued body-self relationships. That is, people and
the particular stories they tell, as potential guides or narrative maps, can
provide a sense of communal consciousness and legitimacy, that can be
transformative and therapeutic. The journey metaphor involving *guides* is
further reflected in the following comments.

Brett: You've talked a lot about how you've changed, can you tell me more?

Doug: Well, after the accident I was pretty messed up. I never thought at that point that I would be here right now. But, while the *journey* to where I am right now hasn't been easy, I've managed to *turn the road* … One reason for this, and my whole change in who I am … and me not wanting to return to my old self, is to do with the *guidance* people have offered me, and the fact that they listened to me, even when I was in real turmoil … Disabled people, and non-disabled people taught me that disability isn't necessarily the end, and the social view of disability that I was exposed to showed me *a different way* to live, and that it is possible to change yourself, individually and as a group, while also living a great life … As I've said, the problem isn't me per se but largely a societal issue. So in that respect, the *guidance* and *advice* offered to me since becoming disabled has helped me resist the tragic role given to disabled people and the expectation that we all want to walk again, which for me just isn't the case now.

Clearly, for David and Doug, journey metaphors and the quest narrative operate in tandem to shape their post-SCI experiences and their identity construction as disabled men. As the comments above reveal, becoming disabled through sport, for these men, is reframed, with the aid of metaphor, as a challenge and an opening to other ways of being. These comments also signal a *developing* self in action in which the direction of their lives concerns them as well as the character of the self they shape, rather than simply commit to specific prior activities and prior identities.[16] Instead, as the metaphors illuminate, these men commit themselves to growing and developing in the future. When restoring a developing self, the men emphasise reconstructing their ability to shift and change as well as to explore new identities as possibilities emerge.

It would seem, therefore, that for David and Doug, constructing experience partly around the notion of a journey is extremely helpful in terms of their ability to explore different identities and reconstruct different body-self relationships. Indeed, metaphors, such as those connected to a journey, are currently key cultural resources that people may draw upon as a way to mediate a disruption to their life following a traumatic event. That is, the meanings associated with certain metaphors, born of relations within a given culture at a given time, help enable the reconstruction of self. Thus, when life must be reorganised following a disruptive life event, journey metaphors may provide a transforming bridge between the image of the old life and the new one because they help re-frame and re-structure meaning.

With the help of the journey metaphors, David and Doug also seem to suggest that while institutions and environments are not awash with counter-narratives on which to build alternative identities, notions of self, and forms of embodiment, reconstructed self stories may be built by accessing counter-narratives about disability and impairment. This can be achieved, for example, by listening to the stories told by other people, gaining access to a social model story-plot, and having others legitimise this plot. As Nelson (2001) argues, with the help of people who legitimate them, the immediate purpose of a counternarrative is to repair or reconstruct identities that have been damaged by oppression.[17] These stories come into being through a process of on-going engagement with the narratives they resist. In particular, they operate at three levels of resistance: they *refuse*, *repudiate*, and *contest* a master narrative.[18] That said, counternarratives do not spring from the individual mind but are social creations. As such, they often start small, like a seed in the crack of the pavement, but partly via resistance and legitimisation, they are capable of displacing surrounding chunks of concrete as they grow.

Closely linked to these suggestions are those of Swain and French (2000), who pointed out both the therapeutic and transformative possibilities of what they termed an *affirmative model of disability* [19]. Building on the libratory imperative of the social model, this is a non-tragic narrative of disability and impairment which encompasses positive social identities, both individual and collective, for disabled people grounded in the benefits and life experiences of being impaired and disabled. As such, it offers a challenge to the mainstream medicalised stories that people often attempt to fit their lives, and the lives of others into by deviating from standard plots and dominant personal tragedy stories of disability, providing new narratives, and legitimising the replotting of one's own life.

Importantly, over time and stimulated by different circumstances, affirmative stories, metaphors as mediators of disruption, and available counter-narratives, operate in ways that empower David and Doug to alter the trajectories of their lives, infusing their history with new meaning and complexity. This enables them to enhance not only *their* experiences, but also the experiences of *others* as they inhabit different bodies throughout their lives. Thus, for them, SCI becomes defined as an opportunity, albeit a difficult one, to develop both different and differently valued body-self relationships and forms of embodiment.

6.   Conclusion

In this article, an attempt has been made to illuminate the salient and most common metaphors used by fourteen men who have become disabled through sport. We have also aspired to reflect on the possible functions and meanings imparted by these metaphors in relation to the process of reconstructing body-self relationships and identities over time. Despite all the men drawing upon metaphors to help come to understand and impose order on their embodied experiences, important differences were identified in the actual metaphors the men used and the influences of these in reconstructing body-self relationships. We have suggested that the differences are due, in part, to the power of the restitution, chaos, and quest narratives to shape experience in general, and the metaphors used in personal accounts, in particular.

Within the restitution narrative, sport and war metaphors predominate. That these are foregrounded years after a traumatic SCI, is indicative of the narrative resources the men currently have at their disposal, and is testimony to their power in Western cultures, and sporting subcultures in particular. Likewise, the form and plot of the stories told draws from a limited repertoire of cultural narratives that revolve around notions of heroic masculinities and a restored and entrenched self that has its reference point firmly in the restorable body. All of which, makes it difficult to develop different senses of self and explore alternative body metaphors and narratives.

The chaos narrative, in contrast, leads to life being metaphorically storied as choking, in solid darkness, an emotionally brittle object, and its emotions are entities within a person. In this scenario, characterised by narrative wreckage, constructing any sense of self or exploring any other identity becomes extremely problematic as the individual is entrapped in chaos and has limited opportunities for telling stories and relationally constructing different metaphors, which are important aspects in any act of restorying a life. Finally, we suggested that journey metaphors are clustered around and related to the quest narrative, providing the opportunity for body-selves to be restored in ways that link the individual to a sense of progress and counter-narratives associated with the social model of disability and an affirmative story. In combination, whilst neither easy nor straightforward, these enable a developing self and a more communicative body to emerge that is willing to explore different identities and possible selves as the need arises and circumstances allow.

Having described and reflected upon the kinds of metaphors that cluster around and relate to the restitution, chaos, and quest narratives, it needs to be acknowledged that the findings presented here are illuminative rather than definitive. Just what metaphors other disabled men, and women use, how are they performed and understood, and the outcome of the metaphors in terms of the functions and meanings imparted by them, requires further exploration. Moreover, the metaphors identified here were produced in the context of an interactive interview. Whilst such a focus on metaphors used in this context is revealing, research in which metaphor is examined in different contexts and conditions is needed. As we hope to have shown in this chapter, metaphors matter and need to be taken seriously.

Notes

[1] G. Lakoff and M. Johnson, *Philosophy in the Flesh: The Embodied Mind and Its Challenge to Western Thought* (New York: Basic Books, 1999), 118-136.

[2] E. El Refaire, "Metaphors we discriminate by: Naturalised themes in Austrian newspaper articles about asylum seekers," *Journal of Sociolinguistics*, 5, 3 (2001), 368.

[3] S. Low, "Embodied metaphors: Nerves as lived experience," in *Embodiment and experience*, ed. T. Csordas, (Cambridge: Cambridge University Press, 1994), 143.

[4] Ibid.

[5] See A.C. Sparkes and B. Smith, "Sport, spinal cord injury, embodied masculinities and the dilemmas of narrative identity," *Men and Masculinities* 4, 4 (2002): 258-285 and A. Sparkes and B. Smith, "Men, sport, spinal cord injury and narrative time," *Qualitative Research* 3, 2 (2003): 295-320.

[6] A. Lieblich, R. Tuval-Mashiach, and T. Zilber, *Narrative Research* (London: Sage, 1998), 16-17.

[7] A. Frank, *The Wounded Storytelle: Body, Illness and Ethics* (Chicago: The University of Chicago Press, 1995), 77.

[8] K. Charmaz, "Struggling for a self: Identity levels of the chronically ill," in *Research in the Sociology of Health Care: A Research Manual*, ed. J. Roth and P. Conrad, (Greenwich: Connecticut, JAI Press Inc, 1987), 302.

[9] P.F. Murphy, *Studs, Tools, and The Family Jewels: Metaphors Men Live By* (London: The University of Wisconsin Press, 2001), 78.

[10] Frank, 94.

[11] D. Kleiber and S. Hutchinson, "Heroic masculinity in the recovery from spinal cord injury," in *Talking Bodies: Men's Narratives of the Body and Sport*, ed. A. C. Sparkes and M. Silvennoinen (University of Jyvaskyla: SoPhi, 1999), 152.

[12] Ibid., 152.

[13] Low, 143.

[14] Frank, 137-167.

[15] Ibid., 117.

[16] Charmaz, 302-303.

[17] H.L. Nelson, *Damaged identities, narrative repair* (Ithaca: Cornell University Press, 2001), 6.

[18] Ibid., 169-172.

[19] J. Swain and S. French, "Towards an affirmative model of disability," *Disability and Society*, 15,4 (2002), 578-581.

Bibliography

Charmaz, K. "Struggling for a self: Identity levels of the chronically ill." In *Research in the Sociology of Health Care: A Research Manual*, edited by J. Roth and P. Conrad, 283-321. Greenwich: Connecticut, JAI Press Inc, 1987.

El Refaire, E. "Metaphors we discriminate by: Naturalised themes in Austrian newspaper articles about asylum seekers." *Journal of Sociolinguistics* 5, 3 (2001): 352-371.

Frank, A. W. *The Wounded Storyteller. Body, Illness and Ethics.* Chicago: The University of Chicago Press, 1995.

Kleiber, D. and Hutchinson, S. "Heroic masculinity in the recovery from spinal cord injury." In *Talking Bodies: Men's Narratives of the Body and Sport*, edited by A. C. Sparkes and M. Silvennoinen, 135-155. University of Jyvaskyla: SoPhi, 1999.

Lakoff, G. and Johnson, M. *Philosophy in The Flesh*. New York: Basic Books, 1999.

Lieblich, A., Tuval-Mashiach, R. and Zilber, T. *Narrative Research.* London: Sage, 1998.

Low, S. "Embodied metaphors: Nerves as lived experience." In *Embodiment and experience*, edited by T. Csordas, 139-162. Cambridge: Cambridge University Press, 1994.

Murphy, P. F. *Studs, Tools, and The Family Jewels: Metaphors Men Live By*. London: The University of Wisconsin Press, 2001.

Nelson, H. L. *Damaged identities, narrative repair*. Ithaca: Cornell University, 2001.

Smith, B. and Sparkes, A. C. "Men, sport, spinal cord injury and the construction of coherence: narrative practice in action." *Qualitative Research* 2, 2 (2002): 143-171.

Sparkes, A. C. and Smith, B. "Sport, spinal cord injury, embodied masculinities and the dilemmas of narrative identity." *Men and Masculinities* 4, 4 (2002): 258-285.

Sparkes, A. and Smith, B. "Men, sport, spinal cord injury and narrative time." *Qualitative Research* 3, 2 (2003): 295-320.

Swain, J. and French, S. "Towards an affirmative model of disability." *Disability and Society* 15, 4 (2002): 569-582.

Note on Contributors

Brett Smith, PhD is a Research Fellow in the Qualitative Research Unit in the School of Sport and Health Sciences at the University of Exeter. His current research focuses on men, sport and spinal cord injury and he is developing work on the lived experiences of becoming disabled through sport (email: B.M.Smith@exeter.ac.uk).

Andrew C. Sparkes, PhD is Professor of Social Theory and Director of the Qualitative Research Unit in the School of Sport and Health Sciences at the University of Exeter. His research interests are eclectic and include: performing bodies, identities and selves; interrupted body projects and the narrative (re)construction of self; sporting auto/biographies; and marginal lives (email: A.C.Sparkes@exeter.ac.uk).

Bring Me Sunshine:
The Effects of Clown-Doctors on the Mood and Attitudes of Healthcare Staff

Bernie Warren

1   Introduction

In November 2000, Fools for Health began to discuss the implementation of a pilot clown-doctor program on the pediatric unit at Hotel Dieu Grace Hospital in Windsor. The program was launched in the first week of March 2002 and, while not without its initial problems, it is now well established. This chapter looks at the work of clown-doctors on this unit and discusses some of the ways that they affect the mood and attitudes of hospital staff and help to enhance healthcare delivery to 'sick' children and their families.

2   Background and History

Windsor is a city of about 200,000 people. It sits in the shadow of the much larger city of Detroit which, although in the United States, is (on a good day) about a fifteen minute car ride away. Hotel-Dieu Grace Hospital (HDG) provides almost all services for patients under sixteen in the Windsor area, except some day surgeries and long-term in-patient psychiatric care. HDG has a 60+ bed pediatric in-patient unit which provides first line medical and surgical care not only for all the usual suspects of childhood (i.e. upper respiratory and gastrointestinal illnesses, accidental injuries, diabetes, etc.) but also for more problematic conditions (e.g. childhood cancers, cystic fibrosis, rare syndromes/ diseases).

On average children stay for three nights on the in-patient unit although longer stays are not uncommon. If after an initial diagnosis children need more specialised care they are stabilised and then moved to larger centres in London and Toronto, Ontario, and occasionally Detroit. In addition to the in-patient beds there is an outpatient area which accommodates eight day-surgery beds plus daily pediatric clinics, including a pediatric oncology clinic. Recently, the hospital was 'certified' to provide chemotherapy treatments for children with cancer obviating the need for families to drive two or more hours to the London Regional Cancer Centre.

In November 2000, Joyce Chamberlain, the nurse manager of the pediatrics unit expressed an interest in initiating a clown-doctor program. Unfortunately at that time, healthcare delivery in Windsor was being "rationalised", a process which saw four hospitals amalgamated into two Hospital Corporations with specific services allocated to one hospital or the other. It was not until November 2001 that discussions concerning the program resumed. Several months, many meetings and a couple of staff presentations later, we began a six week pilot project in March 2002 and have offered continuous service ever since.

3   Moving Forwards... BB Steps

Clown-doctors are professional performers who are additionally trained in healthcare procedures relevant to the ward they work on. They have worked in hospitals around the world since 1986, although they have a much longer history.[1] Clown-doctors interact with patients, their families and the healthcare team to help promote wellness through the use of music, improvisational play and humour. It is important to note that clown-doctors never work alone and typically work with a partner in what is called a "clown marriage".

The program at 'Peds" began with almost no funding. We barely had enough money to hire one clown. To make the program work, I realised that I would have to volunteer my clown-doctor character Dr. Haven't-a-clue's services twice a week. However, because of my university commitments I needed to find the right partner not only for Haven't-a-clue but also someone mature and skilled enough to act as the "program stupidvisor." I was very fortunate that I had just hired Allyson Grant (Dr. B.B.), a mature, extremely sensitive and talented performer who was just about to graduate from the University of Windsor's BFA Acting program. While her age and inexperience in healthcare was an initial obstacle, her dynamic, vivacious personality both in and out of clown are in large part the reason the program has been so successful.

4   Working in the Hospital

Since the program began, clown-doctors have worked on Pediatrics an average of two and a half days a week and a total of six different clowns have worked on Pediatrics, with Dr. BB and Dr. Haven't-a-clue being the most consistent and longest serving "clown-marriage' on the unit. Each day the team follows the same pattern. After arriving and signing in they go, out of clown, to get the daily census and to receive notes from and ask relevant questions of the in-patient unit's Patient Care Resource Leader (PCRL). HDG has four such PCRL, experienced pediatric nurses who have this responsibility for six weeks at a time. Then the clowns proceed to outpatients and the day clinics to get notes from the oncology nurses and the day clinic secretary.

Getting notes from Debbie (PCRL) on Pediatrics.

Receiving Notes in Oncology Clinic

After receiving notes from the various stations. The pair proceed to the 'clown office' to change into their clown-doctor characters. The process takes about 30-45 minutes. During the process of transformation the partners talk a little about the mood of the ward, the types of problems present that day and possible strategies for working with each patient. Then they warm-up vocally and physically, get into character and leave the room. Once in character they will spend from two to six hours as a clown-doctor at the hospital. At the end of the day, the partners change back into street clothes and make detailed notes about the day's work.

One of the major things that clown-doctors do at HDG is to generally brighten up the hospital. At some point each day they simply walk the hospital hallways. Everywhere they go they smile at nurses, kitchen staff, porters, volunteers, janitors, doctors, patients, family members and everyone else they see. More often than not, the people they smile at smile back. Sometimes the clown doctors stop to talk with people or joke with them.

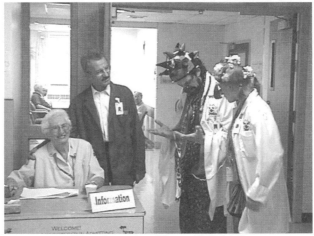

How Long is a Piece of String?

During the SARS outbreak in Toronto in the late-winter and spring of 2003, hospitals in Ontario cancelled all non-essential surgeries, day clinics and even closed many emergency departments. Access to hospitals was restricted to all but a handful of essential personnel. Security guards and nurses stood outside hospitals turning away many angry visitors who were denied access to their sick loved ones. It was very stressful for patients, families and the healthcare staff.

During the initial "hot phase" of the outbreak, the clown-doctors were excluded from the hospital. However, after a few days they were deemed an "essential" service and allowed back in. The first day back, they walked around telling everyone there was an outbreak of "smiles" in the building. It was obviously very contagious because everywhere the clown-doctors went people started smiling! They warned them that they must be careful as the next stage could be a full blown outbreak of laughs! Later, many staff especially the nurses and security staff, commented about how they had helped lighten the load of dealing with the stresses of the situation.

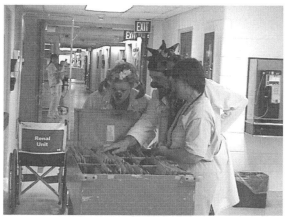

Helping Staff in Hallways

In addition to simply walking the hallways, they go to the cafeteria in clown. There they order, sit at a table and eat lunch in clown. Occasionally they interact with or wave to people. However, they try not to be too large or noisy because while most people enjoy the clowns, in the early stages there were a couple of complaints.

When the weather permits, the clown doctors sit outside in the healing garden and wave at people walking across a glassed in walkway inside. It is amazing to see the changes in people's posture and demeanour when they see these two brightly dressed clowns waving at them.

5   How Clown Doctors Help the Healthcare Team

Recently we conducted some preliminary research on the effects of the clown-doctors on the pediatric nurses. Over a period of several weeks a researcher visited the unit and recorded the interactions of the nursing staff. In addition a selected group of nurses were asked to comment on the effect of the clowns on their work. Each nurse was also asked to self rate their daily stress level. Finally the researcher also noted the general mood of the unit at the beginning and end of a shift and whether the clowns were present or not.

Waving in the Healing Garden

Several points emerged from the work. It would appear that when clowns are on the ward, nurses talk and interact more often with each other, with patients and with a patient's family. They smile more often and report a lower level of stress. The information gathered from this simple research supports findings gathered from the work of clowns in Europe. However, I would suggest that a more thorough study would need to be carried out to corroborate these findings.

One of the simplest ways they help the nursing staff is by brightening up a patient's room. With infants and young children, this might include singing a song or the use of finger puppets or very simple "peek-a-boo" style play. This type of work is particularly helpful to the staff when they are able to help calm a crying or agitated baby before the parents call for a nurse.

Baby Clapping

May We Come In?

With older children, the clown doctors try to help the child take their mind off their illness. One day we were preparing to work with a fifteen year old girl, with a very rare form of cancer. In addition, on this particular day, she was in a reverse isolation room as she was dealing with an infection and high fever, one of the side effects of her low white cell count. Outside her room we were putting on all the isolation room gear (mask, gloves etc.) trying to decide how to approach the girl. We looked in through the class doors and she seemed depressed and lethargic. We were hesitant, as previous interactions had been 'mixed' to say the least.. We realised that her mother, who had previously acted as "gatekeeper," was not there. We started slowly, and in retrospect we realised that *we* were worrying too much about her illness, focusing too much on her illness rather than thinking about the "well' parts of her. She, luckily, had other ideas. We ended up engaging with her in a most amazing and somewhat risqué fantasy play that she directed and controlled, in which she imagined auditioning boys to take with her to Paris, where she would be wined and dined and eat lots of chocolate. When we left her mood had changed and she was smiling.

This type of intervention which allows the child to think about life beyond the illness may be helpful. Children, especially hospitalised children, need fantasy images, which provide structures in a language they understand, to help them work though their own trials. Their fantasy life is an essential outlet, a release from the day to day traumatic realities of their hospitalization. Hospitalized children often choose a story or an image that acts as a healing metaphor for them. In many cases these healing metaphors build resources for the child, helping them to build what

Tomkiewicz refers to as "Resilience". By and large it is easier for the healthcare team to work with a non-depressed child.

Hold Still. This Won't Hurt a Bit.

Much of what the clown-doctors do could be considered "diversional therapy" where we help to act as a 'distraction' during minor bedside procedures, such as when a nurse inserts or removes an intravenous drip or draws blood.

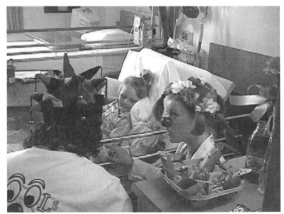

At the Bedside

One day we were working with a young seven year old boy who had been in a very severe car accident which, among other things, left him with a large gaping wound in his abdominal area. This wound needed to be drained and packed regularly. This was not a pleasant experience for the nurses or the boy. The whole time the nurses were working on the boy,

Dr. Haven't-a-Clue proceeded to do belly-button surgery on Dr. BB. This is a clown schtick which uses a toilet bowl plunger, a pink gauze scarf and a lot of sleight of hand. Both operations were a complete success and the nurses profusely thanked us afterwards for helping to make the process go so smoothly.

One time a developmentally delayed boy was already screaming. We had been asked to help, and even though we know better we entered the room midway through a procedure. He was kicking while the nurses were trying to draw blood from his toe with a very thick gauge needle. His mother was blocking her child's view of us in an attempt to stop him from looking at the procedure. We tried our best but he could not see us and he did not know it was us singing. He kept on screaming (albeit a little muted at times). At the end of the procedure we felt we had failed but later, outside the room, we said to one of the nurses "sorry we couldn't help very much in there" and she replied "By being there and singing you helped to calm us, which made everything easier ..."

On a different occasion we were more successful. A stubborn ten year old boy, who had been particularly aggressive to the nurses, was to have an IV inserted. We went to the treatment room with him. It was a very small space so we stood almost on top of one another and for ten minutes we sang to this boy, constantly keeping eye contact with him. We also used finger puppets and through circular movements of these puppets and the singing of soft songs we lulled the boy into a 'quasi-hypnotic' state. As one the nurses said: "I thought this was going to be really hard, but you almost put him to sleep."

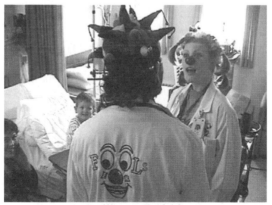
Smiling at Bedside

One day Dr. Tilly and Dr. BB were stopped on their way down to lunch by the head of emergency, who asked them to come with him immediately to see if they could help nurses who had been unsuccessfully trying to insert an IV for a very distressed autistic child. When they arrived, the clown-doctors were greeted by blood on the sheets and a child who would not stop moving. For twenty minutes they sang a medley of every upbeat song they knew, trying to keep the song's beat lively but themselves and the patient still. The procedure was successful and when finished the nurses were so relieved that after thirty minutes of noise and agitation, everybody (patient, parents and staff) was finally at peace. All the nurses said thank you so much.

This event led to the head of emergency asking the clown-doctors to visit ER whenever they can. So now the clown-doctors work regularly in the Emergency room and they have even been paged over the public address system. Although there are very strange looks throughout the hospital when people hear: "Dr. BB, Dr. Haven't-a-clue please go to Emergency immediately."

Since March 2003 the clown-doctors have been working once a week with a little girl (she just turned five) who has an inoperable brain tumour. One day we worked with an oncology nurse to help the girl have her port flushed, (I should mention that none of the clown-doctors signed on to watch blood and bodily fluids. More so, most of us as people are very squeamish. However, we are "clown doctors" and we therefore must take all the medical aspects in stride.) As the tube was inserted and the blood began to flow, we sang songs with this girl and, as part of one song, we got the girl to raise her hands above her head and wave, which facilitated the procedure. The nurse commented that the girl was much more cooperative and compliant. The very next day we worked with her again, and she wanted to play doctor, with the clown doctors as patients. It was amazing to see the detail with which she proceeded to play at inserting an IV line, flushing Dr.BB's port and giving her chemotherapy.

Recently, Dr. BB and I were training a new clown, Dr. Hoppy-Go-Lucky. Dr Hoppy and I entered a room where a young girl was crying softly. Her dad was on the bed stroking her hair. I asked "would you like us to visit with you today?" She looked up, still crying she shook her head. I took a pause and asked, "Would you like a song before we leave?" She looked at me, thought for a moment, and again shook her head, but she was no longer crying. I said goodbye and we turned to leave, as we did she gave a brief smile and a small wave.

When I left the room I felt we had been rejected and somehow unsuccessful., Later that day, however, when we all sat down to write our notes, I realised that the interactions with this girl epitomised what the clown work is all about. For a brief moment we had taken that child's mind off her illness. We had managed to make her smile and had empowered her. She was able to reject us and for that brief moment she was in control. This is crucially important to a hospitalised sick child who has so little control over what is happening to them.

6   Final Thoughts

One day Dr. BB and Dr. Haven't-a-clue were having lunch when Mr. Deane (who had recently arrived as the new hospital CEO), along with the senior nursing sister (HDG was a religious institution formerly operated by nuns) and a senior unit manager sat down to eat with us. These administrators were not hesitant to be seen with two clowns and had actively sought us out. They wanted to talk to us but they also wanted to talk to the people behind the nose. Something that is hard to do because once in character, people think and act differently. For example, I can play musical instruments but Haven't-a-clue cannot remember notes. On the other hand, while I stumble over the French language, Dr. Haven't-a-clue speaks it fluently, although not always meaningfully!

Anyway as we sat there, with Allyson and I half in and half out of our clown-doctor characters, the conversation turned to research and the value of the clowns on the ward. We tried as best as we could to talk about the research and how clown-doctors seem to reduce patients' need for various medications such as antidepressants, anti-anxiety drugs and painkillers. Mr. Deane listened thoughtfully. When we had finished he said,

> "I don't need to see the statistics to see the good you
> do in this hospital.... everywhere you go you bring
> sunshine ... not just to the pediatric unit but to the
> hospital as a whole"

End of the Day

Notes

[1] Bernie Warren, "Treating Wellness: How Clown Doctors Help to Humanize Health Care and Promote Good Health" in *Making Sense of Health, Illness and Disease,* ed. Peter L. Twohig and Vera Kalitzkus (Amsterdam and Atlanta: Rodopi, 2004), 201-16. See also Caroline Simonds and Bernie Warren, *Le Rire Medicin: Journal du docteur giraffe.* Paris: Albin Michael, 2001.

Bibliography

Simonds, Caroline and Bernie Warren, *Le Rire Medicin: Journal du docteur giraffe.* Paris: Albin Michael, 2001.

Warren, Bernie. "Treating Wellness: How Clown Doctors Help to Humanize Health Care and Promote Good Health." In *Making Sense of Health, Illness and Disease,* Ed. Peter L. Twohig and Vera Kalitzkus. Amsterdam and Atlanta: Rodopi, 2004, 201-16.

Note on Contributor

Bernie Warren, PhD, is a professional clown doctor and a professor in the School of Dramatic Art, University of Windsor, Canada. He is also the director of the 'Fools for Health' clown doctor programs.

Part 3

Reframing Clinical Encounters:
Narrative, Literature and Video

Narrativising the Body:
Fragmentation and Unification in Jed Mercurio's *Bodies*

Jarmila Mildorf

The late twentieth century has seen a growing number of literary texts written by 'physician writers', i.e., doctors who also write literary texts. Examples are, among others, Samuel Shem's *The House of God*, Atul Gawande's *Complications,* Oliver Sacks' *Awakenings*, David Widgery's *Some Lives! A GP's East End*, Richard and Enid Peschel's *When a Doctor Hates a Patient*, the story collection entitled *Recognitions* edited by Carol Donley and Martin Cohn, and the work of William Carlos Williams. One of the most recent publications in Britain is Jed Mercurio's novel *Bodies*,[1] which depicts the experiences of a young unnamed hospital houseman, who starts a career in an English city hospital. Bodies are not only the eponymous central theme of the novel, they also function as a recurring metaphor for a fragmentary and fragmenting clinical practice which leads to the gradual disassociation of the young man's life. In this chapter, I first wish to investigate the metaphor of the body in Mercurio's novel by taking into account Anthony Giddens' notion of fragmentation and unification in modern society.[2] Secondly, I will consider the role narrative has to play as a unifying and defragmenting discourse mode not only within the novel but also on a metatextual level. If one accepts the view that narrative constitutes one cognitive mode of making sense of the world, as scholars in disciplines as varied as Artificial Intelligence,[3] social and cognitive psychology,[4] sociology,[5] sociolinguistics[6] and narratology[7] have claimed, then doctors' literary narratives can be viewed as means of making sense of their work and lives and as devices for conveying their meanings to the 'outside' world, so to speak.

Narrative has always played a role as a unifying principle, as Ana Celi and María Cristina Boiero show in their research on Native American storytelling: "Indian stories and ceremonies ensure the survival of the belief in the essential unity of the whole and show how events and experiences are related to one another."[8] Prickett argues along similar lines when he points out that narrative is used to overcome "the twin twentieth-century problems of subjectivity and pluralism"[9] and that, as a consequence, areas like religion, science and history have seen a growing number of competing narratives which all attempt to describe and make sense of the world. According to Prickett, however, this leads to an ever-increasing pluralism of narratives, which ultimately again fragments our world view: "But not merely are our stories of the world partial, incomplete and fragmentary, no amount of scientific progress will settle political, philosophic, moral or religious questions."[10] Applied to physicians' stories about their work and lives, this means that, in sum, they will also not convey a coherent picture of medical practice. Nevertheless, I contend that, on an individual level, doctors create "enclaves of self"[11] by narrating and 'narrativising' the body, and spaces of freedom in the artistic realm where medicine is recontextualised and rewritten. Young claims that patients can reintroduce themselves as persons into medical consultations through the insertion of personal stories:

> Stories are sealed off from the occasions on which they occur – here, the realm of medicine – as events of a different ontological status. For that reason they can be used to reinsert into that realm an alternate reality in which the patient can reappear in his own person without disrupting the ontological conditions of the realm of medicine.[12]

Likewise, physicians' stories can be said to reinsert the medical world into the world of the lay patient and thus become instruments for the mutual interpenetration and permeation of domains which have hitherto been regarded as marked by insurmountable conflict and tension.

1.   Fragmentation and Loss of Self

In *Modernity and Self-Identity*, sociologist Anthony Giddens argues that modernity with its indefinite range of possibilities and the openness of the world fragments as well as integrates, and thus poses a dilemma to the individual:

> On the level of the individual right up to that of planetary systems as a whole, tendencies towards dispersal vie with those promoting integration. So far as the self is concerned, the problem of unification concerns protecting and reconstructing the narrative of self-identity in the face of the massive intensional and extensional changes which modernity sets into being.[13]

At the same time, abstract systems and the diversity of expert knowledge have a deskilling effect on the individual and in a sense expropriate us in many areas of everyday life. Medicine is one arena where the body is fragmented in examinations and where the self is thus estranged and objectified. As Katharine Young puts it: "Medicine translates me bodily from the realm of the ordinary in which I am a self into the realm of medicine in which I am an object."[14] In Mercurio's novel, even the young doctor himself is caught up in the institutionalised cynicism and the fragmenting practices of medicine. This is typically depicted in images of the body. The hospital, for example, is frequently referred to as "vaults", in which the young doctor loses himself:

> Ahead of me a straight white corridor drops away to a set of doors and through the glass of the doors I see another straight white corridor stretching to another set of doors. In the glass of those second doors I make out a third straight white corridor and all together the corridors and the doors are an ever diminishing series of arrows pointing me deeper in and I feel like I'm falling.
>
> I'm falling through layers of brick, concrete and glass. In the weatherless vaults of corridors and stairwells outsiders dwindle.[15]

Just as he 'falls into' the architectural 'body' of the hospital, the doctor becomes absorbed into the hospital routine and the medical community, which drains his energy and leads to the breakdown of his relationship with his girl-friend, Rebecca. Interestingly enough, the couple's disagreements are intricately linked to a communication problem between the young doctor as a medical professional and Rebecca as an 'outsider' to the profession. Thus, when the doctor tries to explain some of the difficulties he encounters in his job, he cannot find the language to express himself: "I've no stamina for the explanation. With civilians I need to find a language in which to describe the job and it's a language I've wearied of sifting for."[16] At this stage, the young doctor has not yet developed the narrative skills granted to him at the end of the novel which help him bridge the gap between the medical and the non medical world. The separation of these two worlds is clearly demarcated by seemingly incompatible linguistic codes: "Those of us who work in the interior constitute a society twice removed, once from the outside world and once again from the borderlands of the hospital. As I push through the door it releases conversation rich with the jargon that identifies our enclave and it makes me feel at home."[17]

Things reach a crisis point when the doctor becomes guilty of overlooking a patient's pulmonary embolism because he takes her for a Munchhausen, i.e. a person suffering from a psychiatric condition characterised by the simulation of disease in order to gain medical attention. The fact that the young man cannot divulge his guilt to his girl-friend and that, when he finally does it, she is not able to understand him, is also presented in terms of bodily and mental distance: "Rebecca's body lies turned to me or away from me but in either case always on her side and her slow breaths slide into the gutter between our pillows like oil seeping into pavement cracks. She sleeps while the Breathless Lady lives on in my thoughts."[18] As in many other instances in the book, the doctor's memories of what happened at work sever him from people in the non-medical world and render it increasingly difficult for him to participate in 'normal' life. Again, the problem is also linguistic, as can be seen in the doctor's rendition of a dinner outing with Rebecca, a solicitor, an estate agent and others[19]:

> They're normal with normal jobs. Their shop talk revolves around the size of offices and the size of expense accounts, holidays booked, openings elsewhere. I'm on a different plane and I discuss work with other doctors in jargon no civilian can comprehend or is meant to comprehend. Already I'm starting to feel I don't belong with civilians or they with me.[20]

This incapability to communicate with the outside world is accompanied by a gradual loss of sensitivity. The doctor comments: "Once I feared how much all this would affect me. Now I fear how little it does."[21] When the protagonist finally breaks up his engagement, his loss of emotionality is epitomised in his incapability to express feelings physically: while his girl-friend bursts into tears, he can only "feel nothing" and he remarks cynically: "That's my job, isn't it? To feel nothing"[22].

Fragmentation is most visible in the way doctors name their patients in the novel. Rather than using proper names, they attach labels which refer to a specific physical condition or the diseased body part of a patient. Patients are called "Vague Yellow Woman," "Breathless Lady," "Grey Meat" or "Young Headache Man," for example. Examinations of patients and emergencies are portrayed with a mixture of minute details of the patient's affected body parts, specialised medical jargon and cynicism which evokes and at the same time suppresses laughter. Consider the following example where a patient suffers a respiratory arrest:

> The nurse brings a working laryngoscope and the sister a slimline endotracheal tube and the anaesthetist struggles for ten minutes before he succeeds in ramming it through the swollen tissues of the Wheezer's throat into his lungs, though by then at least he's got his breath back. We pump in 100 per cent oxygen hard via the Ambu bag. His heartbeat returns a few minutes later. By then his brain's been starved of oxygen for nearly half an hour.
>
> When we stop squeezing the bag no reflex prompts him to gasp for air. The anaesthetist taps him on the forehead like knocking on a door. 'Anyone at home?'[23]

The cynicism that marks the entire novel reveals an ambivalent stance towards medical practice. While medicine tries to deal with health problems by objectifying the body, it cannot avert itself from the threat posed by illness, disease and, ultimately, death. Jean Baudrillard observes that:

> Therapeutic scientificity and efficiency presuppose the radical objectification of the body, the social discrimination of the sick, and hence a process of mortification. [...] Mortified, the patient is also deadly, taking his revenge as he can: by means of its functions, its specializations and its hierarchies, the clinical institution as a whole seeks to preserve itself from contamination from the already-dead. [24]

The young doctor also experiences this threat and, with a tone of resignation, he summarises:

> Doctors have no more power over life and death than any other living organism. All we do is bear closer witness. Everything we feel and everyone we know will one day be extinct. And when I gaze into my own face in the mirror I see nothing that promises me any different. I see a face and I don't know if it's one in bloom or one in decay. [25]

The doctor's cynicism can thus be interpreted as an indirect means of self-defence in the process of trying to eradicate the symbolic difference between illness and death. It also facilitates communication about experiences which are basically unspeakable.[26]

The fragmentary and fragmenting nature of medical examinations is probably best visualised in the description of a CT scan, where the patient's body is virtually 'sliced up' into pieces:

> We retire to the control room and from behind plate glass we watch his head creep inch by inch through an invisible guillotine of X-rays. [...] The gallery of images appears on a transparency. The scan has sectioned the Young Headache Man's brain into planes like a butcher slicing ham.[27]

Technology is used to fragment the body in order to discover illness and also to reduce the symbolic power of death. As Philippe Ariés puts it: "Death has been dissected, cut to bits by a series of little steps, which

finally makes it impossible to know which step was the real death, the one
in which consciousness was lost, or the one in which breathing stopped."[28]
While passages like these are possibly disturbing because of their
presentation of allegedly bare facts through provocative imagery, they also
make for gripping drama. James Owen Drife contends that surgery

> is physical and it makes people faint. Gritty truth has
> always been fashionable in narrative from Charles
> Dickens to Irving Welsh, and surgeons are in regular
> contact with blood and guts. The operating theatre is a
> place of drama...[29]

This dramatism also pervades the depiction of the young doctor's private
life, most notably his sexual affairs. After his separation from his fiancée,
the young doctor begins an affair with an attractive nurse, Donna, and the
initially merely physical relationship gradually develops into more.

2.   The Healing Power of Sexual Bodies

While the protagonist's sexual encounters are also presented with
careful attention to physical detail, sexual bodies, in contrast to the sick
bodies of the hospital wards, are experienced by the young man as having
a sensory healing power that reunifies body and soul. The following text
passage illustrates this emotion:

> She registers the tenseness of my body and pulls me
> close so her pelvis rubs against mine. In the softness of
> her lips and skin and breasts I relax. I feel my body
> joining hers and with this feeling springs an erection
> that she senses as it pushes into her crotch and it makes
> her smile.[30]

The narrator-protagonist's descriptions of his sexual acts are synaesthetic
orchestrations of merging bodies: all the senses, from tactile to visual to
auditory to olfactory, are involved in the evocation of the touch of skins,
body smells, etc. Physical boundaries become blurred when the narrator
talks about "confluent mouths" and "confluent loins."[31] While medical
practice disintegrates the body into its individual parts, sexuality enables
the experience of the body as a whole and, more importantly, the
transcendence of self to incorporate another self. Thus eroticism facilitates
communication which need not be conveyed through words or, as Michael
Hardt writes:

> The erotic points us toward the vital continuity
> extending across the surfaces of being. It breaks down

or dissolves the separateness, the self-possession, the discontinuity that exists among individual entities and things. It strips them naked, empties them, and puts them in common. Eroticism is thus a state of communication that testifies to our striving toward a possible continuity of being, beyond the prison of the self. The limits or boundaries of individual entities become open thresholds that feel the pleasures – the rise and the recess – of flows and intensities[32].

One must concede, however, that the sex the doctor experiences as recreational also becomes increasingly forceful, if not violent, in the course of the novel, culminating in Donna's request to "Just fuck me, just fucking rape me."[33] Thus, sexual intercourse becomes a physical means to combat desensitisation and fragmentation, a struggle which can also be seen in the frequent interruption of scenes of sexual encounters by the doctor's flashbacks to medical procedures which keep re-surfacing even in situations when he wishes to put them aside.

In Mercurio's depictions of sick and sexual bodies as well as of the 'body' of medical institutions and the medical community, the metaphor of the body is used to illustrate the development of the protagonist's self from disassociation to integration. Bodies are thus not only narrated but they are also narrativised, i.e. they are made into narratives *per se*, narratives which recount the fragmentation of a young doctor's life through modern medical practice and its unification in a meaningful personal relationship. Significantly enough, this unification is only fully accomplished when the "naked and divine communion"[34] between the young doctor and Donna, the "physical language"[35] of their relationship, is supplemented by their sharing of personal life stories.

3.   Narrative as Unifying Discursive Practice

During a short holiday at a village near a lake, Donna and the doctor for the first time have the chance to spend more than only a few stolen hours together. Apart from making love, they now also find the time to engage in storytelling. Thus, Donna relates an incident at work where a young woman's cancer of the cervix had been missed in previous examinations and was only discovered at the delivery of her baby, which finally led to the woman's death a short time after. This story is elicited by the young doctor's request that Donna tell him why she had changed her mind and started an affair with him despite her engagement with another man. This pattern is repeated when Donna likewise asks him: "Tell me something you've never told anyone else."[36] The doctor replies with the story of his failed attempt to kill an arsonist who had murdered a mother and her children, through providing the wrong medication. What is

significant in this exchange of life stories is that both Donna and the
doctor are for the first time able to disclose their innermost secrets to
someone else without having to face lack of understanding. Donna admits
that she never told this story to her husband and she explains: "How'd he
ever understand?"[37] Narrative thus becomes another point of convergence
for Donna and the doctor and the additional mutual understanding that
both gain from this experience ultimately induces Donna to promise to
leave her husband for the doctor.

There are other instances throughout the novel where the young
doctor attempts to recreate himself through storytelling. When he starts to
have qualms about his job and asks himself whether he really wants to
stay in medicine, for example, he draws an analogy by means of an
anecdote from his childhood: "When I was a little boy I remember finding
rabbits crammed in a hutch and out of mischief releasing the latch but
none of them ran away. Instead their paws scratched at the straw under
them in panic, backing into each other, cowering from the opening.
They'd been caged since birth."[38] The story functions as a simile, likening
the rabbits to doctors who have stayed in the profession for too long.
While the doctor recalls this story in order to reflect on his own situation,
the anecdote also becomes an illustration of the doctor's dilemma for the
reader: "I can stay here, the only place I know, the only place I can be a
doctor, or plunge into the big scary unknown. I'm staring out of the rabbit
hutch."[39] By telling stories, the doctor can place himself in the foreground
of the narratee's and, by implication, the reader's, awareness, which is
denied to him in his job. The role of a doctor is technical, which is often
expressed in the image of the scalpel, and it is spatially restricted to the
background of other people's lives: "I must always be the scalpel that
glints and cuts and never becomes blunt. I must always be that blur in the
back of the scene, present for an instant then appearing no more in the
narrative of other people's lives."[40] It seems that the doctor can overcome
his isolation mainly through narrative.

Although the novel is in large parts reminiscent of postmodern
writing, e.g. in its strings of seemingly unconnected episodes in the
hospital, there are pivotal events which run like a red thread through the
narrative and finally achieve closure. Thus, the incident with the
Breathless Lady is solved in the end when the doctor reveals the truth
about his fatal mistake to the patient's family. Interestingly enough, the
novel thus culminates in a storytelling situation:

> In the little house I sit in their living room and to the
> Breathless Lady's family I tell the truth about what
> happened that night when I was called to see her and I
> made a mistake and because of my mistake she died.
> They listen in silence and the first time I sob one of the
> women offers me a tissue but I say, 'It's OK,' because I

made sure I brought a handkerchief. Though often I'm
staring into the floor and I'm wiping tears from my face
I carry on until after an hour I've told them everything. I
say, 'I'm sorry.' At last I've finished and they've heard
every part of everything I've done.
Now I look up. Now I look up to be judged.[41]

The narrative helps the young doctor regain his self and, what is more, his
self-esteem. At the same time, he is finally allowed to enter the foreground
of other people's lives by visiting them at home. Rather than hiding
behind the hospital and medicine as an institution, he steps outside,
assumes responsibility and agency and thus places his role as doctor on a
new footing.

4.   Narrative Metatext in *Bodies*

As far as the role of narrative is concerned, the novel operates
analogously on a metatextual level. While narrative offers a means to
unify and defragment the protagonist's experiences of medical practice,
this process is time and again discussed and reflected in the doctor's own
narrative and is ultimately enacted by the novel as a whole. As I
mentioned above, one of the main problems the young houseman faces is
how to communicate his experiences to the outside world. Frequent
references to language and to divergent linguistic codes point towards a
seemingly unbridgeable gap between the medical world and the life
worlds of other people. Part of the problem, the young doctor argues, is
the fact that people do not wish to have a greater insight in the gritty truths
of medicine: "You realise no one from outside is watching. No one is
watching me examine patients and talk to relatives and write up notes and
fill in charts. They're not watching because they don't want to see what I
see. They let the interior be my world."[42] On the other hand, the young
doctor has also not found a means of conveying this "interior" world to
outsiders yet, which is picked up by Donna when she says: "Maybe, even
if you take the deal, one day you'll be able to get your message across
some other way, some other way that doesn't even occur to you now."[43]
Baudrillard contends that medicine imposes a prohibition of speech on
patients:

In any case, if the priest was nothing but a vulture, today
this function is largely fulfilled by the doctor, who shuts
speech off by overwhelming the dying with care and
technical concern. An *infantile* death that no longer
speaks, an inarticulate death, kept out of sight. Serums,
laboratories and healing are only the alibi of the
prohibition of speech.[44]

Focusing on the (dying) patient, Baudrillard seems to overlook that doctors too are subjected to this prohibition of speech, that they are prevented from speaking the unspeakable except in their own professional community. The question that arises therefore is how doctors can overcome this prohibition in order to communicate with outsiders. The ending of the novel would suggest that it is indeed storytelling which could be the "other way" of getting one's message across. While, throughout the novel, the doctor has been an effective, yet imperceptible and temporary "instrument" in the "narrative of other people's lives,"[45] his own life narrative becomes an "instrument" to propel him to the foreground of the Breathless Lady's family and, ultimately, to anyone who reads his story.

Likewise, Jed Mercurio as the author of *Bodies* rewrites to some extent his own role as former physician and creates a new space for medicine in the realm of the literary text. Narrative is used to make sense of medical practice, even if this sense-making also involves criticism and self-reflexivity. At the same time, the world of medicine or better, one picture of that world, is conveyed to the reader, and we are invited to peep into a professional area from which we are normally excluded or to which we are only partially admitted as patients and laypersons.[46] That narrative plays an important role in medicine and that one should therefore pay closer attention to it has been attested by a number of scholars in recent years. Roger Munger, for example, concludes his study on pre-hospital care narratives in emergency medical services (EMS) by stating that "narrative is especially well suited for reflection on experience and for documenting that experience. Narrative encourages writers to create order out of chaos, see relationships, and seek closure for a sequence of events."[47] By reflecting not only on their narratives but also on their narrative practices, Munger argues, EMS professionals are better able to understand their work and ultimately to improve their service provision. That literary narratives also have a place in medicine is cogently argued by Kathryn Hunter. She maintains that:

> Years of experience taking care of patients may foster the clinical wisdom necessary to handle difficult cases well, but meanwhile for physicians, as for all of us, the vicarious experience offered by narrative increases familiarity with the range of human character and the life outside office and hospital to which medicine aims to restore them.
>
> In particular, literature is a source of knowledge about the operation of values through time.[48]

While narrative allows us to learn about people and life in general, it also offers the possibility to express feelings and experiences which may otherwise be difficult to communicate. The fact that doctors in the past as well as in recent years have undertaken the project to write literary texts[49] indicates that they embrace this possibility and make use of the spaces of freedom available in literature. Medicine is thus recontextualised not only for the doctors themselves but also for their audiences, which may ultimately lead to enhanced mutual understanding and acknowledgement. This, I think, is particularly important in our fragmentary and fragmenting modern world, where medicine is still regarded by most people as a hardcore scientific enterprise. As Drife points out:

> Medical science has currently been hijacked by mathematicians, and many of today's doctors feel that a concept has no validity unless it comes festooned with "p" values. Narrative, however, is an art. The craft of surgery lies somewhere between science, on one side, and art on the other.[50]

One can only hope that more doctors will gradually come to realise the significance of art and, more specifically, narrative art, in their daily work practices. Writing in this context has the power to make medicine more human or, as William Carlos Williams famously put it in his autobiography:

> I found by practice, by trial and error, that to treat a man as something to which surgery, drugs and hoodoo applied was an indifferent manner; to treat him as material for a work of art made him somehow come alive to me.[51]

Notes

[1] Page numbers refer to the following edition of the novel: Jed Mercurio, *Bodies* (London: Jonathan Cape, 2002).

[2] Anthony Giddens, *Modernity and Self-Identity: Self and Society in the Late Modern Age* (Stanford: Stanford University Press, 1991).

[3] Roger C. Schank, *Tell Me a Story: Narrative and Intelligence* (Evanston, Illinois: Northwestern University Press, 1990).

[4] Jerome Bruner, "The Narrative Construction of Reality," *Critical Inquiry* 18 (1991): 1-21. Michele L. Crossley, *Introducing Narrative Psychology: Self, Trauma and the Construction of Meaning* (Buckingham, UK: Open University Press, 2000).

[5] Catherine Kohler Riessman, *Narrative Analysis* (Newbury Park: Sage, 1993).

[6] Deborah Schiffrin, "Narrative as Self-Portrait: Sociolinguistic Constructions of Identity," *Language in Society* 25(2) (1996): 167-203. Barbara Johnstone, *Stories, Community and Place: Narratives from Middle America* (Bloomington: Indiana University Press, 1990).

[7] David Herman, *Story Logic: Problems and Possibilities of Narrative* (Lincoln: University of Nebraska Press, 2002). Vera and Ansgar Nünning, (ed.), *Erzähltheorie transgenerisch, intermedial, interdisziplinär* (Trier: Wissenschaftlicher Verlag Trier, 2002).

[8] Ana Celi and María Cristina Boiero, "The Heritage of Stories: A Tradition of Wisdom," *American Studies International* 15(2) (2002): 60.

[9] Stephen Prickett, *Narrative, Religion and Science: Fundamentalism versus Irony 1700-1999* (Cambridge: Cambridge University Press, 2002), 3.

[10] Ibid., 257.

[11] Katharine Young, "Narrative Embodiments: Enclaves of the Self in the Realm of Medicine" in *The Discourse Reader*, ed. Adam Jaworski and Nikolas Coupland (London: Routledge, 1999), 428-441.

[12] Ibid., 438.

[13] Giddens, 189.

[14] Katharine Young, "Narratives of Indeterminacy: Breaking the Medical Body into Its Discourses; Breaking the Discursive Body out of Postmodernism" in *Narratologies: New Perspectives on Narrative Analysis*, ed. David Herman (Columbus: Ohio State University Press, 1999), 203. An interesting example of the patient's fragmentation can be found in Salman Rushdie's novel *Midnight's Children*, where the physician grandfather of the narrator examines and courts his future wife through a sheet with a hole in it which displays the part of the body under examination.

[15] *Bodies*, 6.

[16] Ibid., 53.

[17] Ibid., 106.

[18] Ibid., 80.

[19] Interestingly enough, these people are not given any names, i.e., they are simply referred to as "Solicitor", "Estate Agent", etc. This already indicates that the communication difficulties do not occur among individual people but among persons from different walks of life. Thus, an emphasis is laid on the significance of professional jargon.

[20] *Bodies*, 47-48.

[21] Ibid., 95.

[22] Ibid., 105.

[23] Ibid., 200.

[24] Jean Baudrillard, *Symbolic Exchange and Death*, trans. Iain Hamilton Grant (London: Sage, 1993), 183.

[25] *Bodies*, 263.

[26] Samuel Shem's *The House of God*, a novel with which *Bodies* bears great similarities, pushes cynicism even further by classifying patients as GOMERS = Get out of my emergency room, for example. The fact that Shem's novel became something like a 'bible' for medical students not only in the United States but also in Europe indicates that cynicism as a mode of expression appeals to doctors because it corresponds with their experiences.

[27] *Bodies*, 12-13.

[28] Philippe Ariés, *Western Attitudes Toward Death: From the Middle Ages to the Present*, trans. Patricia M. Ranum (Baltimore : Johns Hopkins University Press, 1975), 88, quoted in Joshua Schuster, "Death Reckoning in the Thinking of Heidegger, Foucault, and Derrida," *Other Voices* 1, 1. <www.othervoices.org/jnschust/death.html>

[29] James Owen Drife, "Narrative in Surgery," in *Narrative Based Medicine: Dialogue and Discourse in Clinical Practice*, ed. Trisha Greenhalgh and Brian Hurwitz (London: BMJ Books, 1998), 116. It is maybe not surprising that the author of *Bodies*, Jed Mercurio, is also the man behind the TV series *Cardiac Arrest*.

[30] *Bodies*, 142.

[31] Ibid., 150.

[32] Michael Hardt, "Exposure: Pasolini in the Flesh," in *A Shock to Thought: Expression After Deleuze and Guattari*, ed. Brian Massumi (London, Routledge, 2002), 80.

[33] *Bodies*, 347.

[34] Hardt, 80.

[35] *Bodies*, 342.

[36] Ibid., 347.

[37] Ibid.

[38] Ibid., 179.

[39] Ibid.

[40] Ibid., 178.

[41] Ibid., 358.

[42] Ibid., 262.

[43] Ibid., 349.

[44] Jean Baudrillard, *Symbolic Exchange and Death*, trans. Iain Hamilton Grant (London: Sage, 1993), 183.

[45] *Bodies*, 178.

[46] Janice Galloway's *The Trick is to Keep Breathing* may be an interesting contrast. She writes about her experiences as a patient in psychiatric ward. Galloway is condemnatory about the NHS and the narrative is highly fragmented.

[47] Roger Munger, "Prehospital Care Narratives: A Time fro Reflection and Professional Growth," in *Narrative and Professional Communication*, ed. Jane M. Perkins and Nancy Blyler (Stamford: Ablex, 1999), 163.

[48] Kathryn Montgomery Hunter, *Doctors' Stories: The Narrative Structure of Medical Knowledge* (Princeton: Princeton University Press, 1991), 157.
[49] One only needs to remember writers such as Somerset Maugham, Anton Chekhov, Tobias Smollett. For a more extensive overview of physician writers, consult members.aol.com/dbryantmd/index.html?f=fs. It is also intriguing that medicine has even made an inroad into popular fiction. Thus, former physician and novelist Robin Cook can be said to be to medicine what John Grisham is to law.
[50] Drife, 112.
[51] William Carlos Williams, from *The Autobiography*, quoted in Carol C. Donley and Martin Kohn, eds, *Recognitions: Doctors and Their Stories* (Kent, Kent State University Press, 2002), 3.

Bibliography

Ariés, Philippe. *Western Attitudes Toward Death: From the Middle Ages to the Present*, trans. Patricia M. Ranum. Baltimore : Johns Hopkins University Press, 1975. Quoted in Joshua Schuster, "Death Reckoning in the Thinking of Heidegger, Foucault, and Derrida." *Other Voices* 1(1). < www.othervoices.org/jnschust/death.html>

Baudrillard, Jean. *L'échange symbolique et la mort*. Paris : Gallimard, 1976.

Baudrillard, Jean. *Symbolic Exchange and Death*, trans. Iain Hamilton Grant. London: Sage, 1993.

Bruner, Jerome. "The Narrative Construction of Reality." *Critical Inquiry* 18 (1991): 1-21.

Celi, Ana and María Cristina Boiero. "The Heritage of Stories: A Tradition of Wisdom." *American Studies International* 15(2) (2002): 57-72.

Crossley, Michele L. *Introducing Narrative Psychology. Self, Trauma and the Construction of Meaning*. Buckingham, UK: Open University Press, 2000.

Donley, Carol C. and Martin Kohn, ed. *Recognitions: Doctors and Their Stories*. Kent: Kent State University Press, 2002.

Drife, James Owen. "Narrative in Surgery." In *Narrative Based Medicine. Dialogue and Discourse in Clinical Practice.* Ed. Trisha Greenhalgh and Brian Hurwitz, 110-117. London: BMJ Books, 1998.

Gawande, Atul. *Complications: A Surgeon's Notes on an Imperfect Science.* New York: Picador, 2003.

Giddens, Anthony. *Modernity and Self-Identity. Self and Society in the Late Modern Age.* Stanford: Stanford University Press, 1991.

Hardt, Michael. "Exposure: Pasolini in the Flesh." In *A Shock to Thought: Expression After Deleuze and Guattari.* Ed. Brian Massumi, 77-84. London: Routledge, 2002.

Herman, David. *Story Logic. Problems and Possibilities of Narrative.* Lincoln: University of Nebraska Press, 2002.

Hunter, Kathryn Montgomery. *Doctors' Stories. The Narrative Structure of Medical Knowledge.* Princeton: Princeton University Press, 1991.

Johnstone, Barbara. *Stories, Community and Place. Narratives from Middle America.* Bloomington/Indianapolis: Indiana University Press, 1990.

Mercurio, Jed. *Bodies.* London: Jonathan Cape, 2002.

Munger, Roger. "Prehospital Care Narratives: A Time for Reflection and Professional Growth." In *Narrative and Professional Communication .* Ed. Jane M. Perkins and Nancy Blyler, 151-164. Stamford: Ablex, 1999.

Nünning, Vera and Ansgar Nünning, ed. *Erzähltheorie transgenerisch, intermedial, interdisziplinär.* Trier: Wissenschaftlicher Verlag Trier, 2002.

Peschel, Richard E. and Enid Rhodes Peschel, ed. *When a Doctor Hates a Patient: And Other Chapters in a Young Physician's Life.* Berkeley, CA: University of California Press, 1989.

Prickett, Stephen. *Narrative, Religion and Science. Fundamentalism versus Irony 1700-1999.* Cambridge: Cambridge University Press, 2002.

Riessman, Catherine Kohler. *Narrative Analysis.* Newbury Park/London/ New Delhi: Sage, 1993.

Sacks, Oliver. *Awakenings.* London: Vintage Books, 1999 [1973].

Schank, Roger C. *Tell Me a Story. Narrative and Intelligence.* Evanston, Illinois: Northwestern University Press, 1990.

Schiffrin, Deborah. "Narrative as Self-Portrait: Sociolinguistic Constructions of Identity." *Language in Society* 25, 2 (1996): 167-203.

Schuster, Joshua. "Death Reckoning in the Thinking of Heidegger, Foucault, and Derrida." *Other Voices* 1, 1 (1997).
< www.othervoices.org/jnschust/death.html>

Shem, Samuel. *The House of God*. London: Dell Books, 1981 [1978].

Widgery, David. *Some Lives! A GP's East End*. London: Trafalgar Square, 1992.

Young, Katharine. "Narrative Embodiments: Enclaves of the Self in the Realm of Medicine." In *The Discourse Reader.* Ed. Adam Jaworski and Nikolas Coupland, 428-441. London/New York: Routledge, 1999.

Young, Katharine. "Narratives of Indeterminacy: Breaking the Medical Body into Its Discourses; Breaking the Discursive Body out of Postmodernism." In *Narratologies: New Perspectives on Narrative Analysis.* Ed. David Herman, 197-217. Columbus: Ohio State University Press, 1999.

Note on Contributor

Jarmila Mildorf is lecturer for English literature at the University of Stuttgart (Germany). Some of her previous sociolinguistic research on general practitioners' narrative discourse on domestic violence was published in *Sociology of Health and Illness* and *Narrative Inquiry*.

The Possibilities of Story: Jacques Ferron's "Little William" and the Teaching of Obstetrics

Betty Bednarski

1.   Introduction

"Little William" is a story about childbirth by Quebec physician-writer, Jacques Ferron. Because of the nature of the subject matter of this story and the way in which it is presented, I believe it is of interest to the teacher of obstetrics. An ongoing concern of mine is to explore the place of literary texts in the medical curriculum. What has caught my attention in "Little William" is the immediately identifiable obstetrical issue – maternal posture in labour and delivery – and the fact that it is a story about a doctor being taught a lesson, which frames it very nicely as a teaching tool.

The story first appeared in Montreal in 1961 in a largely physician-subscribed bi-weekly. *"Le petit William"* is the title in the original French. It can be read below in an English translation by Ray Ellenwood.[1] In the pages that follow, which should be seen as the extension of a previously-published essay,[2] I will discuss some of the possibilities for learning that it creates. Included in that discussion will be a few words of introduction about Ferron himself. Just imagine to start with that what you are reading is taking place sometime in the 1940s, in a remote fishing community, somewhere along Quebec's Gaspé Shore ...

2.   *Little William*, A Short Story by Jacques Ferron

In pedes procidere nascentem contra naturam est, quid argumento eos appellavere Agrippas ut aegre partos.   Pliny

The young woman refused to stay on her back. No matter how many times we turned her over, she would look up at us through blurred eyes and then roll onto her side again, tucking her knees up to her stomach, hiding her face in the pillow, sulking her way through labour. I stood near the bed, gloved to the elbows, looking like a priest stalled in the middle of his *Dominus vobiscum.* I was all at sea, being both impatient (it's a fatiguing way to stand) and disconcerted, because for things to be ship-shape according to my rites, the young woman should not have been capsized. The old lady who was helping me didn't say a word, waiting snide attendance. When finally I asked for her advice she said, "Take off your gloves, Doctor dear, and make yourself comfortable." Then she ordered her cohorts to bring a cup of tea. Stripped of my gloves, I was at her mercy.

"Drink up, it'll do you good."

"I'm sorry," I said, "but in the hospital we don't have complications like this. The women are strapped down the way we want them."

"What a shame!" said she.

Before I could open my mouth to object, she asked me how the tea was. Was it good? "Excellent," I replied. She seemed pleased. But not just at my satisfaction.

"Look at the length of those thighs," she said, pointing to our patient. "The late Cotnoir, your predecessor, liked them that that way. I think he was right. Me, I've got short ones and I've never brought a child through my labours, just lucky to save my own skin. That's why I became a midwife. Drink your tea, doctor. The late Cotnoir was in the habit of drinking two or three cups while he was keeping an eye on a patient. Look how well this one's pushing with her head in the pillow. After all, we don't need to see a pretty face to do our little job, do we Doctor?"

I had to agree. But all the same it seemed to me she would be better off if she turned on her back. It was an obsession with me and there was nothing I could do about it. To deliver me thereof, the old woman began telling me how there had once been an English doctor on the Shore.

"A boat brought him, a boat took him away, and in between he set up practice as an accoucheur. People made use of his services. One of my aunts was his assistant. And you know, he had his own special way of doing things: first of all he never put his finger in the proper place, and secondly he made the woman lie on her side, with her knees pulled up to her belly, in the exact same position as this little one here."

With my nose in my cup, I was drinking my lesson, and the old lady did not hesitate to make it clear. I didn't really mind, since I was fascinated by exotic practices of all kinds, and God knows I'd never heard of the English position.

"And did it work?"

She seemed surprised at my question.

"Of course, it worked perfectly."

"Shall we try it?"

"Now, Doctor, that's just what I was going to suggest. There's only one problem…"

But the labour was getting hard and I didn't have time to hear about any problem. Judging from the baby's damp crown, which was now showing, the young woman needed us, even though she was still sulking. We let her sulk, and we delivered her on her side – on her side but turned a little toward the front, with her face in the pillow, which in fact meant from behind. And everything went well. When it was all over, she rolled onto her back and looked up at us through wide, clear eyes as if nothing had happened. We placed the baby next to her. She seemed surprised:

she'd had it with her back turned, and maybe she thought it had just dropped from heaven. That's the big advantage of the English position.

"What's the problem then?" I asked the midwife.

"Why, the poor babe will have to be called William."

"After all," she went on, "he's a little Englishman, so to speak."

Contes anglais et autres, 1964. English translation © Ray Ellenwood, 2004

3.   The Possibilities of Story

What I mean by "the possibilities of story" in the context of medical education is the potential of story – in this case literary story – not only to pass on experience and knowledge in a memorable and meaningful way, but also to provoke, or elicit, a series of useful questionings. In the case of the birth story "Little William" the possibilities for questioning are limitless. Together they constitute a potential for learning I have neither the expertise to fully exploit (I am not an obstetrician or a midwife, not a doctor, not a medical historian), nor the space to fully develop here (this text will be "shorthand" for what is becoming a fairly elaborate extended "lesson plan"). At best I can try to identify for you those lines of questioning that would seem to me to be of most relevance to the teaching of obstetrics, calling on my own expertise as a teacher of literature and on the insights I have gained during my association with a medical faculty. I should add that this is part of an ongoing reflection on the "place" of literature in medicine – very much a work in progress at this point. I hope it will have some very practical applications. You should bear in mind that even though I've spent a great deal of time thinking about this pedagogical potential I've not yet had a chance to see my ideas tested in the context of an actual class.[3]

4.   The Author of the Story and the Circumstances of its Writing

In the still hypothetical learning situation I am imagining, my teacher of literature's instinct is to assume – and encourage – a certain degree of curiosity about the author of the story and the circumstances of its writing. A first line of questioning would therefore allow students to satisfy their need for background information on Jacques Ferron and on his training, his practice, and his attitude toward his profession. It might also serve to draw attention to the phenomenon of the physician-writer and allow for some preliminary reflection on the relationship between writing and medicine, and, in Ferron's case, the profound connections between writing and birth.

In the first instance, it would be important for students to know that Ferron studied medicine at Laval University in Quebec City in the 1940s, qualifying just before the end of World War II. After a short stint as a doctor with the Canadian Army in 1945, he spent two years as a country doctor in the Gaspé, then thirty-seven years as a family physician in the Montreal suburb of Ville Jacques Cartier (now Longueuil), where he practised until his death in 1985.[4] He was a doctor with a profound social conscience. Pierre Vallières has paid moving tribute to him in his essay *Nègres blancs d'Amérique (White Niggers of America).*[5] He was also what you would call a humble sort of doctor, critical of professional arrogance, and when it came to himself, not at all sure he had ever been of any great use. He did, however, admit to feeling a certain satisfaction at having been helpful at births. He enjoyed delivering babies and brought all four of his own children into the world. Childbirth is a frequent theme in his writing. There are scenes of deliveries throughout his work, and in one book he even portrayed his own birth.[6]

In the passages Ferron wrote on childbirth, one is struck by his decidedly "feminist" stance with regard to birthing practices. In a 1975 letter to the Montreal newspaper *Le Devoir*, he denounced what he called "male imperialism" in hospital delivery rooms,[7] and in a 1982 interview he stated his profound conviction that childbirth should be "returned" to those to whom it rightfully belonged, insisting not that men should be excluded, but that women should regain the control they had lost over the centuries.[8] Notable, too, is the prominence given in Ferron's birth writings to the figure of the traditional country midwife. She is a recurring character and in his fictional universe wields considerable authority. One is struck, finally, by his insistence on the importance of the community, of the broad socio-cultural context of birth. In the Gaspé, he prided himself on having practiced a kind of "humble" medicine, "far from the hospitals" – *"loin des hôpitaux"* – and perfectly integrated into the community and the world of the everyday. There, deliveries, like the delivery in the story of "Little William", had taken place at home, and it was the presence of the local country midwife that had symbolized for him the perfect integration of care and community.[9]

Such, then, is the kind of bare-bones background this first line of questioning is likely to provide. It would also be important at this point to touch on the question of autobiography and the relation between Ferron's doctor-narrator and himself. There is, as you might have guessed, an autobiographical element to this story, as there is to most of Ferron's best-known "doctor stories." He is no doubt basing his fictional doctor's experience on a similar experience of his own. This is well-documented, and the teacher could refer the student to the text of the 1982 interview I have already mentioned, in which Ferron alludes to the once-upon-a-time "English doctor", whose boat had had to put in to the port of Grande Vallée (no doubt for some protracted repairs, because he had time to teach the "English position" to the locals, one of whom had subsequently demonstrated it to Ferron himself). He also mentions the Gaspé ritual of the bedside cups of tea, commenting that he himself had never taken to it, much preferring coffee, and always making that preference known (and into that comment we could read a lot).[10] So, while Ferron and his first-person narrator are very much alike, they differ in some significant ways, not least of which is their degree of ignorance – or innocence – with respect to the exotic "English position," or *posture anglaise.*"

5.   The Human Dynamic

Now, it is clear that in the context of medical teaching this story offers an opportunity to learn – just as the doctor-narrator learns – about one of the classic positions for labour and delivery, better known once than it now is, and more familiar in some places than in others. It is, of course, the so-called Sims position or left lateral semi-prone.   An obstetrical issue is at the centre of this story. It is because the doctor's ignorance of the left lateral, and his initial refusal of it, collide with the young woman's stubborn insistence on adopting it, that the story happens. The attitude of doctor to patient is shaped by the anomalous position. The complex interaction between doctor and midwife expresses itself in relation to it. This maternal posture – its characteristics, its variations (what it requires of the woman, and what must be done by the person or persons assisting her), its history (how old it is, where it comes from), its use and relevance today, and its perceived advantages and disadvantages – will, of necessity, be the main focus of any reading shared with students of obstetrics. Yet my teacher of literature's instinct is to first draw attention to what I would call "the human dynamic," the living relationship between three characters – the doctor, the midwife and the patient – that is part of the story's value as story, and precisely what sets it apart from the manual of midwifery, the handbook of obstetrics, or the history of childbirth practices over the last two or three hundred years. In the shifting interaction of this threesome (two birth attendants plus one woman in labour; two women plus one man; two locals plus one outsider), two "couples" stand out: that of the doctor-midwife, and that of the doctor-patient or doctor-parturient.

A. Doctor and midwife

The doctor-midwife couple first. Questioning the text, we realize that we know far more about these two characters than we do about the other one. We see the doctor needing to feel in charge, disconcerted when his authority is questioned and his certainties are shaken – "all at sea." We see him defensive at first, reluctant, then compliant, showing himself capable of adapting to the circumstances. We see the midwife, gently ironic, quietly condescending, with her "doctor dear," a little fearsome too, as she "waits snide attendance." We see her stripping the doctor of his gloves, the symbol of his superiority, dispensing her lesson with her cup of tea, and taming him and making an ally of him by the end. We know that *she* is old. I think it's natural to assume that *he* is young.

These characters are, more than anything, types. Beneath the surface niceties of their polite social exchange can be read all the complexities of the medical-obstetrical profession's historical relationship with traditional midwives – the centuries-old rivalry *and* the collaboration; the resentment and suspicion *and* the mutual accommodations, the often grudging mutual respect. One would direct students' attention to histories that recount some of the ups and downs of that troubled relationship through the centuries. Since the perspective of most such histories is that of the male medical profession, this would be a good point at which to create a degree of critical awareness, raising with students the question of how history is made. In the context of a short story in which a male doctor's authority is challenged by two women, I would refer students to works that "read" the doctor-midwife relationship somewhat differently, from a woman's perspective, describing the transformation of childbirth from an event rooted in female culture into one dominated by male professionals.[11] And since this story – we know it implicitly – is set in Quebec, one would also direct the curious and questioning student to works where information can be found on the role of the traditional midwives in New France and, throughout the nineteenth and early twentieth centuries, in rural and small-town Quebec.[12]

Students might actually be puzzled to find the doctor and the country midwife working side by side in this instance. One would need to explain that in the Gaspé of the period Quebec provincial regulations would have made it illegal for traditional midwives to practice. Government-paid nurses and doctors (Ferron himself was one of these) were sent out into the communities. It was they, officially at any rate, who were responsible for attending births. But the isolation of the region would have made it impossible to completely supplant the old ways. Attachment to the traditional midwives remained strong and long after their official exclusion they continued to be called in by families for reassuring support. Ferron had great respect for these women and valued his unofficial association with them.

What is important in "Little William" is the way in which institutional obstetrics and popular midwifery have come together. They are shown to be reconcilable. Indeed they are inseparable. We discover, just as we do when we study the relationship between oral and written traditions in literature – in the case of fairy tales, for example – that the influences, far from moving in one direction, actually go back and forth. What Ferron's doctor takes from the popular tradition originates in actual fact with the so-called "English doctor," with someone who was not only from a far off country, but no doubt institutionally trained.[13] A practice has gone from the institution through the popular tradition and back to the institution again. In the end it is interdependence that is stressed. Doctor and midwife emerge as partners in a successful delivery. Complicity, not rivalry, is affirmed. It helps that both midwife and doctor are French-speaking Québécois and that their perfect obstetrical collaboration can be "sealed" with an "English" joke.[14]

B. Doctor and patient

An examination of the doctor-patient dynamic is equally revealing. We see the patient, stubborn, non-compliant, disobedient – "sulking" (*"elle boudait son accouchement"*). When considering this word "sulking" (not entirely adequate as a translation of *"boudait,"* it is true, but as close an approximation as could be found[15]), it is important to remember that the narrative point of view is the doctor's. Students would need to be reminded that the perceptions inherent in the word are his. We see the doctor himself, rigid, seeking at first to impose what is the norm for him, what he thinks is best for her and what is convenient for him. The woman knows what she wants. He is not prepared to give it to her, convinced that he knows best. It is the midwife who ensures the woman gets her way by interceding on her behalf. In the end there is a delightful parallel between these two figures who are at first seen to be at loggerheads. In French, Ferron exploits the related meanings of the verb *"délivrer."* "It was an obsession with me. To deliver me thereof (*pour m'en délivrer)* the old woman proceeded to tell me how there had once been an English doctor on the Shore...") Learning requires "unlearning." Both doctor and patient are "delivered" – he of some arrogant misconceptions, she of her baby boy.[16]

I must just say, finally, before moving on to my next line of questioning, that as a female reader (and two-time parturient), I am drawn to this young woman about whom we know nothing. She exists for us because of her resistance. She is silent. She is the only one of the three characters who says nothing. Each of the other two has some degree of narrative autonomy. The doctor is the actual narrator, but the midwife gets to narrate a brief story within his story. The two of them engage each other in conversation too, talking over the young woman's head – behind her back. And because of her posture, this character is not only *voiceless*, she is *faceless* until the very end. I would hope that the questioning kind of reading I am advocating here would arouse curiosity about her, and that in due course the student-reader would sense something of the significance of what we do not know, and what this text, because of its silence, makes us desire to know.

I will return to the question of *"Why?"*– to the question of the reasons for, the "meaning" of, the young woman's posture. At this point, however, in the context of the doctor-patient dynamic, it would be important for the teacher to open up discussion around the notion of maternal choice, since Ferron's story is as much about maternal choice as it is about a particular position. Choice was clearly not an option in the hospitals where Ferron's young doctor was trained ("At the hospital, we don't have complications like this. The women are strapped down the way we want them." "What a shame!" [*"Quelle pitié!"*]). A decidedly prescriptive stance on birthing posture developed, along with modern obstetrics, in the eighteenth, nineteenth and twentieth centuries. Students should be made aware that the degree of freedom given to women in this matter varies greatly from country to country, even from hospital to hospital, and remains to this day a subject of debate.[17]

6.   The Explicitly Obstetrical Content

I come now to the explicitly obstetrical content of this story. This content is rich and would, as I have said, be at the centre of the learning experience I am imagining.

A. The doctor's lesson

The young doctor himself learns a great deal that is of a specifically obstetrical nature. From direct experience, he discovers a birthing posture hitherto unknown to him. He discovers: (1) the actual characteristics of the side position as it is assumed; (2) that it can be maintained in the first and second stages of labour as well as in delivery; (3) that pushing is effective in this posture; (4) that the woman is turning away from the attendants and that delivery consequently takes place from behind, *"par en arrière."*

He also learns from the midwife's narrative. (1) He learns first of all that the position was introduced into the region by an "English doctor" – *"un Anglais"* – and deduces from that its origins in English obstetrical culture. (2) He also gleans from this same narrative a piece of rather mysterious information, through the midwife's allusion to the "English doctor's" habit of never putting "his finger in the proper place." Trained obstetricians will have little difficulty deciding what (for her) "unorthodox" practice the midwife is referring to. But it is a mystery never elucidated in the text and an interesting question for students to research.[18]

It would also be important to draw students' attention briefly to what might be called the "secondary" obstetrical lessons. I am thinking of the midwife's reference to the young doctor's predecessor's preference for "long" thighs, and his habit of drinking several cups of tea while waiting for a birth. Useful discussions could be generated around both of these minor but significant points.[19]

B. The historical and inter-cultural dimensions

As far as the left lateral itself is concerned, quite apart from the practical details, some of the most productive lines of questioning are historical ones, and because of the midwife's narrative of the position's "origins," we are led into the history of obstetrics quite naturally. Just like the midwife's story of the "English doctor," most histories identify this position as originating with a man (or men), and associate it with obstetrical practice in the English-speaking world, in particular the British Isles, where it was the standard obstetrical position until well into the 1960s.

An obvious place to begin any historical enquiry would seem at first glance to be with the eponym, James Marion Sims, who was an American from the deep south, practicing in the southern states and in New York in the second half of the nineteenth century. Even though Sims promoted "his" position for a gynecological procedure (the repair of vesico-vaginal fistula), and not as a position in which to give birth, his name attaches to this day to the obstetrical posture, and at times, somewhat loosely, to its several variations (the French also refer to "*la position de Sims*"[20]). The name being therefore something of an obstetrical misnomer, Sims is relevant to our lesson in only the most tangential way. But a consideration of his career would be interesting for students from a number of points of view. What is useful about Sims' case is, first of all, that it provides an opportunity to bring to students' attention the whole phenomenon of the medical eponym, an opportunity to reflect on this tradition whereby physicians' names are assigned to their "discoveries" – whether these be instruments (there is also a "Sims' speculum"), cures, viruses, bacilli, or even medical conditions themselves. Here, we have the bizarre example of the position of a woman's body being given a man's name. The intention may not be such, but the suggestion might seem to be that Sims is somehow the "inventor," the "patent-holder," perhaps that he can even claim "ownership" of a particular posture for birth. Once again we have a reminder of the particular perspective from which most medical history has been written, and a quite telling example of that so-called male "take-over" of birth and the female body, which so many feminist critics have objected to, and which Ferron frequently denounced. In considering what is, after all, a story about birth and "naming," it seems to me that it would be important to take the time to give this some thought. Sims' career also provides an opportunity to reflect – again, tangentially – on the human cost of the finding of many a medical cure, since his twentieth-century critics – mainly women – have taken exception to his use of female black slaves to perfect, over a period of several years, through repeated trial and error, his ultimately successful and deservedly celebrated surgical technique.[21]

The story of the English doctor opens the way quite naturally to historical enquiry. But whereas the midwife's narrative is mysteriously – and poetically – incomplete (it has the ring of legend to it: "[T]here had once been an English doctor on the Shore. A boat brought him, a boat took him away") – the teacher of obstetrics will want to encourage students to seek answers to questions like: When exactly, where exactly, and in what circumstances did the obstetrical position originate? When and where did its adoption become routine? Is it used anywhere today and, again, in what circumstances? Additional questions might be: To what extent has the position been identified with English culture or Englishness? Is it identified this way by the English themselves, by other cultures and, particularly, by the French? Ferron's story is French. His narrator is speaking, and Ferron himself is writing, out of a French obstetrical tradition, and part of the humour of the story comes from its portrayal of a French perception of an English custom. What, then, have the French said about it in their obstetrical writings? Have they ever adopted it themselves? And what might Ferron have been taught about it at Laval University? What might he have already known when he arrived in the Gaspé?

Having myself gone down what I call "the trail of the English doctor" (I was accompanied on this "trail" by my surgeon colleague, Vivian McAlister of the London Health Sciences Centre, London, Ontario, and we were both amazed at the wealth of material we found), having myself embarked on extensive historical research, much of it comparative, I can vouch for the richness of this line of enquiry. Because of the story's strong inter-cultural dimension, and because of the striking divergence between English and French obstetrical practice as regards maternal posture, it would seem to be a particularly compelling one. Already in the mid-eighteenth century English man-midwives were making the distinction between the dorsal position used in France and the lateral one favoured by the English. In 1742, Fielding Ould of Dublin speaks of the "French" position and the "English" one ("Irish" being subsumed here in the term "English," of course);[22] William Smellie, writing in 1752, calls them the "London" and "Parisian" positions respectively.[23]

One of my own most significant findings is that from the early nineteenth century on French obstetrical writings associate the position unequivocally with "*les Anglais.*" The term "*posture anglaise,*" which Ferron's narrator appears to have invented spontaneously, occurs frequently. It is found in the caption to an illustration appearing in 1887 in the Parisian obstetrician Witkowski's *Histoire des accouchements chez tous les peuples;*[24] and in another book, a French manual of birthing postures dating from 1908, the chapter on the left lateral is also given the title "*Posture anglaise*" – not "*Position latérale,*" not "*Position sur le côté,*" not "*Décubitus latéral,*" but the culturally specific "*Posture anglaise*" (what is more, this is the only chapter in the book to have such a culturally specific title).[25] I have also learned that at Laval University in the1940s the obstetrics curriculum was taught from textbooks from France. The French manual used in Ferron's obstetrics class of 1944-1945, *Précis d'obstétrique* by Maygrier and Schwaab, recommends and presents in detail the classic dorsal position, but the left lateral is given a summary two-line mention, in which it's identified with England (and "some other countries").[26] The textbook also contains an illustration of delivery on the side, which one can only assume Ferron must have seen. There's every reason to believe, then, that although Ferron had had no first hand experience of it, he, unlike his narrator, had at least read about the position before arriving in the Gaspé.

Finally, and perhaps most significantly, I have discovered that the explanation most frequently given by French obstetricians for the English preference for the side position is rooted in cultural stereotype. In an 1864 French medical encyclopedia, for example, a Parisian obstetrician states that English doctors are obliged to respect the prudery of their women, who, he says, carry their sense of modesty "to such extremes in this and other matters."[27] And there is a clear tie-in here with Ferron's English joke. Ferron's story grows out of a particular medical-historical context and culture. It can be seen as a contemporary and particularly French Canadian "take" on a centuries-old Anglo-French obstetrical debate. One of the "uses" of literature in this context, then, is to lead the medical reader naturally into this realm of the "inter-cultural," where one culture's perceptions of another culture's practice are being "read".

C. The advantages and disadvantages of the left lateral

"And did it work?" the curious young doctor asks the midwife ... One necessary stage in this pedagogical reading would be the consideration of the perceived advantages and disadvantages of the lateral posture. Since they are many, and since they vary considerably depending on time and place, students would not only gain historical perspective, but become engaged in an ongoing and subtly evolving debate that goes to the heart of key issues in obstetrics: issues like perineal care, fetal oxygenation, maternal blood supply, pushing, obstetrical intervention, monitoring, asepsis, physician control ...

The main obstetrical argument in favour of the left lateral is now, and seems to have been in the past, that it helps prevent lacerations of the perineum, by lessening the likelihood of overdistension, allowing greater visibility of the perineum, and affording the physician or midwife greater control over the emerging head.[28] Let us take, for example, the question of superior visibility, mentioned time and again in the literature. It is interesting to note the American obstetrician Joseph DeLee, in the 1930s, affirming that same superiority of the left lateral in the very textbook where he nevertheless promotes the use of the dorsal position. This gives rise to a rather strange and paradoxical situation. DeLee's 1938 manual, *The Principles and Practice of Obstetrics*, recommends and describes the dorsal position, but all of his illustrations are of the left lateral. The author explains that in spite of his preference for the dorsal, he has chosen the left lateral for his illustrations because more can be *seen* in this position. I have found in his textbook, by the way, some of the finest "illustrations" of "little William"'s birth.[29] In this connection, I would point out to teachers the wealth of illustrative material on the left lateral available to share with students. Besides being useful as visual aids, textbook illustrations could themselves become a topic for discussion, providing as they do an opportunity to reflect on the subject of medicine's visual representations of birth and of the female body.

I certainly do not have the space here to follow through on all the advantages and disadvantages, all the obstetrical arguments for and against the left lateral. The pedagogical opportunities to be gained from discussing them would, I hope, be apparent, since they do in every case raise such fundamental questions for the obstetrical profession. Take the question of intervention. In very general terms it is probably true to say that the decline in popularity of the lateral position can be associated with an ever-increasing interventionism, in other words with an intensifying of the so-called "obstetrification" of birth. Fetal heart monitoring is more difficult in this position, for example, and surgical procedures are generally assumed to be less conveniently performed. Interestingly, though, whereas nineteenth-century French obstetricians saw the lateral as an obstacle to forceps use, the British defenders of it always insisted on its facilitation of a number of interventions and manœuvres. Students would no doubt be interested to find that illustrations of forceps delivery or of internal version in the lateral position are a regular feature of British textbooks of the late nineteenth and early twentieth century.[30]

7.   The Woman's Point of View

One thing the student will quickly discover from the literature on the left lateral is that apart from allusions to its accommodation of female modesty and, occasionally, to restfulness and comfort (the physiological basis for which it would be important to make clear), scientific writing on the advantages and disadvantages of this position only rarely considers the point of view of the woman giving birth. A French obstetrician writing in the 1860s notes that women who come to adopt this position at any point in their labour are generally very reluctant to abandon it for another one, but he does not go on to ask why this should be so.[31] This brings me back to the silence at the heart of Ferron's story, and to my curiosity about the young woman and the *"Why?"* of the position she has so stubbornly maintained. To question Ferron's text is to come ultimately to question historical narratives of the posture's origins, which, seemingly without exception, trace it back to the mid-eighteenth century and to an "English" man-midwife, or English man-midwives (John Burton of York, Fielding Ould, Benjamin Pugh, Brudenell Exton, have each on various occasions been credited with being "first"). This is an overwhelming tendency, both of traditional histories, recounted from the male medical profession's perspective, and of those that endeavour to retell the history of birthing practices from the woman's point of view. Jo Murphy-Lawless, for example, in *Reading Birth and Death: A History of Obstetric Thinking*, cites Fielding Ould's comment on one important advantage of the left lateral, namely, that with her back to the "Operator" and others in the room, the woman in labour is protected from their "remarks and whispers." In the context of her feminist analysis, this and other "advantages," like visibility of the birth outlet, become associated with the assertion of male professional control.[32] Historically, there can be no doubt that the privileging of the side position in British obstetrical culture was connected with the rise of the eighteenth-century man-midwife (although by the late twentieth century, once it was no longer the standard position, its use had become associated with the influence of women, notably the nurse-midwives responsible for instruction in manual delivery in many hospitals in the United Kingdom and Ireland). In the context of Ferron's story, however, use of the position is seen as patient-driven, and it has come to represent the assertion of female control. Perhaps the question of where the position "originates" does not have to lead back to "England," or to a man?

It is true that the young Gaspé woman may very well have owed her knowledge of the lateral position to the influence of the story's "English doctor." As a result of his practice, she could have observed other women in her community giving birth in this way, or she might already have given birth in the position herself (there is nothing to indicate whether William is her first child). But might she not – might not any woman – conceivably have *"found"* the position for herself? This would be an obvious point at which to have students of obstetrics consider the infinitely problematic notion of *naturalness*. Modern obstetrics has been unsuccessful in its attempt to identify a "natural" position for birth. But the attempt itself has been interesting. It led in the nineteenth century to an obstetrical fascination with so-called "primitive" cultures, and hence with anthropology. As it turns out, nineteenth and early twentieth-century anthropologists have interesting things to say about the "artificial" and "civilized" nature of the lateral position, about its very "unnaturalness," if you will, and they confirm the connection with prudery that the French were insisting upon.[33] And yet, by the end of the twentieth century, renewed interest in the position in the United States is associated with the desire to provide women with a more "natural" birthing experience.[34] In relation to this notion of naturalness, one might refer students to the interesting early nineteenth-century experiment by the German obstetrician Naegele, who arranged for a young and inexperienced primipara to be left alone during labour, and secretly observed what positions she adopted.[35] Or one might direct their attention to a 1986 American study that attempted to determine what positions women in hospital assume in labour when they are "permitted to do so without coertion or instruction." In the latter, the most common position adopted was found to be "the left lateral lying position," though no attempt was made to take into account ethnic or cultural background.[36]

Ultimately, however, one would encourage students to look beyond such clinical studies, beyond historical narrative and beyond anthropology even, to find in their own readers' imaginations the deeper meaning of a preference that may after all not simply be "taught" or "learned." One would remind them that there could be an instinctive element in the young woman's response. The lateral not only provides the much-discussed protection of modesty, relief from fatigue and pain, and a natural corrective in the case of certain anomalous presentations, it is already for many women a familiar position for sleep. It resembles the fetal position with which we associate various forms of regression or denial/withdrawal, and, avoiding as it does "front-on" exposure, it could also indicate an instinctively self-protective response (one midwife I consulted reported having observed a marked tendency to adopt this position among victims of rape or other forms of physical abuse[37]). With her head in the pillows and her back stubbornly turned, the young woman might be manifesting ignorance, unpreparedness, ambivalence, or some powerful inner resistance to the birth event. But, as I have suggested elsewhere, she might also be simply shutting out intrusion, concentrating inwardly, creating for herself a closed and private inner space. In this at once public and intensely private moment, could there not be a need for something like secrecy?[38]

The turned back, the averted gaze, draw me to this woman. I would hope Ferron's story would cause students to pause and consider her psychic space. A revealing exercise – one often used in literature classes, where awareness of narrative point of view is traditionally encouraged and the "uses" of imagination have been well explored – would be for students to re-write the story of "Little William" as the mother's first-person account.

8.   The Political Dimensions of Birth

Sooner or later, the reader of "Little William" must confront the broadly political dimensions of birth. Issues of gender, for example, are never far from the surface, and the teacher might wish to explore with students connections between gender, power and the profession of obstetrics which I have barely touched on here.[39] It would also be important to consider another more overt political dimension of this story, a dimension brought to light by the final "twist" of the "English" joke, when the midwife gives the newborn baby an Englishman's (and, what is more, a conqueror's) name. While that "twist" may seem at first glance to have little to do with issues of childbirth and obstetrics, and therefore to fall outside of the range of our obstetrical lesson's enquiry, it could in fact be shown that there are close textual connections between the two. The story's Latin epigraph, a quote from Pliny the Elder on the relevance of fetal presentation to naming, is particularly significant in this regard.[40] So, too, is the evocation of the moment of crowning (implicit in the French reference to "*le toupet mouillé*," and made quite explicit in the English translation's rendering of this by "the baby's damp *crown*"), which strengthens the association with English royal conquerors. It would be important, then, to have students consider, even briefly, the political implications of the joke. It serves, if nothing else, as a reminder that birth takes place in both a private and a public realm.

It will not be possible to develop this last political line of questioning here. I will simply remind you that in Canada – now, as at the time Ferron was writing – the survival of French culture is far from being assured. In Ferron's writing, as in the Québécois collective consciousness, birth is associated with cultural survival, and the relationship with "Englishness" is fraught with ambiguity. Here is how one critic has read the political significance of the left lateral position in "Little William:" "While she hides her head and turns her back," writes Eileen Sarkar, '*la mère patrie*' [in the person of William's mother] gives birth to generations of *petits Anglais.*"[41]

9.   Conclusion

By identifying these few lines of questioning, I have tried to indicate how much of a scientific and practical nature a curious and critical reading of this brief story is able to reveal. I hope I have also convinced you of the relevance – the usefulness – of those lines of questioning that have the potential to go beyond the scientific and the practical, giving students of obstetrics a sense of historical and cultural perspective and reminding them of the many *meanings*, the enormous individual and collective significance of the event in which they will be called upon to play their small part.

You will have noticed that I have not questioned the relevance of history or of anthropology to the study of medicine, although I know that when it comes to the medical curriculum that relevance is far from being universally accepted. Above all, you will have noticed that I have allowed myself to take for granted the value of literature in medical education, although I know as well as you do that literature does not form, and is unlikely ever to form, a significant part of the curriculum in medical schools. Doctors may well wish to challenge me on the value of literature to their students. Or they may wish to help me articulate more clearly where that value lies. My hope is that those who agree that there *is* value will be willing to engage with me in discussing in more detail this hypothetical learning experience I have envisioned. Perhaps together we can find a way – a realistic and practical way – of integrating it into the work they do.

When considering what mode of integration might work best, I must say I have not simply been thinking in terms of a course in literature and medicine, the kind of course offered now in more and more medical faculties, and for which models and precedents have existed since the 1970s. Such a course is unlikely to be taken by more than a fraction of medical students, and even though I would be delighted to give one, and include "Little William" in the syllabus, I confess that I have been thinking more along the lines of close integration into the case-oriented, problem-based curriculum. I like the idea of *all* students being exposed, even sporadically, to literary texts. Perhaps once per module. What I know about the case-oriented approach leads me to believe that an at once spare and highly concentrated literary narrative like "Little William" could occasionally be substituted for the kind of constructed "case" today's medical teachers provide for their students to analyse. I am also curious to know when might be the ideal moment to introduce students to a story such as this, and whether teachers feel exposure to such material could come with the very first contact with the obstetrical curriculum, or whether it might be better saved for a later stage. I myself like the idea of engagement with literature occurring early on in the medical education process, and being sustained throughout.

Notes

[1] Jacques Ferron, "Le petit William," *L'Information médicale et paramédicale* XIII, 2 (3 October, 1961): 14-15; reprinted in *Contes anglais et autres* (Montréal : Éditions d'Orphée, 1964), 80-83. An earlier version of Ray Ellenwood's English translation appeared in *Impulse* 3, 2 (1974): 11-12.

[2] Betty Bednarski and Vivian McAlister, "Literature and Obstetrics: Reading Maternal Posture in Jacques Ferron's 'Little William'," *Literature and Medicine* 21, 2 (2002): 216-241. The present article makes frequent reference to this essay and should be read in conjunction with it.

[3] The rich pedagogical potential of the story first became apparent to me during the term I spent as Hannah Millennium Visitor in the Dalhousie Faculty of Medicine, in 2001. The text of this article is based on the paper delivered at the second "Making Sense…" conference, Oxford, July 2003. It also incorporates elements subsequently developed for presentation at the annual general meeting of the Association of Professors of Obstetrics

and Gynecology (APOG), Toronto, December 2003, where I spoke on the topic: "Obstetrics in Literature, Literature in Obstetrics: Reading, Writing, Teaching Birth."

[4] A brief overview of Ferron's medical career and his importance as a physician-writer, can be found in a recent article written for a medical audience: Mark Cardwell, "A Literary Giant," *The Medical Post*, November 18, 2003, 32-33. The most comprehensive summary to appear to date is my own study: Betty Bednarski, "Putting Medicine in its Place: The Case of Physician-Writer Jacques Ferron," in *Making Sense of Health, Illness and Disease,* ed. Peter L. Twohig and Vera Kalitzkus (Amsterdam and Atlanta: Rodopi, 2004), 54-84.

[5] Pierre Vallières, *Nègres blancs d'Amérique: autobiographie précoce d'un terroriste québécois,* nouvelle édition revue et corrigée (Montréal: Éditions Parti-pris, 1969), 154-158. Trans. Joan Pinkham, *White Niggers of America* (Toronto : McClelland and Stewart, 1971), 114-117.

[6] Jacques Ferron, "La créance," in *Les Confitures de coings et autres textes* (Montréal: Éditions Part-pris, 1972), 231-260. Trans. Ray Ellenwood as "Credit Due" in *Quince Jam* (Toronto: Coach House Press, 1977), 186-208.

[7] Jacques Ferron, "L'impérialisme masculin," *Les Lettres aux journaux,* ed. Pierre Cantin, Marie Ferron and Paul Lewis (Montréal: VLB éditeur, 1985), 415-416. Discussed briefly in Bednarski and McAlister, 226-227, and in greater detail in Bednarski, "Putting Medicine in its Place, " 10, 11.

[8] Jacques Ferron ct Picrrc L'Hérault, *Par la porte d'en arrière: entretiens* (Montréal: Lanctôt éditeur, 1997), 92.

[9] Ibid., 79.

[10] Ibid., 89.

[11] Jean Donnison, *Midwives and Medical Men: A History of Inter-Professional Rivalries and Women's Rights* (London: Hcincmann, 1977); Jo Murphy-Lawless, *Reading Birth and Death: A History of Obstetric Thinking* (Bloomington and Indianapolis: Indiana University Press, 1998).

[12] Hélène Laforce, *Histoire de la sage-femme dans la région de Québec* (Montréal: Institut québécois de recherche sur la culture, 1979); and "The Different Stages of the Elimination of Midwives in Quebec," *Delivering Motherhood: Maternal Ideologies and Practices in the 19th and 20th Centuries,* ed. Katherine Arnup, Andrée Lévesque and Ruth Roach Pierson (London: Routledge, 1990), 36-50.

[13] While the English translation reflects the assumption that the accoucheur in question was a medical doctor, it should nevertheless be noted that Ferron's text does not specify this, referring to him only as *"un Anglais."* For a reference to a male version of the traditional or country midwife, see Jacques Ferron, "L'accoucheur, personnage insolite," *Voir* 13, 36 (9 September, 1999): 20.

[14] Bednarski and McAlister, 228.

[15] Ibid., 225.

[16] Ibid., 227. See also the chapter entitled"'Le petit William:' une double délivrance," in Andrée Mercier, *L'Incertitude narrative dans quatre contes de Jacques Ferron: étude sémiotique* (Québec: Éditions Nota Bene, 1998), 110-120.

[17] For interesting statistics on maternal choice, see Iain Chalmers, Jo Garcia and Shirley Post, "Hospital Policies for Labour and Delivery," in *Effective Care in Pregnancy and Childbirth,* Vol. 2, *Childbirth,* ed. Murray Enkin, Mark Keirse, Iain Chalmers and Eleanor Enkin (Oxford: Oxford University Press, 1989), 818. See also Wendy Mitchinson, *Giving Birth in Canada 1900-1950* (Toronto: University of Toronto Press, 2002), 184-185.

[18] On the subject of rectal versus vaginal examination, see Bednarski and McAlister, 220-221.

[19] Ibid. 218, 226.

[20] *Dictionnaire de médecine Flammarion,* 4th edition. (Paris: Éditions Flammarion, 1991), 773.

[21] See Thomas Baskett, *On the Shoulders of Giants: Names and Eponyms in Obstetrics and Gynecology* (London: ROCG Press, 1996), 209-211, and Jacalyn Duffin, *History of Medicine: A Scandalously Short Introduction* (Toronto: University of Toronto Press, 1999), 260-261.

[22] Fielding Ould, *A Treatise of Midwifry in Three Parts* (Dublin: Oli. Nelson, 1742), 32-33.

[23] William Smellie, *A Treatise on the Theory and Practice of Midwifery* (London: D. Wilson and T. Durham, 1752), 199-203.

[24] Gustave-Joseph Witkowski, *Histoire des accouchements chez tous les peuples* (Paris: Steinheil, 1887), 365.

[25] René Giron, *Histoire curieuse et critique des postures de la femme en gésine* (Paris: Steinheil, 1908), 74-80.

[26] Charles Maygrier et Albert Schwaab, *Précis d'obstétrique*, 2nd edition (Paris: Octave Doin, 1922), 236. Dr. Pierre Potvin, former Dean, Faculté de médecine, Université Laval, identified this textbook for me.

[27] J. A. H. Depaul, "Des soins à donner à la femme pendant l'accouchement physiologique," s. v. "Accouchement," in *Dictionnaire encyclopédique des sciences médicales,* ed. Raige-Delorme and A. Dechambre (Paris: P. Asselin, 1864), 413. For more references to French reception see Bednarski and McAlister, 222-223, esp. notes 24.-27.

[28] For a fuller discussion of the perceived advantages and disadvantages of the left lateral as they relate to "Little William," see Bednarski and McAlister, 223-224.

[29] Joseph DeLee, *The Principles and Practice of Obstetrics,* 7th edition (Philadelphia and London: W. B. Saunders, 1938), 351-354.

[30] See, for example, Thomas Watts Eden, *A Manual of Midwifery,* 2nd edition (London: J. & A. Churchill, 1908), 494-499.

[31] Joseph-Alexis Stoltz, "Position et attitude de la femme en travail," s. v. "Accouchement naturel," in *Nouveau dictionnaire de médecine et de chirurgie pratiques,* ed. S. Jaccoud (Paris: J.-B. Baillière, 1864), 275.

[32] Murphy-Lawless, 37, 62-63, 80.

[33] George J. Engelmann, *Labour Among Primitive peoples: Showing the Development of Obstetric Science of Today from the Natural and Instinctive Customs of All Races, Civilized and Savage, Past and Present* (St. Louis: J. H. Chambers, 1882), 82.

[34] Hampton W. Irwin, "Practical Considerations for the Routine Application of the Left Lateral Sims' Position for Vaginal Delivery," *American Journal of Obstetrics and Gynecology* 13, 2 (1978): 130, 132. See also Bednarski and McAlister, 238, note 37.

[35] For an account of Naegele's experiment see Edward Rigby, "What is the Natural Position of a Woman During labour?" *Medical Times and Gazette* 15 (1857): 345-346, and Bednarski and McAlister, 238, note 38.

[36] Jerold M. Carlson et al., "Maternal Position in Parturition During Normal Labor," *Obstetrics and Gynecology* 68, 4 (1986): 443-447.

[37] Mme Huguette Boilard, Directrice, Programme de baccalauréat en pratique sage-femme, Université du Québec à Trois-Riviéres.

[38] Bednarski and McAlister, 225.

[39] See Bednarski and McAlister, 226, 232 for discussion of possible gender issues to be explored, and a reference to sexual innuendo in the text.

[40] For a full discussion of the Pliny quotation and of the historical and cultural significance of the name William, see Bednarski and McAlister, 229-231, and Mercier, 114-120.

[41] Eileen Sarkar, "The Uncertain Countries of Jacques Ferron and Mordecai Richler, " *The Canadian Fiction Magazine* 13 (1974): 99. The connections between birth and politics are discussed more fully in Bednarski and McAlister, 232-234.

Bibliography

Baskett, Thomas F. *On the Shoulders of Giants: Eponyms and Names in Obstetrics and Gynecology.* London: RCOG Press, 1996.

Bednarski, Betty. "Putting Medicine in its Place: The Case of Physician-Writer Jacques Ferron." In *Making Sense of Health, Illness and Disease,* Ed. Peter L. Twohig and Vera Kalitzkus. Amsterdam and Atlanta: Rodopi, 2004, 54-84.

---------- and Vivian McAlister. "Literature and Obstetrics: Reading Maternal Posture in Jacques Ferron's 'Little William'." *Literature and Medicine* 21, 2 (2002), 216-241.

Cardwell, Mark. "A Literary Giant." *The Medical Post,* November 18, 2003, 32-33.

Carlson, Jerold M. et al. "Maternal Position in Parturition During Normal Labor." *Obstetrics and Gynecology* 68, 4 (1984): 443-447.

Chalmers, Iain, Jo Garcia and Shirley Post. "Hospital Practices for Labour and Delivery." In *Effective Care in Pregnancy and Childbirth,* Vol. 2, *Childbirth.* Ed. Murray Enkin, Mark Keirse, Iain Chalmers and Eleanor Enkin. New York and Oxford: Oxford University Press, 1989, 815-819.

DeLee, Joseph B. *The Principles and Practice of Obstetrics,* 7th edition. Philadelphia and London: W. B. Saunders, 1938.

Depaul, J. A. H. "Des soins à donner à la femme pendant l'accouchement physiologique," s. v. "Accouchement." In *Dictionnaire encyclopédique des sciences médicales.* Ed. Raige-Delorme and A. Dechambre, 406-420. Paris: P. Asselin, 1864.

Dictionnaire de médecine Flammarion, 4th edition. Paris: Éditions Flammarion, 1991.

Donnison, Jean. *Midwives and Medical Men: A History of Inter-Professional Rivalries and Women's Rights.* London: Heinemann, 1977.

Duffin, Jacalyn. *History of Medicine: A Scandalously Short Introduction.* Toronto: University of Toronto Press, 2000.

Eden, Thomas Watts. *A Manual of Midwifery,* 2nd edition. London: J. A. Churchill, 1908.

Engelmann, George J. *Labor Among Primitive Peoples: Showing the Development of Obstetric Science of To-Day from the Natural and Instinctive Customs of All Races, Civilized and Savage, Past and Present.* St. Louis: J. H. Chambers, 1882.

Ferron, Jacques. "L'accoucheur, personnage insolite." In *Voir* 13, 36 (9 septembre, 1999): 20.

----------. "L'impérialisme masculin." In *Les lettres aux journaux.* Collected and annotated by Pierre Cantin, Marie Ferron and Paul Lewis, 415-416. Montréal: VLB éditeur, 1985.

----------. "La créance." In *Les Confitures de coings et autres textes.* Montréal: Éditions Part-pris, 1972, 231-260. Trans. Ray Ellenwood as "Credit Due" in *Quince Jam.* Toronto: Exile Editions, 1977, 186-208.

----------. "Le petit William." In *Contes anglais et autres,* 80-83. Montréal: Éditions d'Orphée, 1964.

---------- et Pierre L'Hérault. *Par la porte d'en arrière: entretiens.* Montréal: Lanctôt éditeur, 1997.

Giron, René. *Histoire curieuse et critique des postures de la femme en gésine.* Paris: Steinheil, 1908.

Irwin, Hampton W. "Practical considerations for the Routine Application of the Left Lateral Sims' Position for Vaginal Delivery." *American Journal of Obstetrics and Gynecology* 131, 2 (1978): 129-133.

Laforce, Hélène. *Histoire de la sage-femme dans la région de Québec.* Collection Edmond de Nevers 4. Montréal: Institut québécois de recherche sur la culture, 1979.

----------. "The Different Stages of the Elimination of Midwives in Quebec." In *Delivering Motherhood: Maternal Ideologies and Practices in the 19th and 20th Centuries.* Ed. Katherine Arnup, Andrée Lévesque and Ruth Roach Pierson, 36-50. London: Routledge, 1990.

Maygrier, Charles et Albert Schwaab. *Précis d'obstétrique,* 2nd édition. Paris: Octave Doin, 1922.

Mercier, Andrée. *L'incertitude narrative dans quatre contes de Jacques Ferron: étude sémiotique.* Québec: Éditions Nota Bene, 1998.

Mitchinson, Wendy. *Giving Birth in Canada 1900-1950.* Toronto : University of Toronto Press, 2002.

Murphy-Lawless, Jo. *Reading Birth and Death: A History of Obstetric Thinking.* Bloomington and Indianapolis: Indiana University Press, 1998.

Ould, Fielding. *A Treatise of Midwifry in Three Parts.* Dublin: Oli. Nelson, 1742.

Sarkar, Eileen. "The Uncertain Countries of Jacques Ferron and Mordecai Richler." *The Canadian Fiction Magazine* 13 (1974): 98-107.

Smellie, William. *A Treatise on the Theory and Practice of Midwifery.* London: D. Wilson and T. Durham, 1752.

Stoltz, Joseph-Alexis. "Position et attitude de la femme en travail," s. v. "Accouchement." In *Nouveau dictionnaire de médecine et de chirurgie pratiques.* Ed. Sigismond Jaccoud. Paris: J.-B. Baillière, 1864, 275-276.

Rigby, Edward. "What is the Natural Position of a Woman During Labour?" *Medical Times and Gazette* 15 (1857): 345-346.

Vallières, Pierre. *Nègres blancs d'Amérique: autobiographie précoce d'un terroriste québécois,* nouvelle édition revue et corrigée. Montréal: Éditions Part-pris, 1969. Trans. Joan Pinkham as *White Niggers of America.* Toronto : McClelland and Stewart, 1971.

Witkowski, Gustave-Joseph. *Histoire des accouchements chez tous les peuples.* Paris: Steinheil, 1887.

Note on Contributor

Betty Bednarski is a Professor of French and the Coordinator of Canadian Studies at Dalhousie University, Halifax, Nova Scotia. She has published widely in the field of Quebec literature and is well known for her translations of works by physician-writer Jacques Ferron.

Patient Narrative Videos:
Learning from the Illness Experience

Karen Christopher and Gregory Makoul

1.   What do these Videos Capture?

Many medical curricula include courses or modules that focus on applying the biopsychosocial model and on learning communication skills. A fundamental goal of such offerings is helping trainees develop a sense of how health problems affect patients' lives. This is difficult to achieve. To foster insight into patient perspectives on the illness experience, a series of patient narrative videos was conceived by Dr. Gregory Makoul, who directs the Program in Communication and Medicine at Northwestern University's Feinberg School of Medicine.

Gwen, a middle-aged grandmother with chronic joint pain, gets on her stationary bicycle with great effort telling us that today she starts her exercise regimen doing fifteen minutes on the cycle. After a minute and a half she declares "I'll slow it down now" and by the two-minute mark she has stopped and is getting off the bike saying "that's riding the bike." Gwen also announces that just before she started on her current diet, she had a lot of pie and most of a cheese cake, saying: "I got all the junk food I wanted in me before I started the diet." In her doctor's office, the camera is trained on the leg she is presenting to the doctor. She states that her knee has been hurting her. The doctor's white coat fills the screen as he questions her and causes her to yelp in pain upon examination. His response to her: "That's your kneecap. Your kneecap's grinding away. That's where your pain is coming from." In spite of the fact that his back is between Gwen and her camera, we get a picture of the way she is treated by this doctor.

David is a physician dying of pancreatic cancer. When he and his wife, Nancy, begin the tape he appears vibrant, but as time goes on it becomes clear the cancer is killing him. They talk to each other in front of the camera about things they say they would not have spoken about otherwise, and they thank the camera and call it a silent therapist. Their discussions range from his thoughts of suicide, an option he rejected, to her need to be independent because she will have to be on her own soon. David and Nancy show concern about how the words they speak will affect the other. Small gestures and expressions provide a sense of how deeply they feel about the decisions they are making from day to day. David talks about how he sees his illness from a holistic standpoint like the general practitioner that he is. He contrasts this with the way his surgeon friend with the same illness saw cancer as an enemy and wanted to cut it out. Later, David's four grown children appear on tape to speak about their father's situation and for some of them it is the first time they speak their feelings out loud. We see very clearly how each patient, and each family member, responds to illness in a different way.

Ann, a mother and an artist and a person with manic depression, relates that doctors and staff at the hospital contributed to her state of panic and hysteria when she was trying to commit herself for psychiatric reasons. She describes them as reflecting her own anxiety back at her rather than presenting her with a kind of calm assurance. Her main concern is that hospital staff seemed not to value her understanding of her own needs. She says "if only they could imagine their way into a world in which everything was so heightened, just so overwhelming, that they could somehow understand that if I was speaking to them, it was at great cost, and that the words I said cost me something, that everything that came out of me had to be measured so it wouldn't deplete me too much or wouldn't move me to tears." She analyzes the body language of her doctors and posits a theory of how it has affected her ability to accept treatment. Though she needs help she has a highly developed understanding of her mental illness and she expresses her condition through visual art. It becomes clear through her words and images that she has struggled greatly and that her struggle is ongoing.

AJ was a 42-year-old book editor working in Manhattan who, at the start of her taping, identified herself as a lesbian living in Brooklyn. The onset of Parkinson's, at the age of 37, had disrupted her professional career and she was struggling with the notion that someday soon she would to have to go out on disability. At the same time, she was going through an identity crisis she was only partially able to articulate. As she talks it is possible to detect a fondness for a fellow Parkinson's sufferer she knew only through e-mail correspondence. She describes him to the camera as "particularly compassionate." By the time she was done with her video journal (a year later) she had left her job, her Brooklyn home, and her female partner for a life in California with a male partner, the fellow "Parkinsonian" of whom she had spoken with so much devotion in the early days of her video journal. She now says she is most comfortable with other people with Parkinson's. She claims to be troubled at the possibility she might be cured one day. She has been through so much change. "I don't know what I'll do if that happens." And though AJ appears an articulate and forthright individual, she stumbles and stammers as she talks into the phone when she has to call her various doctors, eventually stopping to write down what she wants to say so that she can read it into the phone.

Karen, an actress and video maker diagnosed with Type I diabetes at the age of 32, expresses exasperation with the doctor who tells her upon diagnosis that it is no "big deal," that her life does not have to change, saying: "Not change my life? This is hugely changing my life, so let's not pretend it's not changing my life." She shows us how diabetes has forced her into a routine. For instance, she now has the same thing for breakfast every day, in the same bowl. From eating to exercise to glucose tests and insulin shots we get a sense we see how her days proceed. She offers her own theories about what facilitates the processing of blood sugar, among them an idea about "arm energy" (vacuum cleaning stairs and shovelling snow process a lot of sugar). We see that she is combining these lay theories with instructions from her doctor. As her story unfolds it becomes apparent, both to the viewer and to Karen, that she is in the midst of a bout of depression. Karen discusses her decision to see a therapist, her reluctance to take the anti-depressants offered by her GP, and her frustration with the restrictions imposed by her health maintenance organization (HMO). The tape ends with Karen talking emphatically about the importance of doctors who seem to like their patients; doctors who listen, seem willing to answer questions, and are not afraid to say "I don't know."

Mary, a full-time mother of three and a Type I diabetic from the age of 11, is tightly controlled, and it is apparent that this control affects many different aspects of her life. In her most compelling request to the camera, addressing directly the people she imagines will watch her tape, she asks that a doctor never say: "I know how you feel." She insists that, since everyone's diabetes is different, there is no way anyone knows how another feels, and she begs: "Just don't say it."

We have made three tapes on living with diabetes. Two of them demonstrate clearly and compellingly that demographically similar people react very differently to what, from a biomedical standpoint, is the same underlying disease. Indeed, when Sara made her tape she came across as rather bitter at times. Karen told of discovering, during the period she had the camera, that she was clinically depressed. The women honestly and articulately present not only their nutrition and injection routines but also how diabetes has affected their relationships and conceptions of themselves. Mary, on the other hand, has lived with diabetes since the age of eleven. As a mother of three, she focuses mainly on her family and her ability to function as a good mother insisting her disease does not overshadow the lives of her children.

2.   How does the Patient Narrative Video Process Work?

People become involved with this project through word-of-mouth or referral. In general, we give patients a small video camera, tapes, and a tripod, show them how to use the equipment, and ask them to take it home in order to share their thoughts and feelings (i.e., "Tell us what your life is like.") taking as much time as they need. After a couple of months, or more than a year in some cases, patients come back with somewhere between two and eight hours of video, which we view and log. We then work to produce a twenty to thirty minute version of the patient's story. We review a rough draft with the patient to ensure that we have not distorted his or her perspective and then produce the final copy. There is never any outside narration added to the tape; the finished version remains entirely in the patient's voice. We have completed several patient narrative videos since 1996, including patients living with chronic pain, diabetes, fibromyalgia, manic-depression, pancreatic cancer, and Parkinson's disease.

We do not pay patients for their participation, in part because we want to reduce the incentive for "performance." The patients offer their narratives because they feel the videos will help people better understand "the world of the sick."[1] Thus far, it appears they are correct: These videos have been shown to medical students, residents, academic and community physicians, medical educators, communication scholars, and film festival audiences in a variety of contexts, each time proving a powerful trigger for reflection and discussion.

The process of making a patient narrative video seems to benefit the patients as well, a point that has been articulated in some way by all of the patients. Storytelling allows the narrators to be in control of their stories, sequence and impose order on a series of life events, and generate a personal meaning system that helps predict the future. Thus, not only can stories help people position themselves within a context and maintain a sense of control over their lives, but they may also help position patients to participate in their own care. More specifically, the process provides a forum for "rehearsing" one's narrative which, as demonstrated by Greenfield, Kaplan and Ware,[2] can lead to significant improvements in both physician-patient communication and health. More recent research focusing on narrative has demonstrated significant improvements in health status.[3] We are interested in the therapeutic value of narratives, particularly in terms of enhancing the communicative coherence necessary for patients to describe their lives to themselves and to health-care professionals.

3.   How does Narrative Affect the Healing Process?

Above all, the onset of disease provides an opportunity for, or a necessity to, change. All of our video subjects express this and it is safe to say it is true for the wider public as well. The disruption of a life in progress and the insistence from without that patterns, habits, and routines must fall in line with new treatment plans or with decreased capacity is a destabilizing event in anyone's life. Identity is disrupted and comfort dislodged. Study into the nature of narrative and its place in human life shows that "narrative ameliorates disruption: it enables the narrator to mend the disruption by weaving it into the fabric of life, to put experience into perspective."[4] By looking at individual stories from the illness experience, it is possible to say that these stories are less about illness than they are about "a life disrupted by illness."[5] There are "complex negotiations and contestations that often surround illness, ones that extend far beyond the illness itself into the very fabric of everyday social life."[6]

In medical encounters, the patient's story must be translated into a medical story. Recognizing that these medical stories – whether entries in patient charts or formal case histories – frame the way patients are seen and treated, Oliver Sacks notes the importance of maintaining a sense of the patient's narrative:

> There is no subject in a narrow case history; modern case histories allude to the subject in a cursory phrase ("a trisomic albino female of 21") which could as well apply to a rat as a human being. To restore the human subject at the centre – the suffering, afflicted, fighting, human subject – we must deepen a case history to a narrative or tale; only then do we have a 'who' as well as a 'what,' a real person, a patient, in relation to disease – in relation to the physical.[7]

Certainly there is some skepticism in the medical community about whether a patient's account is particularly reliable, especially if it has been carefully crafted into a well-told narrative. The potential unreliability of narrative lies in the fact that a perfectly sculpted story, complete with beginning, middle, and end, does not necessarily reflect true life any more than a sterile list of defects describes an illness experience. Those studying the relationship between narrative and healing struggle with the problems of definition. What is a true story and how is it useful? Lived experience, it is argued, cannot be contained within a narrative structure because it does not have an end while it is being told. It is ongoing and transitory and is a chaos of uncontrollable meanings including everything that is and is not a coherent story.[8]

In the field of narrative analysis there are (at least) two approaches to the idea of the relationship between lived experience and articulated narrative. One argues that not all stories are coherent and so rather than looking at narrative as always being a tightly wrapped package we have to accept that it includes the fragmentary and the less-than-coherent within the scope of narrative. Another argument is that lived-experience itself is not so far from narrative form and that narrative in fact serves as a "fundamental way of making sense" of human life. And further, that what Cheryl Mattingly refers to as "emergent narratives" may involve a host of unspoken information that must be observed rather than read as text. [9]

This means that for narratives to be most useful in understanding life lived, they must include nonverbal methods of meaning making. They must be what Mattingly refers to as "improvisational and embodied stories"[10] as well as coherent narratives. From this point of view our homemade videos are a hybrid between lived-experience and fully sculpted story. The subject supplies the raw material which, though fragmentary, contains the seeds of a story in the way that all human life contains those seeds. This includes both the consciously and unconsciously provided material delivered by the subject. It includes the moments when a word would not come to mind or the wrong one did, as well as when the eyes fluttered and the brave face flickered into vulnerability for a moment. The bitten lip, the sideways glance, the language of hands and shoulders, and even positioning of the body in space all tell parts of a story as involuntarily as a sneeze. The video editing process uses the narrative techniques of selection and focus to assemble these fragments into a story that reflects and communicates an individual's lived experience.

4.   Why Video?

When a person picks up a pen to write or sits down at the computer, she or he is likely impaired by the impulse to write well. But more than this, if someone is putting down in words the story of his or her condition, the stylistic conventions of written stories infiltrate the language used and influence the dynamic. Furthermore, writers at nearly all levels tend to feel pressure to make a complete story. Given the fragmentary nature of a video journal, the whole story is less of an issue. The patients are asked to document any part of life they want and not to worry about making sense because we will make sense of it later in the editing process. This freedom from a linear approach allows patients to make entries in a real, immediate, and less inhibited way.

Because television is considered low culture (we are speaking of American television here) there is a sense now more than ever that anyone can do it. Video has become a regular feature in the lives of most people and there is a high degree of comfort with it. The almost completely automatic quality of today's camcorders makes taping an easy task for any amateur, and some of these amateurs are pretty savvy. In footage by a person with Parkinson's disease, camera placement illustrates her understanding of the location of her condition – when she places the camera to introduce herself as a person with Parkinson's all we can see is her clutching and wavering hand. We hear that her first sign of Parkinson's was the deterioration of her handwriting and the gyrating hand becomes a painful symbol of her loss.

Watching the finished video, a viewer is likely to pick up on subtle and perhaps repressed material that might never see the surface if it were left up to written word. Little mannerisms or expressions tell many things patients might not like to admit or recognize. It may take a relatively experienced literary analyst to pick up on this kind of thing in print, but the video image is more easily accessed since it more closely mirrors real-life. It may even be easier to read the video image than the live patient in front of you because the presence of the person in the room can be distracting or even a bit intimidating.

5.   How does the Story come Together?

When we get the video material, we view it with an eye toward determining the main concerns of the patient. At this point we are making choices based on what we see on the screen. A patient with fibromyalgia may not be aware of how many times she spoke of twisting her ankle or needing her mother's help, though it becomes apparent when reviewing the footage. So we are making decisions that the patient may not have made consciously, and yet those decisions are rooted firmly in the content of the material itself. We are looking for issues specific to patients' medical conditions that concern them and affect the way they conduct their lives. We are also proceeding with keen awareness of the audience for these tapes and what we are trying to convey to them. The most common request of the subjects of our videos is for doctors to hear and see them not as diseases but as people living with disease.

When putting together a tape, we are attempting to make a document that has a coherent narrative. It is important that the viewer understands what is being said by the patient. This does not, however, mean that we are tying up a nice package with all of the questions answered. An important goal of the video series is to start conversations about what patients are going through. Sometimes an offhand comment made by a patient sets off alarm bells in the viewer and stimulates the need to know more. In one of the tapes a woman says as an aside that her husband used to help her with her injections in her arm but "he didn't want to be married to a diabetic" so now she pushes the syringe against the wall. Divorce is not mentioned anywhere else in the video and so the comment is left hanging and with questions unanswered. Often, during discussion that follows, someone will ask: "Did her husband really leave her because of diabetes?" Perhaps this is not a question that can be answered but it speaks to the attention to detail of the person who asked it, just as the statement in question speaks to the way the patient is feeling about her lot. Attention to this kind of off-hand comment can be instructive and can lead to helpful solutions to the life problems encountered by people living with disease. Discussion following the video is tremendously helpful because medical students or doctors, or whoever might be in the audience, learn very quickly that each person in the room reacts differently to the material. This observation, in and of itself, reinforces the notion that each patient reacts differently to health problems.

6.   Why are Patient Narrative Videos so Powerful?

The transcript below is an excerpt from the patient narrative video, *Karen: A Woman with Diabetes.* It has certainly lost something in the translation from video, which contains considerable information in the visual image as well as the tone and timing of the spoken word. But some sense of the content is intact and it gives a fair idea of what is communicated in the following piece.

(The image shows Karen sitting at a kitchen table preparing to test her blood sugar. We hear her voice.)
My first doctor kind of bugged me. He was into making it seem like diabetes was no big deal: "you aren't going to have to change your life at all." All we'd do is figure out how much insulin I should take and that would be that. But, until that time, I'd probably best stay away from sugar – a little bit. And, I don't know, it just seemed too vague to me and a little disturbing. He tried to get me on some pills and other things, first, which I guess was a good thing, but eventually, obviously, it wasn't working out –
(We hear a series of chirpy beeps from the glucose monitor; the result is high; the number 257mg/dl can be seen on the screen of the glucose meter.)
uhhh!
(She places her forehead on the table next to the glucose meter in a gesture of despair.)
I can't understand how it can be 257. Really.
(She looks straight up into the camera.)
Really I can't.
(There are a few moments of silence as she looks back to the glucose meter. She looks up at the camera. She reports the warning message on the screen of the glucose meter.)
Check ketones. I believe I ate a normal amount of food today.
(She blinks as she looks into the camera. There is another lengthy silence as she looks back down at the number on the meter.)
This seems outrageously high, I mean, I normally don't get this high. And this is before dinner . . . I haven't eaten dinner yet.
(There is a pause as she looks into the distance.)
I was experimenting with making some cookies *(grimace)* making some cookies sweetened with barley malt to see how they'd be. But I didn't eat that much. I ate a tiny little bit of the batter.
(She thinks a moment looking down and then away. We can see that she is swallowing, we can hear the sound as her fingers rub hard against the bottle of test strips she is holding.)
Anyway, umm, he said, oh, he was just into making everything like it was no big deal and I was thinking: not change my life?

(The image has cut to her sitting in her bathroom preparing to take an insulin injection.)
This is, like, hugely changing my life! So let's not pretend it's not changing my life, I mean, I'm going to change my life here, I've got to change my life. You know, for four months I was on other medications that weren't working so my sugars were pretty high, they were, well, a low blood sugar for me was, like 275, and they were mostly, like, 400, 300. And finally I got on insulin. Finally, I had to say: "give me the needle! Put me on insulin!" Because I was feeling so lousy and once I knew what the lousy was from, you know, and this other stuff wasn't working, I just, well, I've no reason not to want to stick a needle in my stomach, or wherever. I need insulin. Clearly I need insulin. So I asked to be put on insulin. He put me on insulin and then I was fine. But of course it took some time getting used to it. Obviously.
(The image cuts back to the shot of Karen sitting at the table with her meter.)
One time I was on the phone with somebody, my blood sugar was very high so I wanted to wait an extra 15 minutes before I ate so I was gonna wait 45 minutes after my shot. And so I was talking to somebody on the phone and I forgot about the time. So it was an hour after my shot and I started feeling it. So I said oh my god, I'm late. I'm supposed to eat. I have to get off the phone. And so I hung up the phone and I was on my way to the fridge to get something to eat and I got distracted or something and I forgot that I was supposed to eat and I called someone else. I got on the phone again. And I'm sitting there on the phone and all of a sudden I realize there is sweat pouring down my sides. I have got this raging shakiness throughout my entire body. My chest feels like it's vibrating and it's like champagne in my spine, you know, and it's like a small electrical reaction throughout my entire body and I was really freaking out. So I had to eat something quick, something quick-acting, fast.
(The picture fades out and then in on an extreme close up of her face as she speaks directly to the camera. Only a fragment of her face is in the frame in a given moment and as she moves the focus shifts and readjusts.)
One of the big problems that I have is that I get very moody. I can be really fine and happy at one point and then, seemingly for no reason, I get very upset and feel like crying and everything's terrible and it seems like there's no reason for that. But if I think back almost every time that happens there was an incident right before it where I denied myself a little treat. And it seems really pathetic and small and stupid that that could be so upsetting but for some reason it is. I have these little diabetic cookies and I like them. But obviously I can't eat very many of them and I really shouldn't have one after dinner because I just had dinner and I had enough carbohydrate but I'd just really like to have just a tiny little cookie and it's not even a great treat, I mean it's not even sugar or anything like that.

(There is frustration in her voice and we can hear that she is fighting back tears.)
But I guess, well I just tell myself: "no you can't have one." Then I think: can't I just this once? and I'm thinking: no it can't be just this once. So I decide not to have one and then the next minute, about something completely different, I start to feel very upset.
(A long pause.)
Somebody pisses me off . . . if there's anybody around . . . or, I don't know, just anything, it could be anything, and I just kind of flip. It's really a small thing. But it feels really big.
(The picture fades to black.)

As the subject of this patient narrative video, Karen has appeared in classrooms after some screenings to answer students' questions. They ask how she's managing her diabetes now, whether she's still depressed, what symptoms she had before she was diagnosed, what her doctor does to make her feel he likes her, what could have made the initial diagnosis easier to cope with. For the most part, students are compassionate and express gratitude that she has shared her experience with them. Many come to shake her hand when the class is over and to thank her for her time. After one screening she attended, before she was introduced to the room (though in plain view, only a couple of students recognized her as the person in the tape), one student asked: "How do we know she wasn't depressed before the onset of diabetes?" This stopped the room for a moment and then Karen was introduced as the best authority on that question.

The student looked at her intently as she answered that she'd always been happy-go-lucky before the onset of disease and then, once suffering symptoms and diagnosed with an incurable disease, she had lost the feeling of being a lucky person. She explained she had never really known she'd felt lucky until she stopped feeling lucky. This may have been a defining moment for this student. The video was an excellent trigger for this question and allowed a chance for this student to see from a perspective other than his own. We can't know exactly what led him to ask this question. But it triggered the opportunity to discuss his thoughts and to wonder whether illness changed the patient or some underlying condition was brought to the surface by confrontation with hardship. Patients are complex; their reactions to illness are complicated and individualistic. And that's the point. The first step toward understanding is to listen with an open mind to the presentation of a patient's reality and give credit to the patient as the expert on her or his own condition.

## 7.	Conclusion

The opportunity to hear from patients through patient narrative videos gives medical trainees and practicing physicians an idea of issues present in a person's life that rarely come out in an office meeting. Upon hearing that a diabetic's finger bled when she massaged her hand in a Tai Chi class, one doctor reflected that it made him think about the fact that a patient like this is constantly reminded she is sick. He wished he had known this kind of detail before, and it gave him ideas about different kinds of questions to ask all his patients. Whatever reactions result from the viewing of these patient narrative videos , what is important is that they heighten awareness of – and sensitivity to – how patients experience illness. If the condition of the person is important, then treating the body is a necessary but not sufficient step toward healing. It is necessary to understand not only the location of the illness and its biomedical remedy or repair, but also the psychosocial world in which the physical body exists. These videos offer a window onto that world and provide a way to see through to the person living with disease. In addition, the videos serve as something of a mirror, reflecting and sometimes clarifying the illness experience for the patients who make them.

Notes

[1] Eric J Cassell, *The Healer's Art: New Approaches to the Doctor-Patient Relationship* (New York: J.B. Lippincott, 1976), 25-46.

[2] S Greenfield, S Kaplan, JE Ware Jr. "Expanding patient involvement in care. Effects on patient outcomes." *Ann Intern Med,* 102 (1985): 520-8.

[3] JM Smyth, AA Stone, A Hurewitz, A Kaell, "Effects of writing about stressful experiences on symptom reduction in patients with asthma or rheumatoid arthritis: a randomized trial." *JAMA,* 281 (1999):1304-9.

[4] Gay Becker. *Disrupted Lives: How People Create Meaning in a Chaotic World* (Berkeley and Los Angeles: University of California Press, 1997), 166-67.

[5] Cheryl Mattingly and Linda C. Garro. "Narrative as Construct and Construction," in *Narrative and the Cultural Construction of Illness,* ed. Cheryl Mattingly and Linda C. Garro, (Berkeley and Los Angeles: University of California Press, 2000), 27.

[6] Ibid., 18.

[7] Oliver Sacks, *The Man Who Mistook His Wife for a Hat* (New York: Touchstone, 1998), viii.

[8] Cheryl Mattingly, "Emergent Narratives," in *Narrative and the Cultural Construction of Illness and Healing,* ed. Cheryl Mattingly and Linda C.

Garro, (Berkeley and Los Angeles: University of California Press, 2000), 181-211.
[9] Ibid., 204.
[10] Ibid., 189.

Bibliography

Becker, Gay. *Disrupted Lives: How People Create Meaning in a Chaotic World*. Berkeley and Los Angeles: University of California Press, 1997.

Cassell, Eric J. *The Healer's Art: New Approaches to the Doctor-Patient Relationship*. New York: J.B. Lippincott, 1976.

Greenfield S, Kaplan S, Ware JE Jr. "Expanding patient involvement in care. Effects on patient outcomes." *Ann Intern Med*, 102 (1985): 520-8.

Mattingly, Cheryl, "Emergent Narratives." In *Narrative and the Cultural Construction of Illness and Healing*. Ed. Cheryl Mattingly and Linda C. Garro, 181-211. Berkeley and Los Angeles: University of California Press, 2000.

Mattingly, Cheryl, Linda C. Garro. "Narrative as Construct and Construction." In *Narrative and the Cultural Construction of Illness*. Ed. Cheryl Mattingly and Linda C. Garro, 1-49. Berkeley and Los Angeles: University of California Press, 2000.

Smyth JM, Stone AA, Hurewitz A, Kaell A. "Effects of writing about stressful experiences on symptom reduction in patients with asthma or rheumatoid arthritis: a randomized trial." *JAMA*, 281 (1999):1304-9.

Notes on Contributors

Karen Christopher works as video editor for the Program in Communication & Medicine at Northwestern University's Feinberg School of Medicine. She earned her BA degree from Pomona College in Claremont, California, and an MFA in Film & Video from Columbia College Chicago. She has been a member of the performance group Goat Island for 14 years, performing and giving lectures and workshops at universities and arts organizations in the USA and Europe. She teaches part-time in the Film & Video Department of Columbia College Chicago. She is the subject (and camera operator) of the video *Karen: A Woman with Diabetes* which won a Holly Harrington-Lux Creative Design award as well as the Silver award from the HeSCA Media Festivals of the Health Sciences Communication Association.

Gregory Makoul, PhD, is associate professor and director of the Program in Communication & Medicine at Northwestern University, where he oversees communication education for the Feinberg School of Medicine and communication research for the Division of General Internal Medicine. Dr. Makoul is a fellow of the Oxford Centre for Ethics and Communication in Health Care Practice, and a member of Northwestern's Robert H. Lurie Comprehensive Cancer Center. His research, conducted both in the United States and England, focuses on communication, decision making, and health promotion in medical encounters, as well as communication skills teaching and assessment. In 2003, Dr. Makoul received the American Academy on Physician and Patient award for outstanding contributions to the literature on the theory, practice and teaching of effective health care communication and related skills. He earned his PhD in Communication Studies at Northwestern University.

Salutogenesis in General Practice:
How to use the Potential of Doctor-Patient Communication to Promote Health

Ottomar Bahrs, Susanne Heim, Vera Kalitzkus,
Peter F. Matthiessen, Hermann Müller

1   Introduction

Salutogenesis is a concept now used in the context of patient centred medicine focusing on the health promoting resources of patients rather than on pathogenic factors. The aim of our project is to foster a salutogenic orientation in general practice, especially with chronically ill patients. Therefore two interdisciplinary quality circles were implemented discussing and analysing this topic for three years (2003 – 2005).[1] The goal of our project is to identify those factors in general practice that hinder or foster the promotion of salutogenic factors especially in the treatment of chronically ill patients. In this paper we would like to show the potential of interdisciplinary quality circles working with video documentations from the participants' practice both for medical training and research in primary health care.

2   What is Salutogenesis ?

The term has been coined by Aaron Antonovsky[2] in his aim to understand what keeps people healthy. It is derived from the Latin word "salus" that means health or well-being. The salutogenic model is not to be seen as substitute, but as complementary to the pathogenic orientation of the biomedical model, as it draws attention to the so far neglected facets in the pathogenic model. Instead of concentrating on singular pathogenic factors, the salutogenic model looks at the complex conditions fostering a person's well being.

The following paragraphs contrast these two approaches to health and illness in order to highlight their special features and differences. In daily medical practice – especially in general practice – there is, of course, overlap and also reflections from practitioners about various coping strategies and health promoting factors in a patient's life world.

A. The Biomedical Model and Pathogenesis

Biomedicine regards itself as pure natural science. Biomedical knowledge is conceptualised as "proven," "timeless" and "objective" (with the exception of new medical findings). The object under question is regarded as existing outside and independent of the researcher, who discovers and characterizes its qualities.[3] This is the basis for its claim of objectivity. The following assumptions belong to the core of the biomedical model:

- Body and illness are regarded as "natural" phenomena
- Biomedical practice and research is objective, neutral and scientific
- Diseases are universal and defined as deviation from the biophysiological norm.

Disease in biomedical terms is conceptualised as a defect of biological and chemical processes of the body that need to be 'repaired' and restored to the biomedically defined norms. These biomedical norms for the human body are most obvious in all the tables of standards for various biological parameters such as weight, blood pressure, cholesterol, blood sugar and so on. These strictly defined norms, however, are only of limited validity as the biological parameters show huge variations, as for example in blood pressure, lung volume or other parameters. Napoleon Bonaparte, for example, is believed to have lived with a pulse of 40, being in a state of full health. A pulse of 40, George Canguilhem reflects, is a severe deviance from the average pulse of 70 – still for Napoleons organism this was "normal."[4] Concerning co-morbidities, patients with Type II diabetes mellitus are considered better of with a lower blood pressure than the average population. The meaning of deviance from such biomedical norms for any concerned individual cannot be drawn from the numbers alone, for they could indicate either harmless variation or serious risk.[5]

With the emergence of positivistic-oriented medicine in the nineteenth century, the focus of medicine shifted from the *subjective description of illnesses* by the suffering individual to the search for *objective biomedical facts*. Through this transition, the patient's body was transformed into a passive object for medical inquiry. Furthermore, with the Cartesian distinction between the body and the psyche/soul, patients learned also to regard their own bodies as objects.[6]

In medical diagnosis, the patient's illness narrative is translated by the doctor into the objective salient facts, which become signs of a pathological process. Medical anthropologist Arthur Kleinman explains that, for this translation to occur, *illness as experience* has to be decoded into the *disease as biological pathology*. There is no room for questions about the meaning of the illness for the individual. Kleinman states:

> Biomedicine banishes purpose and ultimate meaning to religion, yet most patients and practitioners struggle to make sense of illness with respect to great cultural codes that offer coherent interpretations of experience.[7]

The lived body, the life world or "Lebenswelt" of the patient and its effect on the health conditions are neglected.

B. The Salutogenic Model

Central to salutogenesis is to regard the whole person in its social and biographical context. The main assumptions of the pathogenic and salutogenic model can be summarized as follows:[8]

	Pathogenic model	Salutogenic model
Conception of health and disease	Dichotomy	Continuum
Applicability of the disease conception	Pathology of an illness Reductionistic	History of the ill person and his being ill, holistic
Health- and Illness factors	Risk factors, negative stressors	"Healing" resources, sense of coherence
Intervention	Use of healing devices	Active adaptation, risk reduction and development of resources

Instead of seeing health and disease in opposition to each other, the salutogenic model understands health and illness as two poles on a continuum. Even when healthy, the body has to react to pathogenic factors in its surroundings – being healthy is therefore not a static condition, but in a constant flux and flow. Even in illness, the bodily reactions towards self healing can be regarded as salutogenic resources. Man can therefore be seen *as more or less healthy* or *more or less ill.*[9]

The biomedical model describes disease as an entity that exists independently of an individual person and that can be characterized by a specific aetiology. This conceptualization is reductionistic as it focuses on the biophysiological or biopsychological processes. In contrast, the salutogenic perspective looks at the history of a person and their illness – a view that can be characterized as holistic because of its attentiveness to the biographical and social context.

As mentioned above, the pathogenic model concentrates on deviations from norms and risk factors, both of which it tries to eliminate. The "healing resources" of a patient and the meaning the specific disease or illness episode for the individual is not taken into account.

As therapy the pathogenic model implies the use of healing devices – interventions from outside to eliminate the pathogenic factors. From a salutogenic point of view one looks at the healing resources of a person, his potential for active adaptation to new circumstances as well as his or her potential for habitual changes for risk reduction and the development of resources.

The question that needs to be asked according to Antonovsky is: What keeps people more healthy and less ill on the health/illness-continuum? Antonovsky drew attention to the psychosocial factors influencing a person's ability to keep healthy. He identified key factors in persons who stay well even under strained circumstances, for which he coined the term 'Sense of Coherence' (SOC). The SOC in a person's life is comprised of a:

- sense of comprehensibility,
- sense of manageability,
- sense of meaningfulness.

Antonovsky understands SOC as "a global orientation that expresses the extent to which one has a pervasive, enduring though dynamic feeling of confidence that one's internal and external environments are predictable and that there is a high probability that things will work out as well as can reasonably be expected."[10]

Of course a persons' well being is also influenced by his or her life circumstances like family or social support and personal traits such as humour, love, spirituality and happiness – aspects that are also dealt with in other contributions of this volume.

3   Salutogenesis in General Practice

The general practitioner (GP) or family doctor has a distinctive professional identity that differs from that of medical specialists. The GP can be described as a generalist rather than a specialist and is quite often the first and the last medical professional dealing with a patient. GPs attend to patients over a long period of time and deal with various illnesses, instead of a specialists' episodic intervention with patients having particular diseases or conditions. As GPs deal with patients and their families over years, sometimes over generations, they can have intimate knowledge of the social and biographical background of the patient. GPs are therefore well-positioned, in the ideal case, to deal with the whole person rather than one isolated "defective" part of the body.

The work of GPs in Germany compared to other European countries is characterized by both higher work loads and greater physician discontent. At the same time, patients' expectations of general practitioners are also higher than in countries without a gatekeeper system, as a Europe-wide comparative study showed.[11] Time is scarce and communication is central. The results of the study showed that patient-centred consultations with scope for participation and time ultimately save resources. Hence, the question is how to improve doctor-patient communication and relationships, so that the patient's and physician's time is best used and create an encounter that is health-promoting for the patient?[12] Our project aims therefore to:

- identify situations and patterns of communication that foster the self help potential of patients ("good practice");
- identify situations and patterns of communication that hinder the salutogenic potential of patients ("hindering structures");
- develop exemplary cases into teaching- and training materials for medical practitioners and medical students.

It is especially important to activate the salutogenic potentials of patients with chronic conditions, as their whole life is affected by the illness. In addition, many chronic conditions can be influenced positively by a patient's life style (such as diet, physical activities and so on). Chronically ill patients make up a large proportion of a general practitioner's clientele but these individuals may also take more time. At the same time, the GP has intimate knowledge of this clientele, which presents the opportunity both for deeper analysis and effective improvement.

4 The Interdisciplinary Quality Circle "Salutogenesis in General Practice"

A. Method

In the project, two interdisciplinary groups in Göttingen and Witten-Herdecke (Germany) are working towards the promotion of a salutogenic orientation in primary health care. The two groups are comprised of general practitioners, non-medical health experts, patient representatives and social scientists. In the monthly group discussions (three hours) video documented physician-patient encounters in general practice are analysed with the goal of identifying unused potentials in the consultations. Especially helpful is the wide range of expert knowledge from the various participating disciplines. Group discussions permit new aspects and scopes of meaning to emerge that might lead to improvements in the specific setting.

The project is indebted to qualitative research methods, using mainly structural hermeneutic and sequential analysis, following the approach of sociologist Ulrich Oevermann.[13] Structural hermeneutics tries to reconstruct latent structures of meaning ("latente Sinnstrukturen") contained in a specific case or encounter. The material for analysis are recorded texts or protocols such as, in our case, the video documentations of consultations. Each sequence is analysed separately to identify all possible meanings in the discussions. For validation and to access the wider socio-biographical context of the encounter we also conduct biographical interviews with doctors and the respective patients. Structural hermeneutics draws on common sense and knowledge of everyday life. This makes the method well-suited for identifying professional patterns of understanding and thus valuable as a tool for raising awareness of patterns connected to special settings. Structural hermeneutics is a way to gather all elements of one specific case together in a non-contradictory way. This should enable a comprehensive reality-near case understanding and respective therapeutic action.[14]

Working with an analytically distant view gives the general practitioner necessary independence to take into account the taken-for-granted aspects in a specific case and/or doctor-patient encounter. This aspect is further supported by the group discussions in the peer-review groups that provide a multiplicity of perspectives. The following objectives are the goal in the group meetings of the quality circle:

- Analysis of the meaning of difficulties in the doctor-patient relationship for problems in the implementation of a therapy.
- Identification of hindering and/or fostering patterns in communication and behaviour of the medical practitioner.
- Identification of hindering and/or fostering patterns in communication and behaviour of the patient.

We are concentrating in our project on two groups of chronically ill patients: patients with Type II diabetes mellitus and patients with asthma and/or chronic obstructive pulmonary disease (COPD). The project is financed by a German health insurance company (AOK), whose interest in the topic is connected to the Disease Management Programs (DMPs) and discussions regarding implementing evidence based medical guidelines in Germany. The question of patient-centred medicine is dealt with only marginally through the DMPs, as they are informed by the biomedical model. This is cause for uneasiness as the individual doctor-patient communication and encounter is central for healing. There is also some question of whether DMPs are compatible with a salutogenic orientation in general practice or not.

How is this method of analysis applicable to general practice? Salutogenic resources can be fostered in the doctor-patient interaction especially via acknowledgement of the individual human being suffering from an illness rather than seeing "cases" representing a disease. In the direct encounter this can be accomplished through active listening. Active listening gives the patient the feeling that dealing with health and illness is worthwhile (*meaningfulness*) and that he or she is acknowledged and appreciated as a unique person. It allows the patient to gain better access to the subjective meaning of his symptoms and complaints (*comprehensibility*). Active listening further allows the experience that risks and problems can be controlled and that the general practitioner can have a supportive function in developing resources and a sufficient social network (*manageability*). Without going deeper into the theoretical approach we would like to exemplify our method by illustration of the work in the quality circle and a particular case study.

B. The Quality Circle in Göttingen: Development and Progress

Physicians participating in the Göttingen quality circle include twelve general practitioners (with specialisation in diabetology, surgery and complementary medical therapies, such as Traditional Chinese Medicine, homeopathy or acupuncture, as well as psychotherapeutic methods). Participants from the non-medical sector, one breathing therapist, an nutritionist, a physiotherapist, and a patient representative. The participants' motives for joining the group were to:

- Improve patient compliance;
- Foster effective daily practice;
- Improve their own work related satisfaction;
- Improve communication;
- Reach patients emotionally.

The monthly meetings started in March 2003, each focussing on a video documented doctor-patient consultation from one of the participant's practice. Each general practitioner documented a whole week of consultations in his practice, from which the social scientists chose one example for use in the quality circle.

The participants developed an open and trustful atmosphere in the circle in a very short time, allowing both discussion of controversial data and self reflexive insights through collegial supervision. Participants emphasized the meaning of this quality circle for their daily work and life: apart from the insights concerning the topic of the circle, they draw strength from the peer review aspects and collegial supervision and see the circle as an important tool for personal development that they do not want to miss.

C. Analysis of One Consultation: A Man with Diabetes Mellitus, Type II[15]

The video under discussion has been recorded in a GP's practice in a small rural town near Göttingen. The 38 year old physician, we call him Dr. Panahi, was born in Iran and lived in Germany since the age of

18. At the time of the recording, Dr. Panahi had been working in this practice as an assistant for three months. As he has special training in diabetology, his boss, a GP himself, often asks that he examine patients with diabetes. In this video, the person with diabetes is a 65 year old man, a former bus driver who is now retired, and who has been patient in this practice for thirty years (and is a second generation patient in the practice). Five years ago he was diagnosed as having diabetes mellitus, type II and treated by oral insulin therapy. The new physician and the patient have known each other for only two months. The goal of the recent consultations has been an improvement of the patient's blood sugar level. The doctor's aim is to change the therapy from oral medication to insulin injections. The patient, on the other hand, is obviously afraid of injections and has therefore objected to this change.

As can be seen in the initial sequence of the consultation, the communication between patient and doctor is dominated by an examination of, and discussion about, the blood sugar level. The patient has a so called diabetes journal, where he jots down his blood sugar levels regularly. They begin the consultation by discussing the high and low levels of blood sugar in respect to the patient's lifestyle and activities. On the one hand, this is necessary to improve the physical condition of the patient; on the other hand, we believe that having the biomedical parameters as the starting point of the discussion, subordinates the subjective state of being and the life world of the patient. Furthermore, with writing a diabetes journal the patient is socialized into the biomedical world view, thus learning to handle his illness correctly. But at the same time the patient is also subjugated under the biomedical perspective as individuals learn to implement the biomedical control over their own body.

The non-verbal analysis also showed the characteristics of the encounter. Patient and doctor appeared as creating a dance, in which both partners try to persuade each other from their opinion. The patient was characterized as "holding his point of view in a flattering way." In the verbal analysis this characterization has been confirmed, but also revealed an ambiguity in the patient between "compliance" and "strong individualism." The verbal as well as the non-verbal analysis revealed a joint negotiation between the partners, which is nevertheless infused with ambiguity. Still, the strategies of patient and doctor fit with one another: the doctor is non-directive and defensive in his action; the patient is active and on the offensive, but shies away from conflict. In this way, both partners are satisfied with the interaction, although it ultimately resulted in achieving the medical goal of injected insulin therapy.

The quality circle's analysis of the consultation revealed the emotional aspects, especially fear, in the doctor-patient interaction as key problem. As the doctor gave an explanation about dealing with a very low blood sugar level, the patient reacted by narrating the experience of an acquaintance who suffered from such a condition and noted that this possibility frightened him. The doctor, on the other hand, did not respond to that hint from the patient's side, which might prove vital for any changes to therapy and the patient's ability to deal with his fear. The group proposed alternative ways of interaction and pointed out the importance to pay attention to the hidden aspects in an encounter. The discussion in the quality circle led to a heightened sensitivity among the participants for the underlying structure and neglected potentials in the encounter.

In a further step, one could look at the biographies of the patient as well as the doctor in order to identify clues for the denial of fear. In this case, doctor and patient still were able to build a reliable partnership and cooperation. Especially in cases where the partnership between doctor and patient is not working, biographical case analysis can identify hindrances that might lead to difficulties between the partners. These analyses can also identify resources that can be strengthened to foster the well-being of the patient (as well as the doctor).

Notes

[1] The monthly meetings of the quality circles and workshops of the project are acknowledged and accredited by the General Medical Council of Lower Saxony (Ärztekammer Niedersachsen).

[2] Aaron Antonovsky, *Unraveling the Mystery of Health. How People Manage Stress and Stay Well* (San Francisco: Jossey-Bass, 1987).

[3] Georg L. Engel, "How Much Longer Must Medicine's Science Be Bound by a 17th Century World View?," in *The Task of Medicine. Dialog at Wickeburg*, ed. Kerr L. White (Menlo Park, California: The Henry J. Kaiser Foundation, 1988), 113-136. It has to be acknowledged that there is a change in medicine in the recent years. With evidence based medicine and the range of complementary therapies that found their way into medical practice, medicine became more pragmatic and has to incorporate various paradigms. See for example Peter F. Matthiessen, "Perspektivität und Paradigmenpluralismus in der Medizin," in *Hilft der Glaube*, ed. Brigitte Fuchs, Norbert Kobler-Fumasoli (Münster, Hamburg, London: Lit, 2002), 3-34; Urban Wiesing, *Wer heilt, hat Recht? Über Pragmatik und Pluralität in der Medizin* (Stuttgart: Schattauer, 2004).

[4] George Canguilhem, *Das Normale und das Pathologische* (Frankfurt: Ullstein, 1977), 121.

[5] Claus Buddeberg, Jürg Willi, *Psychosoziale Medizin* (Berlin: Springer, 1998), 363.

[6] Michel Foucault, *The birth of the Clinic: an Archaeology of Medical Perception* (London: Tavistock, 1976 [1963]).

[7] Arthur Kleinman, *Writing at the Margin. Discourse Between Anthropology and Medicine* (Berkeley: University of California Press, 1995), 50.

[8] With reference to Jürgen Bengel, Regine Strittmatter and Hildegard Willmann, *What Keeps People Healthy? The Current State of Discussion and the Relevance of Antonovsky's Salutogenic Model of Health* (Köln: Federal Centre for Health Education, 1999), 32.

[9] Antonovsky 1987.

[10] Antonovsky, ibid.

[11] Van den Brink-Muinen et al., *The Eurocommunication Study – An International Comparative Study in Six European Countries on Doctor-patient communication in General Practice* (Utrecht, 1999).

[12] Ottomar Bahrs, "Mein Hausarzt hat Zeit für mich – Wunsch und Wirklichkeit. Ergebnisse einer europäischen Gemeinschaftsstudie," *GGW* 1 (2003), 17-23.

[13] Unfortunately there is only one publication in English about his work: Ulrich Oevermann, Tilman Allert, Elisabeth Konau, Jürgen Krambeck, "Structures of Meaning and Objective Hermeneutics," in *Modern German Sociology. European Perspectives*, ed. Volker Meja, Dieter Misgeld, Nico Stehr (New York: Columbia University Press, 1987). For further information see the homepage of the Institute: Institut für hermeneutische Sozial- und Kulturforschung e.V. (IHSK), <www.ihsk.de. The implementation of the methodology for the practice of clinical sociology is explained in Ulrich Oevermann, *Klinische Soziologie auf der Basis der Methodologie der objektiven Hermeneutik – Manifest der objektiv hermeneutischen Sozialforschung* (Frankfurt: Institut für Hermeneutische Sozial- und Kulturforschung e.V., 2002). (www.objektivehermeneutik.de).

[14] Marcus Siebolds, "Die Kunst der Falldeutung. Hermeneutische Fallarbeit als Grundmodell professionellen Handelns," *Der Hausarzt* 12 (2000), 25-29.

[15] The results of the analysis according to the method of structural hermeneutics can be given here only in a very condensed style. There is also not enough room to document the methodological process of the analysis in detail and how the hypotheses are validated and cross checked with the documented text. For methodological background see also Ulrich Oevermann, Tilman Allert, Elisabeth Konau, Jürgen Krambeck, "Die Methodologie einer ‚objektiven Hermeneutik' und ihre allgemeine forschungslogische Bedeutung in den Sozialwissenschaften," in *Interpretative Verfahren in den Sozial- und Textwissenschaften*, ed. Hans-Georg Soeffner (Stuttgart: J.B. Metzler, 1979), 352-434; Ulrich Oevermann, "Struktureigenschaften supervisorischer Praxis. Exemplarische Sequenzanalyse des Sitzungsprotokolls der Supervision eines psychoanalytisch orientierten Therapie-Teams mit dem Methodenmodell der objektiven Hermeneutik," in *Therapeutische Teams*,

ed. Benjamin Bardé, Mattke Dankwart (Göttingen, Zürich: Vandenhoek und Ruprecht, 1993), 141-269.

Bibliography

Antonovsky, Aaron. *Health, Stress and Coping: New Perspectives on Mental and Physical Well-being.* San Francisco: Jossey-Bass, 1979.

Antonovsky, Aaron. *Unraveling the Mystery of Health. How People Manage Stress and Stay Well.* San Francisco: Jossey-Bass, 1987. [German translation from 1997: Salutogenese. Zur Entmystifizierung der Gesundheit. Tübingen: DGVT.]

Bahrs, Ottomar, Ferdinand M. Gerlach, Joachim Szecsenyi, Edith Andres ed. *Ärztliche Qualitätszirkel: Leitfaden für den Arzt in Praxis und Klinik* Köln: Deutscher Ärzte-Verlag, 2001.

Bahrs, Ottomar. "Mein Hausarzt hat Zeit für mich – Wunsch und Wirklichkeit. Ergebnisse einer europäischen Gemeinschaftsstudie." *GGW* 1 (2003), 17-23.

Bengel, Jürgen, Regine Strittmatter and Hildegard Willmann. *What Keeps People Healthy? The Current State of Discussion and the Relevance of Antonovsky's Salutogenic Model of Health.* Köln: Federal Centre for Health Education, 1999.
Buddeberg, Claus and Jürg Willi. *Psychosoziale Medizin.* Berlin: Springer, 1998.

Canguilhem, George. *Das Normale und das Pathologische.* Frankfurt: Ullstein, 1977 [1972].

Engel, Georg L. "How Much Longer Must Medicine's Science Be Bound by a 17th Century World View?" In *The Task of Medicine. Dialog at Wickeburg.* Ed. Kerr L. White, 113-136, Menlo Park, California: The Henry J. Kaiser Foundation, 1988.

Foucault, Michel. *The birth of the Clinic: an Archaeology of Medical Perception.* London: Tavistock, 1976 [1963].

Kleinman, Arthur. *Writing at the Margin. Discourse Between Anthropology and Medicine.* Berkeley: University of California Press, 1995.

Matthiessen, Peter F. "Perspektivität und Paradigmenpluralismus in der Medizin." In *Hilft der Glaube*. Ed. Brigitte Fuchs and Norbert Kobler-Fumasoli, 3-34. Münster, Hamburg, London: Lit, 2002.

Oevermann, Ulrich. "Struktureigenschaften supervisorischer Praxis. Exemplarische Sequenzanalyse des Sitzungsprotokolls der Supervision eines psychoanalytisch orientierten Therapie-Teams mit dem Methodenmodell der objektiven Hermeneutik." In *Therapeutische Teams*. Ed. Benjamin Bardé and Mattke Dankwart, 141-269. Göttingen, Zürich: Vandenhoek und Ruprecht, 1993.

Oevermann Ulrich. "Die objektive Hermeneutik als unverzichtbare methodologische Grundlage für die Analyse von Subjektivität. Zugleich eine Kritik der Tiefenhermeneutik." In *'Wirklichkeit' im Deutungsproze*. Ed. S. Müller-Doom and T. Jung, 106-1089. Frankfurt: Suhrkamp, 1993.

Oevermann, Ulrich. *Klinische Soziologie auf der Basis der Methodologie der objektiven Hermeneutik – Manifest der objektiv hermeneutischen Sozialforschung*. Frankfurt: Institut für Hermeneutische Sozial- und Kulturforschung e.V., 2002 (http://www.objektivehermeneutik.de).

Oevermann, Ulrich, Tilman Allert, Elisabeth Konau, Jürgen Krambeck, "Die Methodologie einer ‚objektiven Hermeneutik' und ihre allgemeine forschungslogische Bedeutung in den Sozialwissenschaften." In *Interpretative Verfahren in den Sozial- und Textwissenschaften*. Ed. Hans-Georg Soeffner, 352-434. Stuttgart: J.B. Metzler, 1979.

Oevermann, Ulrich, Tilman Allert, Elisabeth Konau, Jürgen Krambeck. "Structures of Meaning and Objective Hermeneutics." In *Modern German Sociology. European Perspectives*. Ed. Volker Meja, Dieter Misgeld and Nico Stehr. New York: Columbia University Press, 1987.

Siebolds, Marcus. "Die Kunst der Falldeutung. Hermeneutische Fallarbeit als Grundmodell professionellen Handelns." *Der Hausarzt* 12 (2000), 25-29.

Van den Brink-Muinen, A., P.F. Verhaak, J. M. Bensing, O. Bahrs, M. Deveugele, L. Gask, N. Mead, F. Leiva-Fernandes, A. Perez, V. Messerli, L. Opizzi, M. Peltenburg, *The Eurocommunication Study – An International Comparative Study in Six European Countries on Doctor-patient Communication in General Practice*. Utrecht, 1999.

Wiesing, Urban. *Wer heilt, hat Recht? Über Pragmatik und Pluralität in der Medizin*. Stuttgart: Schattauer, 2004.

Note on Contributors

Ottomar Bahrs (PhD), the head of the project, is a medical sociologist, working in the Department of Medical Psychology, University of Göttingen (Germany), since 1996. His special field of interest is in health promotion and medical training. He was part of a Europe-wide comparative study on doctor-patient communication (EUROCOM study), initiated and implemented the concept of quality circles in the medical profession, specialising in video based training modules. Susanne Heim (M.A.) studied literature and health promotion. Since 1999 she has worked in the field of health promotion, self help and patient rights. Vera Kalitzkus (PhD) is a medical anthropologist. She has been collaborator in a research project at the University of Göttingen on the cultural dimension of new medical technologies and completed her doctoral thesis on organ transplantation in Germany in 2002. She is currently employed by the Society for Promoting Communication in Medicine (GeMeKo e.V.) in Göttingen. Peter F. Matthiessen (MD, PhD), professor for medical theory at the University of Witten-Herdecke, is head of the study group in Witten-Herdecke. He has worked for many years in the field of complementary therapies. The organizational and analytical work in the Witten-Herdecke quality circle is done by Herrmann Müller (PhD), a sociologist specialized in the area of biographical research and structural hermeneutics.

Acknowledgement

The project "Salutogenesis in General Practice" is funded by the AOK, a German health insurance organization. It is a cooperational project between the *University of Göttingen*, the *University of Witten-Herdecke*, the *EFNMU Witten-Herdecke* (European Federation of Natural Medicine Users) and the *GeMeKo e.V.* Göttingen (Society for Promotion of communcation in medicine).

Many insights into salutogenesis as well as the specific case studies grew out of the meetings with the quality circles in Göttingen and Witten-Herdecke as well as the methodological workshops with the social scientists and specialists in biographical analysis *Wolfram Fischer* (Ph.D, professor at the University of Kassel), *Martina Goblirsch* (M.A.) and *Bruno Hildenbrand* (PhD, professor at the University of Jena), for which we are very thankful.

Part 4

Making Sense of the Art of Dying

Ars Moriendi: The Lost Art of Dying

Jon E. Cutler

Lux Aeternam – I heard a voice from heaven saying unto, Blessed are the dead who die in the Lord, for they rest from their labours: even so saith the Spirit.

Light eternal shine upon them, Lord we pray: with saints and angels ever dwelling, for Thy mercy's sake, may they rest in peace. Grant them rest eternal, Lord our God, we pray to Thee: and light perpetual shine on them forever.
The Burial Service, 1662 Book of Common Prayer

1.

John Rutter, composer and conductor put this piece to music with other pieces from The Burial Service of 1662 Book of Common Prayer to form his major work entitled The Requiem. Rutter wrote, [a citation needs this " in the beginning. If it is more than 3 lines long, it needs to be formatted differently. Where is the end of the quote? Add full reference as endnote] 'I wanted to write: intimate rather than grandiose, contemplative and lyric rather than dramatic, and ultimately moving towards light rather than darkness – the lux aeternam of the closing text… For me it stands as a clear sign of humanity's quest for solace and light amidst the darkness and troubles of our age. Art, Andre Gide said, must bear a message of hope… The Requiem was written in 1985 and dedicated to the memory of my father, who had died the previous year.'

23rd December 2001

My father died.

Shakespeare has Julius Caesar reflect:

Of all the wonders that I yet have heard,
It seems to me most strange that men should fear;
Seeing that death, a necessary end,
Will come when it will come.

Death belongs to the dying and to those who love them. But how is it that at one time people believed in the concept of ars moriendi, the art of dying? There was no choice but to die the best way possible, at peace with God. Today the art of dying is lost. There are only techniques to sustain life, exercises in futility. Is life just all about being sustained?

6 Months before - 25th June 2001

Murray (my father) went to the doctor a month ago because he had blood in his urine. His appointment was 11:00 that morning. That evening he did not come home. We called his office and his cell phone, but there was no answer. We called the police and the local hospitals. There was no sign of where my father could be.

My brother and I went to look for him. It was more to do something because I felt so out of control. We searched all the possible places, nothing. We went back to our folk's place around 9:30 that night. There was my dad. He was only home by a few minutes.

He forgot the make of his car and where he had parked it. He even forgot how to reach us. The only thing he remembered was asking a stranger if he could take him home. It was as if the fog lifted for that moment that he remembered where he lived. This stranger was kind enough to bring my father home. Wow, we were really lucky that this was a kind person.

It could have been a lot worse. My brother and I figured out that Murray wandered the streets for over nine hours. That must have been so horrible. I cannot imagine how frustrated and afraid my father felt. I just hope that he was so out of it that he did not feel those things.

Medical insurance system sucks. Murray now has to wait a month before he can get an MRI.

24th July 2001

The day of the MRI comes. My father has to immediately check into the hospital because of the results. I am with my father when I get the call. The doctor tells me over the phone, "I have good news for you and I have bad news for you. The good news is that your father may have 18 months to live and the bad news six months."

Everything goes blank. I try to hear what else the doctor is saying but cannot. I catch a few of his words, brain cancer.

I try so hard to move but nothing happens. I start to cry and I have to leave my father. How am I to tell my father about his death sentence? How am I to tell my mother, who has been with this man for 52 years? How can I squeeze what seemed previously an endless lifetime into six months? Death rarely, if ever, acts according to our plans or even to our expectations.

I end up saying to my dad that he has a brain growth, that the doctor does not know what it is and he needs to take a biopsy. As I am signing the papers (I have power of attorney) for surgery, the doctor is silent. I feel his hopelessness. There I stand feeling lonely and helpless, feeling so separated from the world.

2

This feeling jolted me out of my everyday existence immersed in mundane diversions. What I experienced with the process of my father dying was a number of unpalatable truths: my bodily functions tie me to the finite; the awareness of my smallness and the awesomeness of the universe; I am one of many – no more, no less; the universe does not acknowledge my specialness; the world continues nonetheless; there are certain stark absolute dimensions of existence that are beyond my influence; and most of all the knowledge of death gnaws incessantly at the edge of my consciousness. In the end I am alone.

Irving Yolam, a psychotherapist, calls this jolt a 'boundary situation,' "when the curtain of reality momentarily flutters open, and we catch a glimpse of the machinery backstage."[1] A boundary situation acts as a catalyst that moves us from living in the world of things and in the everyday chatter of life to the state of mindfulness of being[2] or defamiliarization:

> In these moments, which I believe every self-reflective individual experiences, an instantaneous defamiliarization occurs when meanings are wrenched from objects, symbols disintegrate, and one is torn from one's moorings at-homeness. In these moments of deep existential anguish one's relationship to world is profoundly shaken.[3]

Heidegger describes this experience as 'uncanny' (not at home). We lose our sense of balance and familiarity in the world. When a person is immersed in being 'at-home' (dasein) in his own world he has lost the connection with his 'existential situation.' He is in the everyday, or as Heidegger says in a "fallen mode."

> As dasein falls… Everyday familiarity collapses… "Being-in" enters into the existential "mode" of the "not-at-home." Nothing else is meant by our talk of "uncanniness."[4]

There is unbridgeable gulf between each of us, between one person and another. We are all fundamentally isolated from one another and parts of ourselves. It is death that makes us fully realize that no one can die with us or for us. On the most fundamental level dying is the loneliest human experience. Ultimately it is death that separates us and it is the fear of death that isolates us.

Yalom likens it to a vale, "Existential isolation is a vale of loneliness which has many approaches. A confrontation with death … will inevitably lead the individual into that vale."[5]

It is not death but existential isolation, which permeates the basis of our fear. We respond to this threat by constructing a world fashioned in such a way as to conceal it. We constitute ourselves in this concealment by creating layer upon layer of worldly artifacts each instilled with personal and collective meaning. Yalom describes this activity as being "lulled into a sense of cosy, familiar belongingness; the primordial world of vast emptiness and isolation is buried and silenced, only to speak in brief bursts during nightmares and mythic visions."[6]

We create experiences of everydayness, the routine activities of the mundane and petty to steer clear of existential isolation. We create a perceived world of stability through institutions and familiar things, 'an at homeness.'[7] Object and being are integrated.

Looking behind the screen we become aware that there is not another who creates and protects us. Humankind is cursed by this self-awareness. The curse is a profound experience of deep loneliness, separateness and awareness of the universe's cosmic indifference.

Existential loneliness is the primary source of anxiety, a signal that one perceives some threat to one's continued existence.[8] According to Erich Fromm, especially emphasized the sense of helplessness inherent in the human's basic separateness:

> The awareness of his aloneness and separateness, of his helplessness before the forces of nature and of society, all this makes his disunited existence an unbearable prison. The experience of separateness arouses anxiety; it is indeed the source of all anxiety. Being separate means being cut off, without any capacity to use my human powers. Hence to be separate means to be helpless, unable to grasp the world – things and people – actively; it means that the world can invade me without my ability to react.[9]

This threat of separateness, Heidegger goes onto explain, is when one is expelled from being "absorbed in the world." The result is confronting loneliness, mercilessness, and nothingness:

> The world in which I exist has sunk into insignificance. Anxiety is anxious in the face of 'nothing' of the world; but this does not mean that in anxiety we experience something like the absence of what is present-at-hand (objects in the world) with-in-the-world. The present-at-hand must be encountered in just such a way that it does not have any involvement whatsoever, but can show itself in an empty mercilessness. [10]

3

7th August 2001

My father and I go to the oncologist for the results of the biopsy. The doctor is sitting behind his desk, looking down over my father's charts. Without picking up his head and looking at my father tells him that he has Central Nervous System Lymphoma. I learn quickly to speak in initials, CNS. 'My father has CNS.'

He finally looks up from the charts and tells my father: "Mr. Cutler I have some bad news for you, you probably have six months to live. The only treatment for this type of cancer is radiation with only a 20% success rate." The doctor asks my father if he has any questions. My father is silent for a moment and responds: "There are no questions. You told me the answer: I have six months to live. I better get my things in order." My father looks at me and says, "I guess I have to tell your mother." I look at him and I am silent.

"Since there are no questions, I suggest that you discuss with your son and wife if you want radiation treatment, let me know." The doctor excuses himself only being with us 15 minutes and leaves my father and me, in silence.

I feel that the doctor abandoned my father because of the type of cancer he has. Since there is going to be no 'siege,' treatment, he lost any enthusiasm. The doctor figuratively and literally disappears.

Afterwards I take my father home. During the drive, my father is very practical about how he is going to get things in order.

At home he has my mother sit down, kissed her and said, "We had a good long run for 51 years." She cries.

17th October 2001

Murray is being kicked out of the hospital today because medical insurance will not cover him for any more days. He has to go to a nursing home. I arrange for the nursing home to pick him up this evening.

He cannot go home because mom cannot care for him and my father does not have enough savings to afford around the clock care. I have to be careful how well I parse out the money. I know that my father is going to die but ... Also, my mother will need the money that my father saved. I am between a rock and a hard place. I do not know how people with less income and savings make it?

My mother cannot stop crying and is constantly asking, "Why is this happening to me?" She cannot get out of her own head. I cannot depend on her to give him his medications on time much less care for him. My brother on the other hands refuses to return my phone calls. He refuses to speak to me. Talk about living in denial. I have to make all the decisions.

At least at a nursing facility he gets 24-hour care, a doctor on call and his medications on time. It makes my life a bit easier. The only choice I have is to find the best nursing facility for him. I hope I am making the right choice. I feel guilty!

Thank God for Thierry (my life partner). I could not do this without him. What a great help he is and a great support for me.

On my way home from Friday evening services I go visit my father at the nursing home for the first time. It is around 10:00 at night. There he is in a stark and empty room, lying on a bed. The room is cold in every manner. He is crying and wants to go home. He is yelling for another blanket because he is so cold. I call for the nurse to get another blanket and I wait and wait. I go into an empty room to get some blankets and still the nurse never comes. At that moment I want to take my father home. I know I could not. Seeing him lying on that bed, every thing seems so cold and inhumane. Here lies a man who I thought once knew almost everything, always so confident and reassuring. Now, he is so helpless and vulnerable. It feels like someone is putting their hand down my throat and pulling my stomach through my mouth. After I find the nurse I ask her to give my father something so he could sleep. She does and I leave. I feel so guilty leaving him there. What else can I do? This is one of the supposed better care facilities.

24th October 2001

Ninety days since Murray has been diagnosed. He is in Chestnut Hill Hospital. He was moved from the nursing home because he is constantly vomiting and he cannot stop. I learned that this was due to neurological malfunction because of the cancer. He is getting worse and he sleeps most of the day now.

Each passing day is like a wave. With each in-coming tide a piece of my father is swept out to sea, never to return, losing a piece of him. He can barely remember anything and he is starting to lose his ability to speak. I feel so helpless. Each day, now, I spend mourning my father's death and mourning the death of a close friend.

He is slipping away and I am starting to feel it more and more. Sad, very sad. I do not know how to express this or deal with it. I am so scared. Every time I see him I am so filled with agony and sadness.

I have entered a new portal, a portal of memories. All that I have are more and more memories. What I am so afraid of now is that when the memories of my father start to fade I will have less and less of him.

25ᵗʰ October 2001

Today, my brother and I met with the doctor. The doctor recommends hospice for my father. The end is here. They only recommend hospice if there is no hope. It is only for pain management and for comfort. What a decision to make. Who can ever be prepared to make this decision? We met with the hospice nurse this afternoon. We sit in the atrium of the hospital. I feel the warm of the autumn sun, the light radiating throughout the room. I do not want to move. I want only to continue to enjoy the warmth. I want desperately to freeze time so I can avoid making a decision. I pray only a few more minutes. The time comes and we have to make a choice, hospice. The warmth dissipates quickly. I am afraid and lonely. I am in such a funk. Sad, really sad. It feels so raw. Robert Frost writes:

> They cannot scare me with their empty space
> Between stars – on stars where no human race is.
> I have it in me so much nearer home
> To scare myself with my own desert places.

It is not death but existential isolation, which permeates the basis of our fear.

What I experienced was a rush of dread, lonely dread. At the moment my brother and I made the decision it felt like the ground was shifting. I felt that nothing was at the core of my being. Who was I decide? How could I decide?

I was jolted from my "being at home" in the world. On one level I was forced to look at my own mortality but behind that was the fear that that no thing or no being can help me. Behind death was the fear of existential isolation. This pulls me into the centre of defamiliarization.

4

The terror of death with all of its implications is ubiquitous and of such enormity that most of our life is consumed with the denial or avoidance of it. Death transcendence is a major subject in the human experience – from the most deeply psychological, our motivations, our dreams, our nightmares, our defenses, to the most public of our rituals (funerals, wakes, shiva), cemeteries, our monuments, our theologies, our ideologies, our need to always explore, to be in control.

As such throughout history we have created a world to provide structure and constancy – roles, values, religious faith, ethics, etc. History itself is what man does with death, says Hegel.[11]

However, in our present era our way of life is based on filling time to avoid death: our addiction to diversions, our unfaltering belief in the myth of progress, our drive to 'get ahead,' our yearning for lasting fame. Recently I asked my students to write an essay on "If they only had one month to live what would they do?" The responses were fairly standard such as helping other people except for the one young woman who said she would watch TV so that she does not have to think about death.

We use the world as tool to create the illusion that we are exempt from natural law, death itself, which motivates many aspects of our behaviour such as self-preservation. It gives us the ability to confront danger without being overwhelmed by the fear of extinction. The Psalmist expressed: "A thousand shall fall at thy right-hand, ten thousand at thy left, but death shall not come nigh thee" (Psalm 91:7).

At the same time this causes us to strive for competence, power, and control. By feeling that we can attain control, power and competence, the death fear is further assuaged and belief in one's special qualities further reinforced.[12] Competitiveness, being goal driven, accumulating material wealth, leaving behind imperishable monuments becomes the way of life which effectively covers up the issue of mortality, which gnaws incessantly at the edge of our consciousness.

When the curtain is pulled back and mortality reveals itself, accumulated material wealth, our accomplishments, and our uniqueness inevitability fails to ease the pain. We seek relief from an additional source to denial and avoidance, the belief in a personal ultimate rescuer.[13]

Throughout history, human beings have retained a belief in a personal omnipotent intercessor: a force or being that watches over us, cares for us and protects us. This intercessor might be loving, frightening, fickle, harsh, or angered but nevertheless remains a figure that is always there for us. The belief is that this intercessor will always ultimately rescue us. Human beings, for millennia, have conquered their fear of death through this belief. No culture has ever believed that humans were alone in an indifferent world.[14]

Cultural factors play an important role in how we perceive the 'ultimate rescuer.' In the United States the 'rescuer' can be supernatural but is more likely worldly. Many Americans, living as they do in a highly sophisticated technological culture, believe that technology is our 'ultimate rescuer.' When confronting death, we turn toward the technologies of science to save us. Dying has become "technologized." Displaced by modernity, dying becomes an anathema. Our society deals with death through avoidance and at the same time looking toward the ultimate rescuer, technology to save us from it.

On 5 December 1989, Daniel Goleman, covering the social science beat for the New York Times, gave considerable space to some recent research findings. Goleman reported that psychological researchers have discovered that people fear death. This insight led them to formulate "a sweeping theory," to quote Goleman, "that gives the fear of death a central and often unsuspected role in psychological life."[15]

This sweeping theory is an example of a technological culture, stating the obvious but giving it an air of importance because it is cloaked in research and statistics. This is a perception that we are in control because we control the statistics and tests. Because of this pervasive cultural value our society sees death as a defeat because it is out of our control or as stated by Shakespeare, "it will come when it will come." We do not see "death as a necessary end", an inevitable culmination.

In modern Western culture nature is the callous enemy that can be subdued only by technical means.[16] We look towards the technologies of physical and biological sciences, to slow down the dying process and to provide the potential of conquering death itself.

American culture – its courts, its bureaucracies, its insurance system, the training of doctors, patient's expectations – is organized to support technological treatment. Technologies, according to Neil Postman, create the ways in which people perceive reality.[17] Susan Sontag applied this in her book *Illness as Metaphor*, highlighting that "as a result in America there is a measure of how much harder it has become in an advanced industrial society to come to terms with death. Death is now an offensively meaningless event."[18] This is embodied in Postman's idea of 'Technopoly' , which is "the submission of all forms of cultural life to the sovereignty of technique and technology."[19]

Technologies have always played a central role in the development and transformation of culture. Postman pointed out that embedded in every technology "is an ideological bias, a predisposition to construct the world as one thing rather than another, to value one thing over another, to amplify one sense or skill or attitude more loudly than another."[20] Everything tradition, social mores, myth, ritual and religion– must give way in some degree to the technology. Technologies are not integrated into the culture. They attack the culture. They bid to become the culture; hence, technologies become the thought-world of the culture. Tradition, social mores, myth, ritual, and religion have to fight for their lives.[21]

Aldous Huxley outlined in *Brave New World* that the authoritarian nature of technology (Postman's Technopoly) seeks to eliminate any competition by making the alternative not unpopular but invisible or irrelevant. [22] It accomplishes this by providing us with how art, religion, history, truth, intelligence, and dying will be defined.

Technology is who we are and how we live and die. We are not conscious of how it defines us. We cannot live other than in a technological world, with all its consequences. It has both positive and negative aspects. Medical technology has extended our life spans with a

higher quality of life but the patient becomes the disease, in the process
losing his/her humanity. But to live in a world without modern medicine
or even 'simpler' things such as electricity, plastic, in-door plumbing, etc.,
is inconceivable. Our technologies have formed how we perceive reality
and, therefore, construct the world, how we interact with others, how and
what we believe and determine what is 'wrong' and 'right.'   It is
totalitarian; it is Technopoly.

Thus, there is now only one method to treating illness – the
technological one. The medical culture can only define competence by the
quantity and array of machinery brought to bear on disease.

Every scientific or clinical advance carries with it a cultural
implication, and often a symbolic one. For example, after Laennec
invented the stethoscope in 1816, the physician no longer had to put his
ear against a diseased chest, thereby transforming the relationship
between doctor and patient and establishing the objective physician, who
could now distance himself from the patient.. Diagnosis became linked
less with what the patient believed but more with sounds from within the
body. The result is that physician believed the process to be objective and
free of bias. Seen from the strictly clinical perspective, a stethoscope is
nothing more than a device to transmit sounds. Symbolically, however,
dangling from the doctor's neck it is the evidence of authority and
detachment.

In his book *Medicine and the Reign of Technology*, Stanley
Reiser, states it best:

> So, without realizing what has happened, the physician
> in the last two centuries has gradually relinquished his
> unsatisfactory attachment to subjective evidence – what
> patient says – only to substitute a devotion to
> technological evidence – what the machine says. He has
> thus exchanged one partial view of disease for another.
> As the physician makes the greater use of the technology
> of diagnosis, he perceived his patient more and more
> indirectly through a screen of machines and specialists;
> he also relinquishes control over more and more of the
> diagnostic process.   These circumstances tend to
> estrange him from his patient and from his own
> judgment.[23]

Does the beeping and squealing monitor, the hissings of the
respirator; the flashing multicoloured electronic signals – the medical
technologies – result in a better outcome for the patient? The answer is
both yes and no. The technology of radiation treatment can shrink and
even eliminate cancerous tumours, leading to more positive outcomes. But
radiation therapy and other technologies can prolong life without

enhancing quality of life. Where is the prudence? This is the critical point. The impending outcome is that the problems created by technological solutions can only be solved by further application of technology.

It is the patient who suffers the fate of modern medicine because medicine can only focus on the disease. If the patient were still to die the physician can claim that the operation or the treatment was successful. It is the patient who becomes separated from authenticity by the very medical technology and professional standards that are meant to return people to a meaningful life, especially those who are the hospitalized dying.

I was talking to my family doctor, Dr. Carol Lawlor, who has 15 years experience with these issues. From her perspective she feels:

> Everyone expects to have an MRI even with headaches. Six out of ten MRIs that I order are unnecessary. Why do I order them? Because of malpractice suits! There is no longer that level of intimacy between my patients and me. They have no problem suing. If I don't order a test or an MRI then I am considered incompetent. On top of that I am reimbursed by medical insurance agencies on the basis of what I do, not on the amount of time I spend with patients. This drives up insurance costs making it unaffordable for more people. They become uninsured. The irony is that technology makes it difficult for more and more people to receive medical care. Nontechnological medicine is time consuming.[24]

A Faustian deal has been made with technology and medical technology specifically. It promises a longer and healthier life, a life free from illness and suffering. However, technology is not a neutral element in the practice of medicine: doctors do not merely use technologies but are used by them; technologies create their own imperatives and, at the same time, create wide ranging social systems to reinforce those imperatives. Technology changes the practice of medicine by redefining what doctors are, redirecting the focus of their attention, and prompting a rethinking of how they view both patients and illness.[25]

And a price we have to pay in American culture is the increase in interpersonal estrangement such as from the family doctor as well as the decline of intimacy-sponsoring institutions – the extended family, the stable residential neighbourhood, the church, and the local merchants. Our interpersonal relationship with the dying has been similarly estranged. They have been removed from our lives and have been relegated to the skilled care facilities, ICU, and funeral homes. These are truly new institutions taking into account how long people have been dying.

5

26th November 2001

Dad is coming home to die with dignity, not in some institution. I don't want my father to die alone. I do not want that phone call in the middle of the night. I could not live with the shattered memories of my father hooked to some machine in a cold institution. I do not want my father to be isolated among strangers, abandoned in the last hours. I want him to be surrounded by his family like Jacob was.

> Some time afterward, Joseph was told, 'your father is ill.' When Jacob was told, 'Your son Joseph has come to see you,' Israel summoned his strength and sat up in bed. And Jacob said to Joseph, 'El Shaddai appeared to me at Luz in the land of Canaan, and He blessed me...' When Jacob finished his instructions to his (other) sons, he drew his feet into the bed and, breathing his last, he was gathered to his people (Genesis 48).

I want my father to die a sacred death, ars moriendi, where he is surrounded by his family and that is a blessing.

Skilled care facilities, ICUs, hospitals in general symbolize the purest form of our society's denial of the naturalness, and even the necessity, of death. With all the high tech hope within these places we segregate the sick to better care for them. But we also use these institutions to hide death from view. Philippe Aries, a social historian calls this modern phenomenon the "invisible death." He claims that dying is ugly and dirty. We in modern society can no longer tolerate what is ugly and dirty. Death has to be secluded and to occur in sequestered places:

> The hidden death in the hospital began very discreetly in the 1930's and 1940's and became widespread after 1950... Our senses can no longer tolerate the sights and smells that in the early nineteenth century were part of daily life, along with suffering and illness. The physiological effects have passed from daily life to the aseptic world of hygiene, medicine and morality. The perfect manifestation of this world is the hospital, with its cellular discipline... Although it is not always admitted, the hospital has offered families a place where they can hide unseemly invalid whom neither the world nor they can endure... The hospital has become the place of solitary death.[26]

The cultural symbolism of sequestering the dying is symptomatic of living in a Technopoly. Because we fear a confrontation with death, which would destabilize our "at-homeness" in the world and result in existential isolation, we have created the fantasy of controlling nature. As such we as a culture have put the emphasis in the wrong place. Nature will always win in the end. Death should be a reminder that humankind's control over nature is limited and will always remain so.

However, a hallmark of Technopoly is medical hubris. With the vast increase in scientific knowledge and its technologies, medicine and its practitioners believe they possess ultimate control. They hold to the belief that there is no limit on what should be attempted – today and for this patient.

There are consequences for this arrogance. It is the patient's catastrophic reaction as well as his or her family members when learning that no medical or surgical cure exists. The patient and family face an overwhelming reality, defamiliarization. The patient and his or her family feel angry, deceived and betrayed. Many patients and even family members become angry with the doctor for 'failing them.' The anger is misdirected. It should be directed toward American culture because it sustains the belief that the medical profession and technology is the ultimate rescuer.

And it is Technopoly that fashions a new moral rule. Technopoly demands a smoothly flowing, effectively managed human component. Even dying has to be managed and be efficient, no time for the existential, human groping with life. At whom can I be angry? At the cosmos? At fate?

Medicine, through its technologies, can offer hope that a specific treatment may work, or hope that suffering may be relieved or even hope that a specific cure may be found. But this is valid only when medicine recognizes its limitations and defeats. It cannot be the fantasy of Technopoly as the ultimate rescuer that is central; it must be the dying and the dying person.

While the great technological advances of medicine have brought gains, they have also created loss. Medical technology is created to provide hope but actually takes it away. Over eighty percent of Americans die in hospitals and the dying have lost the only remaining occasion to have the final moments with those being left behind. What is lost is a good death. What is lost is the time of spiritual sanctity. In that we lost the ability how to respond to death.

Our culture has been drained of the potency of its resources to respond because of the debilitating results of Technopoly, progress without limits, rights without responsibilities, and technology without cost. With this the individual constitutes him or herself, their world and their situation within that world. There exists no "meaning," no grand design in the universe and no guidelines for living other than what the individual creates. And we sense that we are microscopic specks within cosmic time and our life activities seem meaningless. The meaning of our life is lost in the great expanse of time. The paradox is "how does a being who needs meaning find meaning in a universe that has no meaning?"[27]

6

19 December 2001

Murray is in the last stages of dying. He can no longer swallow. He has gone from the wasting stage to the stage of not responding. He is just breathing. I do not want to visit him, it is too hard on me.

I could not sleep and last night it came to me as an epiphany, "Out of the deep I have called unto You, Lord: Lord, hear my voice. O let Your ears consider well the voice of my complaint" (Psalm 130). I truly understood what the psalmist meant. What he wrote 4,000 years ago is exactly what I am feeling now. What he experienced is what I am experiencing, "out of the deep I called onto the Lord." He felt the anguish. I feel the anguish. There is a bond of empathy, of connection. We both travel this road together. We are bound through experience that transcends all time. I find comfort and meaning knowing that I am not alone, others have walked this path before me.

A search for meaning implies a search for coherence. What is the meaning of life? It is an inquiry about whether life in general or at least human life fits into some overall coherent pattern.[28] Meaning structures a culture to organize its institutions, to develop its ideals and to find authority for its actions.[29]

Religion has given us assurance that our lives have meaning by lifting us out of the fear of existential isolation by connecting us with powerful spiritual forces. Despite the terrors and uncertainties of existence religion protected early humans from self-defeating fatalism.

Probably for the first time in history religion has lost its plausibility. This is an acute crisis, meaninglessness. We live in a world of double consciousness; we are conscious that the universe has no meaning and yet we are conscious that we need to seek and create meaning. Religion can no longer be imposed. Where do we seek our meaning?

Meaning systems cannot relinquish without some substitute. Hence, religion with its symbols, rituals, and art, has been replaced with efficiency, technical expertise, economic advance, and ecstasy of consumption – a world of functionality. Individuals now pursue meaning through social positions, prestige, material acquisitions, or power. Yalom calls this "the false centring of life."[30] The result is that the symbols, stories, rituals, and the arts, which held significant meaning, have become trivialized if not irrelevant.

Immediately following the events of 11 September 2001, national TV anchors in America started to wear black and speak in hushed tones. Within a week people could not handle the constant viewing of the events of 9/11 and they demanded a return to normal programming. Cemeteries are located in the suburbs no longer on the property of a church. This is symbolic of how we push death to the fringes of our society making it irrelevant.

"All the meanings have vanished," according to Yalom. "A citizen of today's urbanized, industrialized secular world must face life sans a religiously based cosmic meaning system and wrenched from articulation with the natural world and the elemental chain."[31]

When faced with the "boundary situations" of life or the veil of the everyday is lifted, we do not have the means or the tools to engage it. We have no choice but to look toward the symbols of our world, technology, which fall short. We are left without the ability to reintegrate death within our culture and within ourselves. It destroys the foundation of human relationships, empathy.

We live in an era where the art of dying is lost. The great majority of people leave life in a way they would not have chosen because it is simply the nature of the thing that kills them. Our task is to understand the implications and consequences. How has this altered our society: the things we think about? How does this alter the character of our symbols: the things we think with? And how does it alter the nature of our community: the arena in which thoughts develop?

Despite living a human creation it is empathy that makes the possibility of faith happen in a world of technology. Religious faith is the leap of empathy. Religion structures meaning. It creates means for people to feel connected on a transcendent level especially when the curtain is lifted, such as when I was sitting shiva for my father. Religion creates the means through its symbols, narratives, rituals and arts, John Rutter's *Requiem.* Through these means it gives meaning to the past, explanation to the present and guidance to the future.

The art of dying should belong to the dying and to those who love them. The art of dying should be our ability to confront it by learning to accept the anxiety, and the fear. The art of dying should demonstrate to others and to oneself that one can suffer and die with dignity. The art of dying should know that I would not be abandoned to die alone.

The art of dying should be learning how to live life. Victor Frankl, a psychiatrist and a survivor of Auschwitz, puts it succinctly, "meaning of life is something to be found rather than given. Man cannot invent it but must discover it."[32] The lesson in all of this is well known.

Ars moriendi is ars vivendi: The art of dying is the art of living. The honesty and grace of the years of life that are ending is the real measure of how we die. The dignity we create in the time allotted to us becomes a continuum with the dignity we achieve by selflessness of accepting the necessity of death and the camaraderie of death. We all face it alone but when we are faced with it there is a sense of tremendous empathy with others who face this human condition. This is the message of hope.

This message is expressed through symbols, narrative, rituals and art such as *The Requiem*. The hope is even in a world where dying is technologized. There are deaths that belong to the dying and to those who love them. This is Lux Aeternam, eternal light.

7

20th December 2001

I am sitting in COSI, a Philadelphia coffee shop on the corner of 12th and Walnut, staring out the window, writing a few lines and I feel like the grim reaper waiting for my father's death, counting the days if not the hours. It is a cold and overcast day. Today the cold goes right through you.

I am looking at a pigeon in the middle of the street. It is staggering and gasping for breath. It is trying to fly. It cannot and it is dying. It twitched and died. It died in the middle of the street. It just happened. The entire world is going by. Life is going by. A truck just came by and ran over it. It is only a bird but it died without any notice except from me.

Life is so tenuous. It exists for a moment and then it is no more. We are all trying to make it on this planet – people, birds. Cars keep running over the bird. The bird started to become part of the asphalt and it feathers were being disbursed to the winds. What seems to be a homeless man sees the dead bird in the middle of the street. He reaches inside a trashcan took out a piece of cardboard went over to the pigeon. He stops traffic, scoops up the pigeon and places it under a tree on some dirt. He gives this bird a burial.

Here a homeless man as marginalized as the bird by society, showed the greatest but the simplest act of human caring and kindness. All those who walked by never noticing, do they even know they are living?

23rd December 2001

My father died!

Notes

1 Irvin D. Yalom, *Existential Psychotherapy* (New York: Basic Books, 1980), 358.
2 Ibid., 31.
3 Ibid., 358.
4 Martin Heidegger, *Being and Time* (New York: Harper & Row, 1962), 233.
5 Yalom, *Existential Psychotherapy,* 356.
6 Ibid., 358.
7 Ibid., 358.
8 Ibid., p. 163.
9 Erich Fromm, *The Art of Loving*, (New York: Bantam Books, 1956), 7.
10 Ibid., 393.
11 Yalom, *Existential Psychotherapy,* 41.
12 Ibid., 129.
13 Ibid., 129.
14 Ibid., 133.
15 Neil Postman, *Technopoly: The Surrender of Culture to Technology* (New York: Vintage Books, 1993), 144.
16 Ibid., 103
17 Ibid., 7.
18 Susan Sontag, *Illness as Metaphor and AIDS and Its Metaphors* (New York: Doubleday, 1989), 8.
19 Ibid., 48.
20 Ibid., 13.
21 Ibid., 28.
22 Ibid., 48.
23 Stanley J. Reiser, *Medicine and the Reign of Technology* (Cambridge: Cambridge University Press, 1987), 230.
24 Personal communication.
25 Yalom, *Existential Psychotherapy*, 335.
26 Phillipe Ariès, *The Hour of Our Death* (New York: Knopf, 1981), ii.
27 Yalom, *Existential Psychotherapy,* 423.
28 Ibid., *Technopoly,* 423.
29 Ibid., 172.
30 Yalom, *Existential Psychotherapy*, 452.
31 Ibid., 447.
32 Victor Frankl, "What is Meant by Meaning," *Journal Existentialism* (1966) 7: 21-28.

Bibliography

Frankl, Victor. "What is Meant by Meaning," *Journal Existentialism.* 1966.

Fromm, Erich. *The Art of Loving.* New York: Bantam Books, 1956.
Heidegger, Martin. *Being and Time.* (New York: Harper & Row, 1962.

Postman, Neil. *Technopoly: The Surrender of Culture to Technology.* New York: Vintage Books, 1993.

Reiser, Stanley J. *Medicine and the Reign of Technology.* Cambridge: Cambridge University Press, 1987.

Sontag, Susan. *Illness as Metaphor and AIDS and Its Metaphors.* New York: Doubleday, 1989.

Yalom, Irvin D. *Existential Psychotherapy.* New York: Basic Books, 1980.

Note on Contributor

Jon Cutler is a congregational rabbi in Bucks County, Pennsylvania. He also is an adjunct professor at Philadelphia University, teaching philosophy and ethics. He received in rabbinic ordination from the Reconstructionist Rabbinical College, Philadelphia and his doctorate in pastoral counselling from Hebrew Union College, New York.

The Art of Dying: Hodler's Cycle of Paintings of Valentine Godé-Darel

Harold Schweizer

1

     A late cycle of paintings by the Swiss painter Ferdinand Hodler chronicles his mistress Valentine Godé-Darel's fight with ovarian cancer, ending with her death in 1915. Most of the more than 200 sketches and paintings – the majority of them executed between November 1914 and January 1915, and of which I can only present a small number in this essay – mirror the progress of the disease in Valentine's face, from her initial expressions of hope and her gradual acknowledgment of the disease to her resignation and the long torment of dying. From December 1914 until her death at the end of January 1915, she does not return the painter's gaze; her eyes remain closed, her face appears like that of one drowning in her bed. The paintings become a record of her struggle and the impossibility of fleeing from her pain. Death awaits her with a certainty and patience visible already in the first paintings of the cycle. Hodler's artistic interpretations of these stages are rendered with decreasing idealization; the symbolic "play" with clock and roses in one of the early paintings (fig. 145, Feb. 1914) falls utterly away when Hodler portrays his mistress during her last two months. The painter's compassionate – or is it compulsive? – attention to Valentine's suffering during this time inflects the deeply emotional style of many of the paintings. The position of her body on the bed, as Hodler's commentators have noted, increasingly assumes the "severe horizontality"[1] of his depictions of the lake of Geneva outside the window of Valentine's room of a private clinic in Lausanne. Hodler's paintings of the faint outlines of the French Alps across the lake underneath a broad swath of sky elegize in universal terms the merging of soul and matter. "All things," Hodler commented, "have a tendency towards the horizontal, to spread out like water on the earth, even the mountains wear down with age until they lie flat like water."[2] As we shall contemplate the images of Valentine's illness and death, we will see her face painted like a mountain eroding to the serene horizontal of water and earth wherein all things merge.
     While I want to read this cycle of paintings descriptively, as a narrative whereby the images comment on the inexorable development of a terminal illness and the drawn out endurance of suffering, I also want to consider the paintings as works of art. As works of art, I suggest, they interrupt or problematize this narrative commentary raising moral and aesthetic questions: how are we to understand the painter's gaze, the

excruciating precision in the depiction of Valentine's dying, the permission the paintings grant the viewer to witness the intimacy of such protracted suffering? The sequence and temporality of the cycle imply on the part of the painter, and impose on the viewer, a moral deliberateness in facing and witnessing Valentine's suffering. How are we to bear, or to respond to, this moral dimension implicit in our viewing of the paintings?

2

Hodler's painstaking rendition of the stages of Valentine's illness requires – for aesthetic and moral reasons alike – our own close attention to the details of this pictorial narrative. The narrative can be conceived as having its beginnings in two portraits, the first dated in the year 1909 where we view Valentine with her head tossed back, her hat and dress implying a social world altogether different from the solitary, intimate life we will witness in subsequent images. I want to begin, therefore, more purposefully with a portrait painted just shortly before the onset of Valentine's illness in 1912 where she appears in a typical frontal pose, in colours of red, tranquil yet vivacious, symmetrical, complete, harmonious:

Fig. 115 Portrait of Valentine Godé-Darel, 1912

Her eyes calmly return the gaze of the painter or viewer. The red colouring
intimates a fullness or completion not just in aesthetic terms but also in terms of relationship and emotion. The colouring in the next portrait is more complex, given the contrast between the gray background and Valentine's tanned face; her greenish torso already announces – to one

who reads these paintings as narrative – colours that will explicitly mark her illness in subsequent paintings.

Fig. 144 Portrait of the ill Valentine Godé-Darel, 1914

The foreshadowing of her illness in this image is all the more poignant since this is Hodler's first portrait of Valentine after the birth of their daughter Paulette. In comparison with the previous portrait in red, here her head is slightly tilted and her eyes, set in shadows, seem tinged with a depth and melancholy at once questioning and resigned. While in the previous portrait her eyes rest on the viewer lightly if intensely, here they rest heavily as if they were to convey, silently, the burden of her knowledge.

The third painting of this cycle confirms the complex dimensions of Valentine's gaze. From now on, with the exception of a post mortem we

Fig. 145 Valentine Godé-Darel in her hospital bed, February 1914

will view her in successive stages of her illness, after two unsuccessful operations and treatment with X-ray radiation, as a bedridden patient who increasingly must subject herself to the logic of her pathology. Here her face has been consigned to the left of the frame while the two thirds of the image on the right are dominated by the horizontality of her bed. "The dramatic expanse of space that comprises the actual centre of the painting," as Sharon Hirsh observes, "emphasizes the fact that, eventually, the void and the horizontality of death will overcome her."[3]   While inflected with the symbolism of transience, the clock and the three roses at the foot of her bed seem incidental confirming redundantly what her position and her gaze appear powerfully to signal: an acknowledgment of a finiteness we had already thought to see in the depth and complexity of Valentine's eyes in the second portrait. Her hand lies inertly on her upper body in a gesture of an inwardness that will gradually take hold of her. Here, as in subsequent paintings, Hodler's own emotions seem expressed in the almost tactile rendering of Valentine's skin tautly stretched over her increasingly prominent cheekbones.[4]

Valentine's last attempt to return the gaze, and thus to be engaged in a communal acknowledgement of her suffering, appears in the painting where she seems to lift her head slightly towards the viewer, but her arms no longer support her. The pale and at the same time excessively rose colour

Fig. 149 The ill Valentine Godé-Darel, November 1914

of her face and the expression of her eyes show the effort of her straining, also perhaps her fearful realization. The rough lines of Hodler's brush around Valentine's eyes, nose, and jaw dramatize, not least by the haste with which they seem to have been applied, the swift progress of the illness. Time will not stand still. Valentine's eyes petition silently against such subjection to temporal processes beyond her control or understanding. Neither time nor the timelessness of art will save her. The painting appears to withhold the consolations of beauty, which may amount to the painter's expression of solidarity.[5]

All of these predictions seem borne out in the roughly sketched painting in dull brown, depicting Valentine on her side with her face epitomizing a suffering for whose unsharability neither aesthetic idealization nor solidarity can offer remedy. Hodler's rough and hurriedly

Fig. 165 The dying Valentine Godé-Darel, 1915

applied brush strokes seem to want to minimize any consolatory aestheticizing of Valentine's suffering. In the expressive intensity of his lines and the muteness of the colour, Hodler's own emotions seem as much visible as is Valentine's suffering.

While some of the sketches Hodler drew during this time depict Valentine as if on a raft towards her mortal destination, death has already signed her face – beautifully – in the serene depiction of Valentine's head, all in shades of green, as if to suggest a reclaiming of her body by nature.

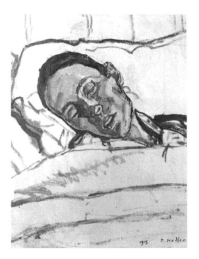

Fig. 160 The dying Valentine Godé-Darel, 1915

The horizontal lines of her bedding announce the horizontal lines of the earth and water outside her window towards which she seems to be sinking. The calm of this scene does not recur in the images where Valentine lies on her back, with her head propped up, the stark materiality of her bones resembling the Alpine mountains and rocks Hodler painted throughout his life. But in spite of such reverberations of earlier paintings

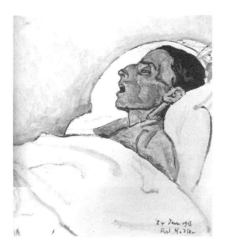

Fig. 173 The dying Valentine Godé-Darel, January 24, 1915

by Hodler where vertical lines powerfully testified to the vitality of the natural world, Valentine's sheets relentlessly flow towards the horizontality of water. Her mouth is open as if each breath marked her endurance of the long time of suffering to death. For the sufferer it is a time comparable to the time in which mountains wear down. Each painting during this last month of her life not only documents the duration of Valentine's dying but also mourns her loss; each painting in this series exhibits, by virtue of the confounding and yet indubitable evidence of this visual record, the incomprehensible phenomenon of dying. The sameness of her position in several of these images permits emphasis of the slight variations of her facial expression, allowing for our notice of the slightly differing depths of her breathing.

Valentine has withdrawn into a universe of suffering uniquely and intimately her own. Before her is no longer her lover but her death, and thus the act of Hodler's exhibition of such intimacy here, if not much sooner, admits the dangers of compulsive, intrusive, or voyeuristic motivations that such paintings would have to negotiate by way of a muting of colours and subduing of drama. Hodler's relentless attention to the smallest changes of Valentine's face and body must not amount to pity but to compassion, it is not a matter of *Mitleid* but of *Mitleiden*, as one of Hodler's commentators puts it.[6] The similarity of the two words in German alerts us to the fact that not only do we have no strictly objective criteria to evaluate such moral imperatives but also that the line between compassion and pity, or watching and witnessing, is difficult to draw.

The painting dated 24 January (fig. 173), is one of the last in which we see Valentine barely alive. She dies the next day. In the painting of her dead body her head is lowered to the level of land, water and sky outside her window and which lines (as we have noted) had begun to form earlier in the way her body flowed into the lines of her gown and sheets.[7]

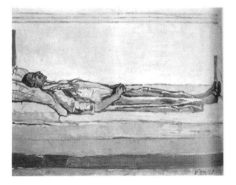

Fig. 179 The dead Valentine Godé-Darel, January 26, 1915

All straining for breath and all passage of time seem to be extracted from this last image of Valentine's dead body stretched out on her bed, the shoes belying her long ordeal, as if death had overtaken her suddenly, mercifully in the midst of an errand. The three blue horizontal stripes in the top part of the image represent, as Hodler explains, the soul floating above the deceased.[9] As Robert Baldwin comments, "one might see the close layering of horizontal bands of glowing color as recalling in more abstract terms the kind of cosmic reconciliation, harmony, and peace allegorized through closely layered, horizontal male and female bodies in Hodler's earlier [symbolic allegories]."[8] And now, even the mountains appear to reflect the emotions of the mournful survivor. Imitating the passage of the dying Valentine to the inorganic world, the mountains lie flat like water.

Fig. 180 Sunset over Lake of Geneva, 1915

In her last appearance in this cycle, we see Valentine once more in a post mortem portrait, resurrected, ethereal, light, and liberated from the material processes to which she had so long and painfully been subject.

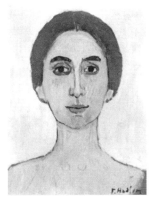

Fig. 182 Portrait of Valentine Godé-Darel (posthum), 1915

3

Let me now proceed beyond these mostly descriptive comments in order to think about some of the questions the paintings raise in the context of this cycle. I would like to do this with a reference to a passage in Walter Benjamin's essay "On Some Motifs in Baudelaire" where he likens a story to an earthen vessel which "bears the marks of the potter's hand."[10] I have referred to the painter's hand only in passing – for example when I remarked on the emotive qualities of Hodler's brushstroke or use of color – without discussing the more complicated dimensions that Benjamin's observations imply. "It is not," he says, "the object of the story" – and I suggest to substitute story with painting–

> It is not the object of the story to convey a happening *per se*, which is the purpose of information; rather it [the story] embeds it [a happening] in the life of the storyteller in order to pass it on as *experience* to those listening." It [the story] thus bears the marks of the storyteller much as the earthen vessel bears the marks of the potter's hand.[11] (my emphasis)

This is not to mean, of course, that we should hasten to translate stories or paintings into autobiography in order to find the marks of the potter's hand. Rather, the important distinction to be noted here is that between information and experience. We look at the paintings – our looking being the equivalent of listening – not to be informed about Valentine's suffering and death, but to acquire in this looking an experience irreducible to information. Since thus our experience in the encounter with these paintings does not inform, or since information is not the essential part of what we acquire in looking at these paintings, commentaries remain suspect or redundant; our experience remains to some important degree incommensurable. As incommensurable, or as irreducible to information, our *visual* experience of the paintings might resemble the *tactile* experience of one tracing the hand of the potter on the earthen vessel – the *tactile* sense emphasizing the emotive or empathic quality of such experience. "It seems to me," writes Jean-François Lyotard, "that the aim of painting, beyond and by means of all the plots with which it is armed ... is to render presence, to demand the disarming of the mind."[12]

To reduce the paintings to information – as if they were merely to document the progress of Valentine illness – is to see them as vessels without the imprint of the painter's hand. (This gives us a sense of why the notion of the original was so important to Benjamin.) How then can we overcome the distances implied in knowledge so as to *feel* the potter's hand? Or, as Benjamin seems to ask, how can we educate our faculty of experience? How, in other words – and this may be pertinent to a gathering of essays such as in this collection – how can we learn not to be informed but to empathize? The answer Benjamin gives is deceptively simple: "To perceive the aura of an object we look at means to invest it with the ability to look at us in return."

"This experience," he goes on to say, "corresponds to the data of *mémoire involontaire* … they are lost to the memory that seeks to retain them."[13] Similarly, as Lyotard writes with reference to the same source in Proust that informed Benjamin, "[I]t happens that a yellow, the yellow in Vermeer's view of Delft, can suspend the will and the plot of a Marcel…. It is this suspension that I should like to call soul…."[14] Hodler's brush, in these terms, becomes analogous to the blind man's cane in Jacques Derrida's *Memoirs of the Blind*, an instrument of intuition or inquiry beyond the means of painterly or linguistic representation. The lines of his brush become, in Derrida's words, a tracing of an invisibility.[15] I mention Benjamin, Lyotard, Derrida – I could add Merleau-Ponty, Kristeva, or Barthes – only to signal that this question of what constitutes the visible in paintings, and how it can or cannot be linguistically transcribed, has been (as various critics have noted) of principal concern for contemporary, mostly French, painting theory.

What seems common to all of these theories is that the invisible aura opened by artistic practice offers resistance against systems or processes – mental, temporal, or material. Such processes are evidently at work – they are thematic – in this cycle of paintings. They are the plots with which this cycle of paintings is armed. They are what informs, what we understand, what is translatable into commentary. And yet, as each painting records, or documents and thus informs us of this process – the process of dying as much as the process of painting – each painting also exemplifies presence, the invisible, or what Benjamin (after Proust) calls *involuntary memory*: it is at once, as Benjamin defines it, something "beyond the reach of the intellect"[16] and "part of the inventory of the individual."[17] The addition of art to the documentary process, or the addition of this intuitive or involuntary form of recognition to the voluntary categories of information, complicates or even confounds the otherwise transparent character of the visible in these paintings.

Given the complexity and opacity thus acquired – and I think of complexity and opacity as virtue – we must draw closer and invest the paintings with the ability to look at us in return. By replacing the distances implied in the aesthetic with the proximities of the ethical, we may feel the potter's hand on his vessel. Each painting, looking at us, solicits from us an attention deficient and yet similar to the attention exacted of the painter faced with the incomprehensible phenomenon of Valentine's suffering. Our *experience* in looking at Hodler's paintings is thus analogous to the experience of listening, to use Benjamin's term, a listening for something unsaid, which no reading can decipher, but which nevertheless must be heard.

All of this is, of course, unverifiable, even if it may begin to circumscribe the moral and emotional dimensions of our *witnessing* of such *intimate* suffering – witnessing demanding proximity and the intimate requiring the experience of one's own self-exposure and vulnerability. Even if, in other words, we cannot decipher the marks of the potter's hand on the earthen vessel, we can feel them. They form but do not inform. To look at a cycle of paintings such as these is to have intimations of a real of which Hodler's brush strokes are traces and to which Valentine's suffering alone could testify.

As we thus find ourselves before this sketch of Valentine's ordeal, we are invited to articulate the *experience* of seeing, to suspended our will, to put our hand on the potter's vessel.

Fig. 159 The dying Valentine Godé-Darel, 1915

Can we see – or rather feel – the serenity of this calm, the subtly expressive left eyelid, the gentle geometry of the chalk lines that emphasize Valentine's face, the vast emptiness of the space on the right, fraught as it is with a sadness and significance for which to find words would be wilful? The tentative nature of such remarks indicates that they are translations of the potter's hand on the earthen vessel, intimations rather than certainties. They are meant to convey not information but experience.

In the context of this collection of essays, tempted as such a project is by facts that inform and thus distance us from the sites of suffering here represented and retold, we must, and that is the point of this contribution, educate our faculty of experience. We must *feel* the potter's, the painter's, the patient's hand. Almost seventy years ago, Benjamin warned in one of his essays, that information had replaced experience and that we were impoverished in experience.[18]

Notes

[1] Sharon L. Hirsh, *Ferdinand Hodler* (New York: George Braziller, 1982), 126.

[2] Ferdinand Hodler, *Ferdinand Hodler, 1853-1918*, ed. Jura Brüschweiler and Guido Magnaguagno (Zürich: Kunsthaus Zürich, 1983), 319.

[3] Hirsh, 122.

[4] Cf. Ibid.

[5] Arthur C. Danto, "Beauty and Morality," in *Uncontrollable Beauty: Toward a New Aesthetics,* ed. Bill Beckley and David Shapiro (New York: Allworth Press, 1998), 34.

[6] Hodler, 370.

[7] Hirsh, 124.

[8] Robert Baldwin, "Hodler and the Problem of Modern Art in Switzerland," Paper Given at the Wadsword Atheneum, Hartford, June 1, 1995,<http://oak.cc.conncoll.edu/~rwbal/UnpublishedTalks/HodlerModernArt.doc> (June 18, 2003), 12.

[9] Hirsh, 124.

[10] Walter Benjamin, *Illuminations*, ed. Hannah Arendt (New York: Schocken Books, 1985), 159.

[11] Ibid.

[12] Jean François Lyotard, *The Inhuman: Reflections on Time*, trans. Rachel Bowlby and Geoffrey Bennington (Stanford: Stanford University Press, 1991), 151.

[13] Benjamin, 188.

[14] Lyotard, 151.

[15] Jacques Derrida, *Memoirs of the Blind: The Self Portrait and Other Ruins,* trans. Pascale-Anne Brault and Michael Naas (Chicago: University of Chicago Press, 1993), 56.

[16] Benjamin, 158.

[17] Ibid., 159.

[18] Ibid., 89.

Bibliography

Baldwin, Robert. "Hodler and the Problem of Modern Art in Switzerland." *Paper Given at the Wadsword Atheneum, Hartford, June 1, 1995.*<oak.cc.conncoll.edu/~rwbal/UnpublishedTalks/HodlerModern Art.doc> (June 18, 2003).

Benjamin, Walter. *Illuminations.* Ed. Hannah Arendt. New York: Schocken Books, 1985.

Danto, Arthur C. "Beauty and Morality." In *Uncontrollable Beauty: Toward a New Aesthetics.* Ed. Bill Beckley and David Shapiro. New York: Allworth Press, 1998.

Derrida, Jacques. *Memoirs of the Blind: The Self Portrait and Other Ruins.* Trans. Pascale-Anne Brault and Michael Naas. Chicago: University of Chicago Press, 1993.

Hirsh, Sharon L. *Ferdinand Hodler.* New York: George Braziller, 1982.

Hodler, Ferdinand. *Ferdinand Hodler, 1853-1918.* Ed. Jura Brüschweiler and Guido Magnaguagno. Zürich: Kunsthaus Zürich, 1983.

Lyotard, Jean Francois. *The Inhuman: Reflections on Time.* Trans. Rachel Bowlby and Geoffrey Bennington. Stanford. Stanford University Press, 1991.

Note on Contributor

Harold Schweizer is Professor of English and Chair of the Department of English at Bucknell University, USA.

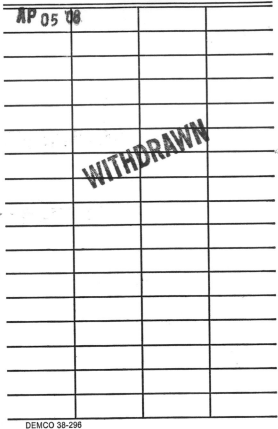